GW00381976

Table of Contents

Disclaimer

The opinions expressed in this publication are those of the authors. They do not purport to reflect the opinions or views of The Paddy Ashdown Forum or any other Governmental or Non-Governmental institution. The designations employed in this publication and the presentation of material therein does not imply the expression of any opinion whatsoever concerning the legal status of any country, area, or territory or of its authorities, or concerning the delimitation of its frontiers.

Foreword

No serious person doubts that as the twenty-first century unfolds, China will exercise an increasingly dominant role in global affairs. That is why this book deserves the attention of any liberally minded individual or group that is thinking about the future, whether near-term or long-term.

What is more uncertain is whether during this century, China will overtake America as the world's pre-eminent economic, political, and military power, and meantime how it will choose to exercise its position in global politics. This series of essays represents a serious and thoughtful attempt to address these questions, by a range of very experienced and knowledgeable colleagues with a broadly liberal frame of reference and a largely European vantage point. There is a range of perspectives among them, for no-one can know with any certainty what the future holds, and you will also see differences of emphasis on the economy, politics, technology, human rights, the environment, and security. Given those differences you may expect some variation in how they believe liberals should think about relating to an increasingly powerful and ambitious China, especially if it continues to be governed for the foreseeable future by the Chinese Communist Party - and as far as that expectation is concerned, there is little dissent.

During the Blair/Mandelson era of British politics a rather superficial economic liberalism assumed that if the Chinese Communist Party could be persuaded of the benefits of the market economy, the outcome would be a more socially and politically liberal China. They were not alone in this expectation. It informed the approach of many of the diplomatic and foreign policy communities in the West. However, this perspective was guided more by wishful thinking than insight, and the truth was much more complex. For the United Kingdom, in particular, there were two consequences of adopting this mistaken view. The first was that soft power resources were withdrawn from other regions, such as Latin America, in favour of China, with the expectation that this would benefit Britain in its relations with Beijing – it did not. The second result was that the focus on economic drivers obscured the fact that China's foreign policy was also informed by other powerful psychological drivers, especially the 'century of humiliation' as it is known in China. While most British liberals view China through the prism of the current human rights challenges faced by the Uighurs and the people of Hong Kong, and have long forgotten about Britain's role in the Opium Wars that led to it possessing Hong Kong in the first place, those historic defeats remain a key element in how China views the United Kingdom.

This book will not give you simple answers to the questions you have about China, for simple answers would inevitably be misleading. Instead, it will help inform you of the complexity of approach that is needed if liberals are to be properly prepared for the coming political changes that will affect all of us, and more especially our children and grandchildren.

It is particularly appropriate that this book should be published by the Paddy Ashdown Forum. Paddy was one of very few leading politicians in the West who was fluent in Mandarin Chinese, and his previous military and diplomatic experience gave him a particularly informed perspective of the region. A well-informed perspective is what liberals need at this time of historical inflection. As the tectonic plates of geo-politics shift slowly but profoundly, liberals need to take some of their attention from constant local campaigning to give space for learning more widely about, and in some cases from, those who operate with a very different frame of reference.

This excellent book is a sign that some leading liberal thinkers have taken up that challenge and I know that you will be rewarded by making time to learn from them.

John, Lord Alderdice, President D'Honneur of Liberal International

Introduction

The story so far: in the beginning, the universe was created. This has made a lot of people very angry and been widely regarded as a bad move – The Restaurant at the End of the Universe, Douglas Adams (1980)

Everyone has an opinion. But is that opinion informed; or not...And how does that opinion fit into the whole? In this volume of essays what you, our dear reader, will ascertain, from the beginning of the very first essay 'China's Governance Structure and System' by Professor Kerry Brown to the last chapter 'China and Global Institutions' by Professor Michael Mainelli, is the depth and breadth of knowledge and understanding that the essayists have on their subject. The range in which they express themselves creates an interesting melodic tone. At times the tone will startle, and at others amuse, above all inform, as the personal opinions expressed are formed from great experience.

Whether you agree with the wisdom that falls off each page is not the point. The point is to encourage debate, dialogue and understanding. Equilibrium in complex systems is vital. That does not mean this book shies away from difficult and complex subjects that create tension. Far from it, for there are individual chapters that may, depending on your experience and point of view, make you mutter under your breath. But, in contrast, there will be other chapters with which you will vigorously nod your head in agreement.

Thus, the book needs to be read and understood in the whole – viewed holistically. To take one chapter, or section, out of context will be to dim the lights and sit in the dark. Taken as a whole, The Rise of China – Fresh Insights and Observations is just that. It shines a light on relationships that are difficult, at times impossible, even unacceptable, but without dialogue there can be no embracing the joyous and opportunistic times of a relationship. There is balance in all things. And to do nothing more than rail against nations is to merely widen the gaps between cultures rather than to build bridges.

Accordingly, this book attempts to advance thinking and actions on our relationship with China since right and wrong are not so simple when all known consequences are taken into account, and unintended consequences considered when siloed thinking and actions are removed to dampen biases based on personal experience, societal cues and burgeoning disinformation that a vast social media spews out dressed as authoritative but can be no more than ill-informed naked hyperbole.

It follows, this book is intended to provide an informed and experienced view on our relationship with China. I use the term 'our' meaning all of us. In one way or another, all our lives are touched by a relationship with China through the effects of multiple interacting investment, organisational, environmental, social and governance ecosystems.

And today, we all find ourselves at a time of crisis – from a pandemic that has inflicted much suffering to the ever-increasing multiple effects of climate change that will continue to inflict ever greater suffering upon the human species and all life that is dependent upon the health of the biosphere. Never at any time before has humankind of all nations got to work together in full cooperation to soothe the ills that mankind in disproportionate amounts has heaped upon our home called Earth.

Consequently, this collection of essays seeks to remove the lid on sound bites, disinformation and clever headlines and create a platform for informed further dialogue for all ages and levels of knowledge and experience. From the enthusiastic student to the most hardened and experienced diplomat. This does not mean that there will not be many who will vehemently disagree with some parts contained in the book, and it is their right to do so. But I hope that in disagreement our dear readers will also find a home for agreement. As a result, we hope you will look kindly upon our humble efforts to bring light where there is darkness and seek to build relationships that will bring balance and an enduring calm upon suffering of all people, indeed all life, for whatever reasons, wherever they may be. That all people will never have to walk alone as we forge forward to build a better, kinder, and more inclusive world where practical action for climate justice trumps fine words and headlines.

Christopher Gleadle, CEO, The Paddy Ashdown Forum

Editors and Contributors

John, Lord Alderdice

John, Lord Alderdice has been a Liberal Democrat member of the House of Lords since 1996 and was the Convenor of the Liberal Democrats in the House of Lords during the Liberal/Conservative Coalition Government. As Leader of Northern Ireland's Alliance Party, he played a significant role in the negotiation of the 1998 Belfast/Good Friday Agreement and when the new Northern Ireland Assembly was elected, he became its first Speaker. In 2004 he retired from the Assembly on being appointed by the British and Irish Governments as one of the four members of the Independent Monitoring Commission (IMC), appointed to close down the operations of the paramilitary organizations. He was President of Liberal International from 2005 to 2009 and continues to serve on its Bureau as a Presidente d'Honneur. His professional background was in psychoanalytic psychiatry in Belfast where, as a Consultant Psychiatrist and Senior Lecturer at Queen's University, he established the Centre for Psychotherapy. He has devoted himself to understanding and addressing religious fundamentalism and long-standing violent political conflict in various parts of the world and is currently a Senior Research Fellow at Harris Manchester College, University of Oxford, and Director of the Centre for the Resolution of Intractable Conflict.

Dr Phil Bennion

Phillip Bennion is a former MEP for the Liberal Democrats UK and served variously on the Foreign Affairs, Employment and Transport Committees and the Human Rights subcommittee. He was spokesperson for the Renew Group on South Asia and an active member of the Parliament's Friends of Kashmir. He nominated Uyghur activist Ilham Tohti for the Sakharov Prize and led the successful campaign to win the award. Phillip is currently Vice Chair of the Liberal International (LI) Human Rights Committee which links liberal politicians worldwide in campaigns to address human rights violations. In this role he raises these issues at the UNHRC in Geneva. He is also a member of the LI Climate Justice Committee. He is a member of the Lib Dem delegation to ALDE Council. Phillip is a former Chair of both Liberal Democrat European Group (LDEG) and the British Group of Liberal International (LIBG). He is Chair and a long-standing member of the Liberal Democrats Federal International Relations Committee. In his day job Phillip is a working farmer in the Midlands with several business diversifications and was previously a researcher in agricultural science. He is an alumnus of Aberdeen, Newcastle and Birmingham universities.

Professor Kerry Brown

Kerry Brown is Professor of Chinese Studies and Director of the Lau China Institute at King's College, London. He is an Associate of the Asia Pacific Programme at Chatham House, London, an adjunct of the Australia New Zealand School of Government in Melbourne, and the co-editor of the Journal of Current Chinese Affairs, run from the German Institute for Global Affairs in Hamburg. He is President-Elect of the Kent Archaeological Society and an Affiliate of the Mongolia and Inner Asia Studies Unit at Cambridge University. From 2012 to 2015 he was Professor of Chinese Politics and Director of the China Studies Centre at the University of Sydney, Australia. Prior to this he worked at Chatham House from 2006 to 2012, as Senior Fellow and then Head of the Asia Programme. From 1998 to 2005 he worked at the British Foreign and Commonwealth Office, as First Secretary at the British Embassy in Beijing, and then as Head of the Indonesia, Philippine and East Timor Section. He lived in the Inner Mongolia region of China from 1994 to 1996. He has a Master of Arts from Cambridge University, a Post Graduate Diploma in Mandarin Chinese (Distinction) from Thames Valley University, London, and a Ph D in Chinese politics and language from Leeds University. Professor Brown directed the Europe China Research and Advice Network (ECRAN) giving policy advice to the European External Action Service between 2011 and 2014. He is the author of almost 20 books on modern Chinese politics, and has written for every major international news outlet, and been interviewed by every major news channel on issues relating to contemporary China.

Sir Vince Cable

Sir Vince Cable was Liberal Democrat MP for Twickenham from 1997 to 2015 and again 2017-19 when he retired. He was Leader of the Liberal Democrats from 2017-19. He served as Secretary of State for Business Innovation and Skills and President of the Board of Trade in the Coalition Government from 2010-15. Before becoming an MP he had a variety of economic roles in the public and private sector and became Chief Economist of Shell. Since retiring from parliament he is a regular columnist for the Independent; author of Money and Power (Atlantic Press); and is to publish a book The China Conundrum in mid-September following a booklet China: Engage. He is Visiting Professor at the LSE, Nottingham and St Mary's.

Lord Tim Clement Jones

Lord Clement-Jones was made CBE for political services in 1988 and life peer in 1998. He is the Liberal Democrat House of Lords spokesperson for Digital. He is former Chair of the House of Lords Select Committee on AI which sat 2017-18 and Co-Chairs the All-Party Parliamentary Group on AI. He is a founding member of the OECD Parliamentary Group on AI and consultant to Council of Europe's Ad-hoc Committee on AI. He is a former member of the House of Lords Select Committees on Communications and the Built Environment and current member of the Select Committee on Risk Assessment and Risk Planning. He is Vice-Chair of the All-Party Parliamentary Groups on Music; Future of Work; Digital Regulation and Responsibility; Ticket Abuse; Performers Alliance; and Writers. He is a Consultant of DLA Piper where previous positions included London Managing Partner (2011-16), Head of UK Government Affairs, Chair of China and Middle East Desks, International Business Relations Partner and Global Government Relations Co-Chair. He is Chair of Ombudsman Services, the not for profit, independent ombudsman service providing dispute resolution for communications, energy and parking industries. He is Chair of Council of Queen Mary University London and President of Ambitious About Autism.

Merlene Toh Emerson (Editorial Team)

Merlene Emerson has a Master of Laws from the University of Cambridge, has practised as a solicitor in the city of London and as partner of a law firm in Singapore involved in project finance and international joint ventures. She is a CEDR accredited mediator and trained in Restorative Justice. She co-founded Chinese Liberal Democrats in 2006 as a bridge between the party and the Chinese & SE Asian diaspora communities in the UK. She stood as a Liberal Democrat Parliamentary candidate in Hammersmith in 2010 and for the Greater London Assembly in 2012 and 2016. Merlene co-founded the Chinese Welfare Trust, a UK charity, in 2008 and was a Director on the boards of RHP, ISHA and Lien Viet Housing Associations. She was editor of the first CLD publication "UK-China Twinned Cities" (2013) and was Chair of the LibDems Race Equality Policy Working Group in 2019. She currently serves on the Finance Advisory Committee of ALDE (Alliance of Liberals and Democrats in Europe) and on the Education and Charities committee of the Worshipful Company of World Traders. Merlene was awarded an MBE in 2016 for political and public service.

Christopher Gleadle (Editorial Team)

Christopher Gleadle is a speaker, writer, and adviser on critical systems thinking and systemic intervention to advance the practical implementation of high performing net-zero strategies. He is CEO of The Paddy Ashdown Forum and Sustainable Viability Ltd. Christopher draws on a diverse professional background from systems software design, paper, automotive, fleet and logistics, and finance where he designed and implemented novel reporting and training solutions highlighting the effects of multiple interacting investment, organisational, environmental, and social ecosystems. How actions of each affects the many. How feedback loops inform better decision making to reduce impact between functions - The 5 Essential Habits To Sustainable Viability. How work on one SDG can impact on another - positively or negatively. Christopher has written and co-authored several books, published 35 articles and written over 150 private reports and policy papers on a diverse range of topics. Contributed to The Greenhouse Gas Protocol (Scopes 1,2,3) as well as keynote speaker and adviser to ASEIC working group on SMEs. Christopher collaborates with European and international think tanks on a diverse range of topics, has conducted deep research and implementation projects from China and Southeast Asia to Europe across many industries and is a member of the China Foreign Affairs working group.

Humphrey Hawksley

Humphrey Hawksley is an award-winning author and foreign correspondent whose assignments with the BBC have taken him to crises all over the world. He has had postings throughout Asia in Colombo, Delhi, Manila, Hong Kong and Beijing where he opened the first BBC television bureau. Humphrey has presented numerous BBC documentaries on Asia, democracy, human rights and global supply chains. His latest non-fiction book is Asian Waters: The Struggle Over the Indo-Pacific and the Challenge to American Power. His is also the author of the Rake Ozenna espionage thriller series which originated when reporting from the US-Russian border during heightened tension. Humphrey has been guest lecturer at universities and think tanks such as the RAND Corporation, the Center for Strategic and International Studies and MENSA Cambridge. He moderates the monthly Democracy Forum debates on international issues and is a host on the weekly Goldster Book Club where he discusses books and interviews authors.

Professor Emil J. Kirchner

Emil Kirchner is Emeritus Professor as well as Jean Monnet Professor Jean Monnet Professor and Coordinator of the Jean Monnet Centre of Excellence at the University of Essex. He received his Ph-D from Case Western Reserve University. He is Chair of the Editorial Advisory Board of the Journal of European Integration, holder of the Order of Merit of the Federal Republic of Germany, a Fellow of the British Academy of Social Sciences, was awarded a Lifetime Achievement Award by the University Association of Contemporary Studies, and has held Fellowships at NATO and the European University Institute, Florence. He has been a visiting professor at universities in various European countries, the United States and China. His recent book publications are (co-author) The European Union and China, Macmillan and Red Globe Press, 2019; (co-editor) EU-Japan Security Cooperation, Routledge, 2018, and (co-editor) Security Relations between China and the European Union, Cambridge University Press, 2016, He has published articles in International Organization, Review of International Studies, West European Politics, Journal of Common Market Studies, European Security, European Foreign Affairs Review and Journal of European Public Policy.

Andrew K P Leung, SBS, FRSA

Andrew Leung is a prominent international and independent China Strategist. 38-year senior Hong Kong government service before and after 1997. China Futures Fellow, Massachusetts Berkshire Publishing Group; Brain Trust Member, IMD Lausanne Evian Group; Gerson Lehrman Group Council Member; Thomas Reuters Expert; Senior Analyst with Wikistrat; Member, Royal Society for Asian Affairs; Former Governing Council Member, King's College London; Former Advisory Board Member, China Policy Institute, Nottingham University; Think-tank Research Fellow, Beijing Normal University, Zhuhai Campus; Advisory Board Member, The e-Centre, European Centre for e-Commerce and Internet Law; Visiting Professor, London Metropolitan University Business School. US-sponsored International Visitor on month-long visit to brief Fortune 50 CEOs, including Steve Forbes, on China post-1989. In 2003, invited by Prince Andrew for private briefing leading to HRH's first visit to China as UK's Ambassador for Trade and Investment. Advised on cross-cultural management in Lenovo's take-over of IBM Computers. Invited as Editor-at-large by MEC International for consultancy on China's energies. Regular speaker on China at overseas conferences. Regular TV interviewee with many international TV channels. Graduate qualifications from University of London, postgraduate qualifications, Cambridge University, PMD, Harvard Business School. Included in UK's Who's Who since 2002. Awarded Silver Bauhinia Star (SBS) in July 2005 Hong Kong Honours List.

Professor Michael Mainelli, MStJ FCCA FCSI(Hon) FBCS, Executive Chairman, Z/Yen Group

Michael is a qualified accountant, securities professional, computer specialist and management consultant, educated at Harvard University and Trinity College Dublin. He gained his PhD at the London School of Economics where he was also a Visiting Professor. Originally a research scientist in aerospace (rocket science) and computing (architecture & cartography), after directing global mapping projects from Switzerland he became a senior partner with accountants BDO Binder Hamlyn, and a director of Ministry of Defence research. During a spell in merchant banking with Deutsche Morgan Grenfell, he co-founded Z/Yen, the City of London's leading think-tank, promoting societal advance through better finance and technology. Michael is Emeritus Professor & Life Fellow at Gresham College, Fellow of Goodenough College, Honorary Fellow of King's College London, Visiting Professor at UCL's Bartlett School, Past Master of the Worshipful Company of World Traders, Freeman of the Watermen & Lightermen, Honorary Liveryman of the Furniture Makers, Water Conservators, Marketers, Tax Advisers, & International Bankers, Honorary Freeman of the Educators, Alderman for Broad Street Ward and Sheriff of the City of London 2019-2021. His third book, written with Ian Harris, The Price Of Fish: A New Approach To Wicked Economics And Better Decisions, won the Independent Publisher Book Awards Finance, Investment & Economics Gold Prize.

Dr Juli Minoves

Dr. Juli Minoves-Triquell holds M.A., M. Phil. And Ph.D. Degrees in Political Science from Yale University and a Lic. Degree in Economics from the University of Fribourg (CH). He is a tenured Associate Professor and the Director of the International Institute (ISI) at the University of La Verne, California. He has been a Visiting Professor at Sciences Po Paris, CIDOB Barcelona and the National Taiwan University of Science and Technology. He was elected as the 13th President of Liberal International (2014-2018) and is currently LI President of Honour. He has served his country, Andorra, in numerous diplomatic and political positions among which Ambassador Permanent Representative to the United Nations and Foreign Minister. He has travelled extensively through the PRC and the ROC Taiwan, in his personal, professional and official capacities.

Dr Yeow Poon (Editorial Team)

Dr Yeow Poon is management consultant working primarily in the public and voluntary sectors. He has worked on a wide range of public administration reform, capacity building, management and leadership development projects in the United Kingdom, Vietnam, China, Lao PDR, Cambodia, Thailand, Myanmar, Bangladesh, South Africa and Greece. He has particular interest in cross-cultural governance, leadership, management and organisation development issues. Yeow was born in Malaysia, attended University in the UK and naturalised as a British citizen. He is the Chair of the Chinese Community Centre - Birmingham, President of England China Business Forum, Chair of Arts in the Yard, Chair of Chinese Liberal Democrats, a Trustee of Chinese Welfare Trust and a core member of Covid-19 Anti-Racism Group. He was The Business Desk Midlands Leadership Award Winner: Public and Third Sector Leader 2018.

Paul Reynolds (Editorial Team)

Paul E M Reynolds works as counsel to government ministers and international organisations globally, on economic, political and security reforms, with particular experience in countries-in-conflict, and those facing insurgencies. These include Iraq, Sierra Leone, Rwanda, Philippines, Sri Lanka, Haiti, and Kosovo. Paul is a former Professor in economic and governmental reform at the University of Westminster in London, and MA Course Director. In China, Paul has worked as an adviser to the Ministry of Finance, the Central Party School and other institutions, including in Hong Kong. Paul has also worked with government ministers in countries on China's periphery, including Mongolia, Kyrgyzstan, Pakistan, Afghanistan, Japan, Cambodia, Myanmar, Kazakhstan and the Russian Far East. Paul selectively supports opposition political parties around the world over pro-democracy reforms and human rights issues. Paul lives in London with his wife and two small children, and has previously lived in Algeria, Canada, France, USA, Japan, Ghana, Cambodia and Bulgaria.

Laurence Vandewalle

Laurence Vandewalle has been the political officer of the EU delegation in Beijing since 2016 and will be based in Hong Kong from September 2021. She was at the European Parliament as their Asian Analyst for the DG External Policies Department from 2013-2106 and was the political advisor and assistant to the Chair of the European Parliament delegation to China before that. A graduate with a bachelor's degree in Chinese Studies from KU Leuven and in International Politics from University of Scranton, Laurence also studied Chinese Language and Literature at Tianjin University and is fluent in 3 languages: Chinese, Dutch, and English.

Chapter 1

China's Governance Structure and System
Professor Kerry Brown

The People's Republic of China (PRC) is, in the eighth decade of its existence, a constitutional republic where one party – the Communist Party of China – enjoys a monopoly on power. This means that while the state constitution, the current version of which was passed in 1982 and which has been revised several times since, sets out the formal structures of governance of the country, in many ways it is simply an administrative document. There is another constitution – that of the Communist Party itself – which indicates where the real political power lies. This division between political and administrative power is a shadowy and complex one. It lies at the heart of how the PRC runs today. There is a Premier, a state council, and a National People's Congress, and all of these administrative structures are reflected down to the most basic unit of administration in the country – the township level. But parallel to these are the Party structures. How these two are interlinked and relate to each other is sometimes easy to see; at other times it is almost invisible. The only thing we can be certain of is that the Party is always present. This means that in some ways the PRC and the Communist Party operate as overlapping but distinct entities – with the Party monopolising what can broadly be described as the political realm, and the country existing as a physical, administrative entity.

How China's Administration Works
The Party, with its 90 million members as of 2021, may seem to be all powerful and ubiquitous. One of the many paradoxes of China however is that the actual formal state machinery is relatively light. China has around 8 million people formally labelled 'civil servants' (gongwuyuan) at the national and provincial levels. In addition to this, there are almost 60 million working for state enterprises – the vast state-owned companies in key sectors like aviation and energy. According to the World Bank, the total of all Chinese public sector employment, including those involved in education, healthcare and other administrative areas, together come to about 46 million.

From an overall employment figure of 770 million, this figure constitutes 13 per cent who can be defined as public sector or state enterprise workers. In view of the fact that in the United States, 16 per cent are employed directly by the local and central state, or a staggering 26 per cent in France, the highly unexpected conclusion is that for a country of its size and complexity, China has too few state workers, not too many.

Civil Servants work within either a central or local network of ministries and bureaus. These are, according to the state constitution, all answerable to the National People's Congress (NPC). This is the country's parliament. It is a parliament like no other. With over 3000 members, drawn from the 31 provinces, autonomous regions (places like Tibet and Xinjiang), and special administrative regions (Hong Kong and Macau), the NPC meets once a year, usually from the 1st March (delayed till May for the pandemic in 2021 (it commenced on May 22 in 2020, but is still happening on March 5 in 2021)). For two weeks it considers budgets and laws. On paper at least it is seen as the highest organ of state power. In reality, it is regarded as a rubber stamp entity, which never opposes proposals, even if sometimes delegates can mark their opposition by voting against motions. A rare occasion in which this proved to be significant was during the opposition to the massive Three Gorges Dam project in the 1990s. Even then, only a third of the 3000 revolted. The dam still went ahead.

The NPC does have a secretariat, a far smaller grouping of 150 members, who continue to work through the year. The annual full NPC mainly listens to the work report of the Head of Government, the Premier (currently Li Keqiang) and then passes the national budget. At provincial and prefectural level too, there are congresses. This whole network operates as a consultative one – there to consider and reflect and give benign feedback. China is not an oppositional, confrontational system. That means public debate on contentious issues almost never happens. Under Xi Jinping since 2012 it has seemingly been wholly eradicated. Instead, the argument by Chinese officials goes, difficult issues are harmoniously dealt with out of public sight, and all that a body like the NPC does is announce the consensus of this.

Government reform in the 2000s did allow more consultation for laws, another responsibility of the NPC, which has to pass these. Bankruptcy and employment laws were passed after large amounts of consultation. It is true that since 2013, there has been a sustained effort to improve the quality of laws, and their implementation, and to make sure that from the start laws are well framed and seen as reliable. In the commercial area, there have been improvements – on the whole, judgements given are clearer and cleaner and more easily implemented because of greater clarity at their origin. Even so, in the areas of criminal and civil law, as things gravitate to more political and contentious issues, the situation changes. The PRC today is still a place where it is very easy to end up in jail for holding unwelcome thoughts and attitudes about political matters.

The NPC meets annually at the same time as another body, which has also existed since the founding of the PRC in 1949 at the Chinese People's Political Consultative Conference (CPPCC). This is also 3000 strong, and is also found at provincial level. It's main difference is that it is an appointed body (in theory, NPC members are elected) and consists of public figures like academics, business people, and prominent individuals. It is mean to embrace the 'Eight Patriotic Parties', all founded before 1949, and all part of the United Front with the Communist Party. The CPPCC as its title says, is purely consultative. The annual convention in the Great Hall of the People at national level beside Tiananmen Square in Beijing is usually one of high theatre, with members of the country's 55 ethnic minorities often paraded in their national dress. This implies that the whole event has limited governance value but strong propaganda utility.

This does not mean that the Chinese government is not sensitive to public opinion and has no ways of actively monitoring it. That so many Chinese are active online now (the PRC is amongst the best covered in terms of smart phones and internet in the world now) means that ostensibly 'private' companies like Alibaba and TenCent are able to harvest vast amounts of data on people, much of which is available to the government if they wish. The government themselves have also been canvassing views on specific issues, either overtly through focus groups, or covertly through keeping a sharp eye on trends that they can see online. This suits the paternalistic nature of the Chinese government – that it is like a watchful parent, making sure it knows how people feel and can say it is taking care of them. While it is known that this process happens, little is really understood about how it operates in practice. One area it does seem to work in is pre-emptively spotting signs of discontent about land rights issues, etc, and emerging protests and then either having officials intervene to try to address the problems, or more aggressively closing issues and activists down by detaining them and stopping their public communication.

The State Council

China is run by the State Council in terms of day to day affairs. The head of this is the Premier. The State Council currently consists of 24 national ministries, and then the ministerial level People's Bank of China and National Audit Office. Under these are a number of organisations and institutions – Xinhua, for instance, the state news agency. In the past, it had at times over 50 ministries. By a process of slimming down and reform, many of these were amalgamated. A Ministry of Transport, for instance, was formed from combining the Ministry of Road, Air and Water Transport and the Ministry for Railways in 2008. These Ministries undertake the same regulatory and administrative functions as similar bodies in, for instance, the UK or Australia. They are headed by a Minister and then Vice Ministers. Most of the time, these are Party members, though on occasion non-Party members have been appointed. The ministries also ebb and flow in terms of their power. The most influential are probably the Ministry of Finance because of its power over disbursement of central funds raised from taxation (fiscally, despite reforms in recent years, China is still a highly centralised country), and an entity called the National Development and Reform Commission (NDRC). This latter is the successor of the state planning agencies that existed from the time of high socialism under Mao from 1949 to 1976. While China has undergone a long process of marketisation and easing up since the Deng Xiaoping reforms of the late 1970s and 1980s, Five Year Programmes are still issued (the 14th of which came into force in 2021). These spell out broad macroeconomic goals – until recently things like GDP growth targets for instance. The NDRC remains in charge of this kind of more lose, but still crucial planning. It has a broad, wide ranging function, and is crucial for other ministries, and for provinces, to keep on side if they want to progress an important plan. The NDRC is in some senses an arbitrator, taking the different objectives of different areas of government and trying to putting them into a holistic plan. The Minister for the NDRC is therefore considered a key government figure.

The State Council operates like a cabinet. It has a secretariat, also, and issues plentiful information. It is also reflected in lower levels of government because there is a bureau and department structure for provinces and entities beneath them that also carve up administration into the same areas as the national body.

Provinces

In some senses, the PRC is a highly centralised country. The main tax raising powers belong to the central state. So too does the power of appointment over the key local party and state officials. One of the informal, and sometimes broken, rules of modern China is that the most important political leaders in provinces are usually outsiders. China is a highly networked society. This is a source of strength, but also weakness. Often strong and entrenched local networks created powerful vested interests and corrupt behaviour. Having someone outside this come in and be the chief power player is one way of addressing this problem.

Chinese dynastic history is characterised by many examples of the tussle between the central government at any particular given time and local ones. The central bureaucracy was powerful, but officials were not numerous. At times, local provinces were more dominant. At others, the centre, whether it was in Beijing, Nanjing, or elsewhere, was. It has been rare for there to be a happy balance. The PRC has been largely one where the central authorities are the most influential. This was partly to address the systemic weaknesses of the Republican era before when the country was subject to chaotic clashes by different provincial power holders. Xi's China is no exception, even though there have been moves since 2015 to move more fiscal power to lower forms of government.

The PRC has one of the most complex systems in terms of divisions of government. There is the central power, and then four under it – provincial, prefectural, county and then town. Nor do these cover everything. Beneath the 40,000 plus separate towns are more than a hundred thousand 'villages'. All of these levels are characterised by parallel structures of administrative committees, doing work like the State Council in Beijing, and then Party Committees. The latter are where key political decisions are made or implemented. These have been in place since the Communist victory in 1949 and illustrate the ways in which the Party was able to effectively dominate the organised political life of the country and ensure that it was the one national organisation that had such extensive reach.

Provinces are often, in geographical and economic size, as large as sovereign countries. Sichuan has over 100 million people. The economy of Guangzhou is more than that of most of the countries in the rest of the world. Each province has particularities. Zhejiang near Shanghai is a Hi-tech leader. Others like Heilongjiang in the Northeast have been heavy manufacturing centres, with strong state-owned enterprise traditions. Fujian is an export hub. Shanghai is dominated by services. Provincial leaders are given some latitude to craft policies appropriate for their specific needs. As long as these do not contradict the political imperatives from the Centre, these are tolerated. Those that prove successful may even be adopted more widely. This was often the way that the Reform and Opening Up process progressed, with initiatives like Town and Village Enterprises created in some areas, and then, because of their success, rolled out to others. Local leaders even on provincial level however, has restraints on how they raise money. In recent years, as Beijing has become stricter on enforcing fiscal policies on them, they have taken to selling land. With this drying up, they now need to look for other sources of revenue.

Village governance in China is still the one area that, despite being out of the formal constitutional structure, has seen the most experimentation in the last four decades. The general breakdown of orderliness into something approaching anarchy in the Cultural Revolution from 1966 in rural China led to the introduction of voting for village leadership positions in the late 1980s. This served to restore at least some of the trust in the system which had been eroded before then. There was never a question of there being a choice of parties in this process. The main liberty was that party and non-party members stood, with the latter sometimes winning. In some areas, the Party arranged that party committees, which ran party affairs, were simultaneously the governance council too – the only thing was that when they governed they had one name, and when they did party affairs they had another! In 1998 a law made elections every three years mandatory across the country. Some described this as the greatest single effort to gather in votes undertaken by any country. But few recognised it as properly democratic. The most that could be accorded to it was that it was a step towards allowing some level of choice about who ran affairs in certain places, even if their higher up managers were always Party people. In some places, figures who were critical of the Party were elected and could take up office. But they had only very local, not even regional or national, reach.

Under Hu Jintao from 2002 to 2012 there were some attempts to have similar style elections at township level. There were even discussions of having inner Party elections for official positions in places like Shenzhen, close to Hong Kong and one of the most advanced and wealthiest areas of the country. By the Xi era, however, even this modest proposal was stymied. For Xi there were other priorities. Elections are due to be held in 2021. There is increasingly talk of only Party members being able to stand. The most active of township elected officials were largely removed from their positions in the previous decade. In this sense, democracy in China has not advanced in the period after 2012. In many ways, it has been reversing.

4

Accountability

A very obvious question about such a monolithic system is how there can be proper accountability when, in the end, only one entity has true power? In the Hu era, there was the notion of 'intra party democracy', where internal elections and voting meant the Party carried at least some diversity and competition over ideas within itself. It is true that the Communist Party sometimes seems of such vastness that it contains clear factions that believe in different things and compete with each other much as separate political parties vie against each other for influence in western systems. Once more, however, under Xi this notion of 'intra party democracy' was shown to be a chimera. In commercial and business issues, as stated above, there was, from a major Plenum in 2013 focussed on rule of law, rather than rule by law, a move to strengthen the credibility and decision-making quality of courts. But in other areas, discipline and uniformity prevailed.

Under Xi, the main means of enforcing decent behaviour and ensuring that officials live up to their stated ethical standards has been through a series of anti-corruption campaigns. These have been almost continuous since the first in mid-2013. While they have varied in intensity, their objective has been the same: to instil a level of obedience by officials within the Party, making them aware that their prime function is to govern and to obey the party, rather than make money and set up their own self-serving networks.

The Communist Party, like the Old Testament God, is a jealous one! It has demanded absolute fidelity under Xi. The causes for this can be found in the previous decade, as rampant growth from the country's entry to the World Trade Organisation (WTO) in 2001 saw GDP quadruple. Officials, never that well paid, became even more visibly poorer while those who 'dive into the sea', as the expression was in Chinese for those who went into business, sometimes became rich. Millionaires, and then billionaires, proliferated. In real estate, in particular, money seemed to grow from the country's ground. Even the most well-behaved and convinced officials and leaders found this constant presence of temptation hard to resist. People who, on paper at least, earned no more than a few hundred dollars a year, were able to purchase luxury brand goods, send their children abroad to elite universities in the US or Europe, or give largesse to extensive family and personal networks.

The result of this was widespread cynicism by the public on the role of officials, and the view that government was merely a huge business, often run for itself rather than for people. Figures like the then Premier Wen Jiabao warned that this one issue could bring the whole edifice down. It had, after all, been one of the chief and most invasive cancers that had caused the Nationalists under Chiang Kai-shek to flee to Taiwan and lose control of the Mainland in 1949. PRC leaders are deeply aware of history. They were not minded to repeat this mistake. From the moment Xi Jinping emerged as the most senior Party leader in 2012 and the head of state in 2013, he made combatting corruption a core priority. Accountability after a fashion has therefore come through these campaigns, ones which while they have not taken in any more than a fraction of those who were guilty of malfeasance and venality, have created enough sense of fear and apprehension to rein other officials in. The anti-corruption campaign has been more effective in the ways in which it has been used as a publicity exercise, gaining the enthusiastic support of the population by showing that once untouchable figures could be taken in, if they went too far, and also within the Party in creating a more prudent and service orientated culture. Websites run by the feared Central Commission for Discipline and Inspection (CCDI), the Party-run graft-buster with huge powers, allow members of the public to report behaviour they find egregious or problematic. This has sustained an atmosphere of fear and apprehension, fortified by a number of subsidiary campaigns which have targeted state-owned enterprises, army personnel, and university leaders.

The anti-corruption campaigns and the ethos derived from them have been designed to allay worries about whether the Party has the discipline to hold itself to account, and expose its governing officials to some kind of restraint and control. One can be sceptical over whether this is really anything more than an elaborate trick. It is still, next to impossible, for a member of the public in China to hold high officials to account. One of the few recourses to justice in the last decades has been the petition system, where citizens are allowed to take their grievances to higher levels of government. But data for successful cases show that less than one per cent of the many million pursued each year actually get actioned. Those who do petition often find themselves treated harshly and accused of being troublemakers. There have been some restraints on the press lifted to allow them to carry stories about official corruption, but these too have proved risky. The Coronavirus pandemic in 2020 saw many accusations of local attempts at a cover up and mismanagement in Wuhan, the city the issue had first manifested itself in. Journalists who had been involved in these stories were dealt with often harshly. China remains a place where those who do wish to hold government figures to account pay a harsh price.

Being a Good Chinese Official: Meritocracy or Patronage?

Because it is a relatively small cohort of people in proportion to the population (see above) becoming an official at any level in China is not easy. There has been evidence in the past of official posts being 'sold' for vast sums of money. Having them is seen as being amongst the most secure jobs, and, in the era where corruption was more open, an easy way to have wide networks to be able to monetarise. Despite this, in the Reform era since 1978 there have been persistent efforts to create a new kind of official. In the Cultural Revolution it was better to be red than to be expert (in a curious precursor of the anti-expert ethos of Britain and America today). But in Deng's China, officials were selected carefully, their technical ability valued, with many of them funded to either travel abroad to study, or to attend one of the many Party schools spread across the country – and, before it was amalgamated with these, the Schools of Governance and Administration.

Contemporary officials in some ways need to balance technical ability alongside the capacity to get on with their superiors and build an enabling network that will help their promotion prospects. This means that the world of officialdom in China is surprisingly homogeneous – mostly male dominated, mostly Han ethnicity, and mostly with a similar outlook because of the large efforts that go into training and streamlining people. On some issues, creative thinking is permissible. Increasingly under Xi, the threat of the wide-ranging anti-corruption campaign means that people often keep their more adventurous ideas about political reform to themselves.

Officials are judged on their ability to deliver economic growth, and their observance of sustainability goals. They are also marked against a score sheet that sees how they deal with dissent, instability and security. Those that are able to keep the wraps on any emerging protest movement that threatens to get out of control (the 2011 Wukan township incident is one of the most studied in recent years) get good appraisals. Those that lost control are almost certainly to either see demotion, or worst. Nor does it seem to matter much what methods they use to enforce this control. Hard or soft, it does not matter as long as order is restored.

In Xi's China officials have never been better educated or better trained. Nor have they been better networked. That means that the current system is a meritocratic one, but also one in which there seems to be a strong role for patronage. China is a country with a relatively small absolute elite. There are about 3000 officials with vice-ministerial status, giving them real powers over decision making, appointment, access to classified material and control over budgets. Having links with any of these figures is helpful. As in any system, high powered figures are often in the business of talent spotting. Xi Jinping himself is a good example, accruing people he regarded as capable and sympathetic to his aims during his long spell as a provincial leader in Fujian and then Zhejiang. Figures like Ding Xuexiang, the current Director of the Political Office of the Communist Party, who served before as Xi's personal secretary in Shanghai, is a good example. In essence, to be expert in China is not a bad thing; but to really excel you need excellence and good networking skills.

Xi Jinping Thought

Since the time of Mao Zedong, every major leader has wanted to leave their ideological imprint on society. Ideology provides the broad framework within which government operates and society develops. Without the ideological changes in the late 1970s and early 1980s which allowed sinified Marxism to embrace elements of the free market and capitalism, it is hard to see how the whole reform process could have happened. Ideological change is the oil that greases the whole vast governance machinery of the country. That is true even today, with the inscription of Xi Jinping Thought into the Party Constitution in October 2017. This was added alongside Mao Zedong Thought, Deng Xiaoping Theory, the Three Represents of Jiang Zemin, and the Scientific Outlook on Development of the Hu Jintao era. The important point was that only Mao and Xi were accorded the privilege of having their ideas labelled `Thought' – a far broader and more ambitious term than any of the others.

In essence, Xi's thought simply reasserts the absolute primacy of the Party and makes it clear that the prime objective of the current system is to make one party rule sustainable. This addresses the fears that the Chinese will go the same way as the USSR, which collapsed in 1991. The means by which this will be achieved were outlined in the Four Comprehensives, issued in 2014. These were the highest level political goals that that party would focus its efforts on in order to achieve its survival:

1. Comprehensively build a <u>moderately prosperous society</u>
2. Comprehensively deepen <u>reform</u>
3. Comprehensively govern the nation <u>according to law</u>
4. Comprehensively strictly govern the <u>Party</u>.

The first refers to the importance of the Party to achieve tangible outcomes. Since the Maoist era, it had shifted to allowing wealth creation, entrepreneurialism and raising living standards for people as the main means by which to gain public support. Communism as an ideology alone no longer worked; the incentive was to show that it could result in a better life. With double digit growth for much of the 1980s up to 2012, this objective has largely been achieved.

Deepening reform, the second, is an acknowledgement that the marketisation and embracing of foreign ideas and capital in the economics realm would continue; there would be no slipping back to a wholly state planned economic model, nor an adoption of more leftist ideas. 'Reform' is a hugely important term in contemporary Chinese political language, and largely refers to the need to be continuously improving, and pushing the country towards modernisation. The third, the reference to law, has already been discussed. China is not about to allow courts and lawyers to challenge the legitimacy of the party state. But it does see value in having more predictability and orderliness in commercial affairs which matter to the huge emerging middle class. Property rights, control of official malfeasance, and strengthening of contract and employment law, and their implementation, have all therefore been priorities. Finally, there is the goal of controlling the Party itself and making sure that it does not behave badly. This is the hardest of all. The anti-corruption struggle has been the key means to enforce this. That has had the mixed results discussed above.

Despite the term 'thought' implying something systemic and articulated, in many ways Xi's ideology is more about an attitude – an attitude of faith and obedience to the Party State, to their benevolence and good intentions, and to them being the only entity that is able to deliver the 'dream' (as Xi has called it since 2013) of a 'strong, powerful country.' In many ways, therefore, Xi Jinping Thought is nationalistic, but also globalist. It supplies the broad framework within which the whole country operates.

The Future
Is this kind of model of governance likely to last? Many have predicted the imminent collapse of the Party system. There have been moments, particularly in 1989, when its fate looked perilous. But in 2021, it has never seemed more secure. There may be deep fissures and cracks that can't be observed in the outside world. The Party state in China, after all, is not keen on transparency. But one could argue that in administrative terms, its dominance, as described in this essay, would be next to impossible to replace without vast turbulence. For those that keenly preach the need for China to change, few can spell out the costs of that change simply as a process where it transits from one order to another. Even if this went smoothly, it would carry some costs. At the moment, the system seems to broadly deliver to a wide enough group of people they want to get their compliance. Beyond this, its nationalistic messaging gets more fervent and probably far wider support.

The removal of time limits to the position of country presidency in 2018 was regarded as a signal that Xi intended to be leader perpetually. It is true that he has presided over a huge centralisation of power, and that the country has become more autocratic since his ascent in 2012. Nor are there signs of any very likely successors, even though in the past there have usually been at least a few clues before a major congress – this one the 20th in 2022. This lack of a successor might mean Xi can rule unimpeded. But it also points to a vulnerability that has been present since 1949 – a system too dependent on one person and susceptible to turbulence and huge change in the transition between leadership generations. That in essence was Deng Xiaoping's great challenge.

It may be that the goal of simply creating a powerful strong wealthy country suffices, and that once this is well achieved, by around 2023 or 2024, then the Xi leadership can look more to the future. Xi himself will be in his seventies then (he was born in 1953) either way, with or without him, the current system in the PRC looks to be deeply entrenched. Those that seek signs of imminent collapse or deep and dramatic reform will have to continue to wait. In 2021, with its eyes sets on celebrating the hundredth anniversary of the PRC in 2049, it doesn't look like this will be happening any time soon.

Chapter 2

What Now?

Dr Yeow Poon

The rise of China has become an enigma for us in the West. China has cherry picked Western political and economic ideologies, added in Chinese characteristics, and in the 40 years since opening its economy became the second largest economy in the world by nominal GDP and the largest by purchasing power parity. It has done so without becoming an open liberal democracy. It has no universal suffrage and no competing multi-parties.

How should liberal Western powers respond to the rise of China? Constructive engagement or a rival to be challenged and constrained? As China develops into a superpower, China is being perceived as a geo-political economic rival challenging the international order (or Western order as perceived by some). The US pivot to East Asia morphed into a trade war, a tech war and now seemingly cold war 2.0.

The narrative in the Western media has also become increasingly hostile towards a more confident and nationalistic China and Sinophobia is on the rise. Accusations of human rights breaches in Hong Kong, Xinjiang and Tibet have led to sanctions against Chinese officials, followed by counter sanctions against Western individuals and entities that China blames for spreading lies. Meanwhile, military manoeuvres in the Taiwan Straits and in the South China Sea risk escalating into something far more serious.

From a western liberal democracy perspective that values individual liberty and freedom of speech as universal and absolute, China is an oppressive state, its citizens brainwashed into obedience or silenced through fear. However, "compared to Western societies, China places much less emphasis on individual rights and significantly more emphasis on the value of the individual in terms of his or her contribution to harmony in society".[1] Given such divergence in values that underpin the foundations of a society what can we do?

Perhaps the starting point is to acknowledge that neither East nor West is perfect and each view the other dimly through the lens of their own history, culture, values and ambitions.

From a Chinese Perspective
When China opened up, the prevailing belief was that as China develops it will naturally adopt liberal democratic values and systems. As this did not happen, various reasons have been put forward to explain the differences in values and outlooks between East and West. In the 'Geography of Thought'[2], the social psychologist Richard Nisbett ascribed the differences to how environmental conditions influenced the social construct of the ancient Greeks and ancient Chinese. According to Nisbett, the ancient Greeks who lived in river valleys separated by mountains developed a more individualistic and objective worldview. On the other hand, the ancient Chinese living in river plains required greater cooperation to share water resources and therefore placed greater emphasis on subjectivity, harmony and relationships.

In the 5th century BC, Confucius and subsequently his followers began to codify the relationships between families, within society and between rulers and subjects into an ethical, social, and political philosophy. The emphasis placed on virtue, wisdom, fidelity, benevolence, and meritocracy had profound effect on the relationship between ruler and subject to this day. The Chinese word for country 国家 means nation-family, unlike western countries where the state is generally perceived as an external intrusive force. The legitimacy of Western countries as nation states depends on the validity of democratic processes that enable citizens to exercise their rights. However, China as a 'family' state draws its legitimacy from "maintaining the unity, cohesion and integrity of Chinese civilisation ... (and) the state is seen as an intimate, as part of the family, indeed as the head of the family".[3]

The importance of the 'unity of the land' in China in contrast to the West can be seen in two popular movies. In the Hollywood movie, Braveheart (1995), William Wallace led a Scottish uprising against the English king. He was captured and, at the moment of his execution, he shouted one word 'freedom'. In the Chinese movie, Hero (2002), the protagonist led a plot to assassinate the Qin emperor, who was successfully conquering one state after another during the Warring States period. When he reached his target, he stopped and sacrificed himself believing that when the emperor succeeds in uniting the land the wars and killings would stop.

One theme that runs through China's history is the way foreign ideas and customs are assimilated with Chinese characteristics. China was conquered twice. Firstly, by the Mongols in the 13th century and secondly by the Manchus in the 17th century. Although each introduced their cultural traits, Confucianism and other Chinese traditions continued and were adopted by the conquerors to consolidate their rule.

When Buddhism was introduced to China in the 2nd century, it struggled to explain Buddhist concepts until it was fused with Daoism as it had similar notions, which eventually gave rise to Chan Buddhism (and then Zen Buddhism when it was transmitted to Japan). Unlike monotheistic religions like Islam and Christianity, Buddhism was more compatible with Chinese traditions and philosophy, and therefore more easily adopted and assimilated. As Buddhism expanded from the 7th to the 10th century, many schools promoted their own philosophies, blending with Confucian concepts such as ancestor veneration and filial piety.

Islam was introduced into China around the 7th century during the Tang dynasty. Although Islam did not spread extensively in China, they were sizeable populations along coastal cities of Guangzhou, Quanzhou and Hangzhou, as well as in the interior such as Chang'an, Kaifeng and Yangzhou. There were inter-marriages and often the men would adopt the names of their Chinese wives or the closest Chinese word that correspond to their Muslim name. Muslims were influential in both the Yuan and Ming courts. As the Ming Dynasty increasingly isolated itself, the Muslims began to assimilate by speaking Chinese and adopting Chinese culture. Chinese language Islamic texts became available in the 16th Century. Nanjing and Yunnan became hubs where Muslim scholars blended Islamic and Chinese literary, philosophical and theological traditions known as Han Kitab.[4] Mosques were built combining Arabic and Chinese architectural features.

Christianity also first entered China in the 7th century and was a major influence in the Mongol Empire, as several Mongol tribes were Nestorian Christian. In the 16th century, the Jesuits began its missions into China. As the Jesuits were learned men, they were accepted in court and even took up Imperial posts at the Bureau of Astronomy. However, there was little or no assimilation between Christianity and Chinese traditions. Attempts by the Jesuits to make Christianity easier for the Chinese to accept by incorporating ancestor worship were rejected by the Pope. During the Ming Dynasty, Christianity and some Buddhist sects were made illegal while Islam and Judaism were acceptable.

In China today, the Chinese Constitution guarantees citizens "freedom of religious belief" and "protects normal religious activities." However, "No one may make use of religion to engage in activities that disrupt public order, impair the health of citizens or interfere with the educational system of the state. Religious bodies and religious affairs are not subject to any foreign domination". The Chinese State recognises five major religions for practice in China - Buddhism, Taoism, Islam, Catholicism and Protestantism – and comes down hard on any religious group that do not conform. Some people view this as enforced sinicisation of religion. Certainly, there are parallels with the myriad ways China has responded to religious influences throughout its history.

The Chinese Constitution also states that women "shall enjoy equal rights with men in all spheres of life: political, economic, cultural, social and familial. The state shall protect the rights and interests of women, implement a system of equal pay for equal work, and train and select female officials." In practice, progress is uneven. The proportion of women, in national state legislature, has increased incrementally to 24.9% in 2020. However, Chinese women's participation in the economy is more pronounced, as two-thirds of the world's top women billionaires in 2021 reside in China. There is also some inconsistency, when five feminists who planned to distribute leaflets to highlight sexual harassment were arrested in 2015. Although several #MeToo cases were profiled on China media, there were also reports of posts being censored.

Homosexuality and lesbian relationships were common in ancient China. The earliest known law against homosexuality was during the Song dynasty in early 12th century, although it appeared the law was not enforced. Same sex relationships were practiced without the persecutions experienced in the West and Jesuit priests wrote of their distress on witnessing what they deemed were wanton acts. Another attempt was made in the 16th century to prohibit same sex relationship and again by the Qing in the 18th century. However, in the early 20th century, intolerance of homosexuals and lesbians gained traction, which some scholars attributed to attempts by the Republic of China to modernise and adopt Western value systems.

Today, China is home to the world's largest lesbian, gay, bisexual, and transgender population.[5] Legal persecution was repealed in 1997. Homosexuality was declassified as a mental disorder in 2001 but the regulations of the National Health and Family Planning Commission were not amended. Hence, some mental health professionals in China still consider homosexuality a disorder that can be treated by sexual orientation conversion efforts. Socially, because of the one-child policy (banned since 2015), there were strong pressures on LGBTQ individuals, as the single child, to marry and reproduce. A recent survey indicated that about 11% of heterosexual participants would not accept LGBTQ family members and 25% if their own children were involved. In the media, LGBTQ programmes are not prohibited but overt displays are usually not allowed. China does not recognise same sex marriage, however, in 2017, a legal guardianship system was enacted to provide some basic rights and protections for same sex couples. A 2019 poll on Weibo indicated that 85% (out of 5 million responses) were in favour of the guardianship system.

Over the course of its history, China has generally absorbed foreign influences, sometimes easily, other times at arm's length and on occasion with violent rejection. China today, since the founding of the Republic in 1912 and the People's Republic in 1949, has been modernising by absorbing and adapting Western ideologies, ideas and systems such as democracy, socialism, Marxism, communism, capitalism and markets, and imbuing them with Chinese characteristics. The resulting governance, economic and social systems we see today are still evolving. From the outside, it appears autocratic, perplexing and opaque, and we don't yet have an adequate name to describe it. The closest is the phrase 'directed improvisation', coined by Professor Yuenyuen Ang to explain how China had escaped the poverty trap.[6]

Sinophobia

Sinophobia began in the 19th century during the Opium Wars, when Chinese culture was perceived as backward and uncivilised, and continued into the 20th century. The Yellow Peril became popular as a racist metaphor. In Australia and New Zealand, in the mid-19th century, Chinese immigrants were described as dirty and disease ridden. There were protests against Asians and Chinese for taking away jobs and legislation was passed to exclude all further Chinese immigration. In Canada, Chinese migrants were subjected to special taxes, not allowed to vote and unable to apply for citizenship until 1947.

In the United States, Chinese migrants were deployed to build the transcontinental railroad, however, similar accusations of uncleanness and taking away jobs led to physical assaults and murders. The Naturalization Act of 1870 prevented Chinese migrants from naturalisation and the 1875 Page Act barred Chinese women from entering the US. In California, the State Constitution in 1879 prohibited state, local governments as well as businesses from employing Chinese people. In 1882 the Chinese Exclusion Act was passed to ban further Chinese immigration. A further act was passed requiring Chinese migrants to carry a resident permit and Chinese were not allowed to bear witness in court. These exclusion acts continued until 1943, when limited migration and naturalisation was allowed.

In The Yellow Peril: Dr Fu Manchu & the Rise of Chinaphobia (2014), historian Christopher Frayling noted[7]:

"In the early decades of the 20th century, Britain buzzed with Sinophobia. Respectable middle-class magazines, tabloids and comics, alike, spread stories of ruthless Chinese ambitions to destroy the West. The Chinese master-criminal (with his 'crafty yellow face twisted by a thin-lipped grin', dreaming of world domination) had become a staple of children's publications."

In 1911, "The Chinese in England: A Growing National Problem", an article distributed around the Home Office, warned of "a vast and convulsive Armageddon to determine who is to be the master of the world, the white or yellow man." After the First World War, cinemas, theatre, novels, and newspapers broadcast visions of the "Yellow Peril" machinating to corrupt white society. In March 1929, the Chinese chargé d'affaires complained that no fewer than five plays in the West End depicted Chinese people in objectionable forms. The popular press warned of the dangers of Chinese men marrying British women as a racial threat to white Britain, and that Triad gangsters kidnapped British women into white slavery.

During the first world war, 96,000 Chinese men served the British Army in the Chinese Labour Corp, and another 40,000 served the French, to provide support at the front and continued after the war with clearing up. Some 3000 Chinese settled in France after the war and there are Chinese cemeteries and memorials at Noyelles sur Mer in France, and in Poperinge and Ypres in Belgium. In the UK, the contribution made by these men was mostly forgotten until the recent World War 1 centenary, and amongst Britain's 40,000 war memorials[8] there is none dedicated to the Chinese Labour Corp.

In World War II, the British Navy had 20,000 Chinese merchant seamen. After the end of the war, in

1946, 2000 Chinese seamen were forcibly deported. Some were rounded up in the streets of Liverpool and others abandoned in foreign ports. About 300 were fathers and their families were not informed.[9] They left behind wives and mixed-race children who never saw their husbands or fathers again. More than 50 years later in 2006, a memorial plaque in remembrance for those Chinese seamen was erected on Liverpool's Pier Head.[10]

Chinese migration to the UK grew from the 1950s onwards, mostly working in the catering trade. During this period, the Chinese became the 'model community', perceived as hardworking, quiet and causing little trouble. There was always an undercurrent of racism, whether spoken in ignorance, jest or in hate, but generally individuals and communities have kept silent. There was however a public protest in London in 2001, when Chinese restaurants were accused by the media as starting the UK foot and mouth disease, which resulted in a spike of racism. Now we have Covid-19 where Chinese-looking people are being blamed and scapegoated.

A You-Gov poll conducted in June 2020 found that people from Chinese backgrounds in the UK are more exposed to racist comments than other minority ethnic groups. 76% of Chinese had a racial slur directed at them compared with 64% for all the Black, Asian and minority ethnic (BAME) respondents.[11] Besides being blamed for Covid-19, the general negativity concerning China arising from geo-political posturing has led to an increase in Sinophobia and hate crime, not just in the UK but also in Australia, Canada, the United States and in Europe.

A common refrain amongst Western politicians critical of China is that they differentiate between the Chinese people, the Chinese State and the Communist Party of China. However, the racists in the street do not. They cannot even distinguish between Chinese and other East and Southeast Asians. Historically, Sinophobia has been expressed as a danger to Western civilisation from the influence of East Asian countries, and as a threat to Western living standards from East Asian migrants. The parallels today can be seen in the clash of civilisations, accusations of genocide and human right abuses, blaming China for the Covid-19 pandemic and the fear of China dominating the world as economic power shifts eastwards. These narratives have a pernicious effect, as public opinions in most Western countries shifted from favourable to unfavourable in recent years concerning China.

So, what now?

When the cold war ended with the dissolution of the Soviet Union in 1991, Francis Fukuyama wrote the 'The End of History and the Last Man'.[12] Western liberal democracy has proven to be fundamentally better and triumphed as the pinnacle of human governance, social advancement and economic development. Globalisation and international rules of conduct, such as trade and human rights, together with agreed global sustainable development goals to control diseases, fight climate change and eradicate poverty, will surely promote the spread of liberal democracy.

As China opened up, Western corporates, abetted by Western governments, transferred their manufacturing base and China soon became the world's dirty factory. Then, as China grew richer, Chinese money was courted for inward investment. There were little concerns for the impact on local industries nor to the strategic interests in their own countries. The stock market, shareholders value and CEO pay rises were all that matters. True, China has infringed on copyrights especially in the early years, it protects its strategic economic sectors and some of its investments abroad are aggressive. Nevertheless, it always takes two to tango.

Yes, there are issues around China's periphery (Taiwan, Hong Kong, Tibet, Xinjiang and the South China Sea) that need dealing with but ... world domination? When the former Prime Minister of Malaysia, Dr Mohammad Mahathir, was asked whether he was afraid of China, he answered "We always say, we have had China as a neighbour for 2,000 years, we were never conquered by them. But the Europeans came in 1509, in two years, they conquered Malaysia."[13] Western fears of China's power appear to be based on their own colonial past, expecting China to do unto others what they have done to others before.

Yes, there are also issues around human rights. Serious human rights allegations have been levelled against China. However, when human rights become a moral crusade or is weaponised to support geo-political aims the resulting war of words turns into a sandstorm that obscures any real abuses that may be taking place. There are those that insist there is clear evidence of genocide, mass sterilisation and forced labour against the Uyghurs in Xinjiang province and there are those that assert the evidence provided is insufficient, dubious or wrong.

Lee Kuan Yew, the first Prime Minister of Singapore, stated: "The ultimate test of the value of a political system is whether it helps that society to establish conditions which improve the standard of living for the majority of its people".[14] From this perspective, democratic governance is understood not as having a system of multi-party elections but of how well the people's needs and interests are met. Perhaps, we should be more mindful of the Maslow hierarchy of needs, putting physical and social needs first before appealing to aspirational desires.

It is not just China; African societies too have their own concepts of human rights, which according to UNESCO were not taken into consideration when the Universal Declaration of Human Rights (UDHR) was made in 1948.[15] Asian or African traditions and philosophies were not considered. Although cultural differences were on the agenda, the Western perception of human rights prevailed, based on the political philosophy of liberalism and on the natural rights of the individual rather than on society and culture. If economic and social aspects of human rights were applied,[16] not just the emphasis on individual liberty, the UK would be found wanting, as over the last 20 years, our society has become more unequal with food banks, homelessness and rising poverty.

Is the adoption of Western liberal democracy the only way to enable peace and prosperity in nations and between nations? How do we, as expressed by Joe Biden, prove that our democracy works, when wealth inequality continues to increase in liberal democracies like the UK and USA? How can it be that after all these years, 'black lives matter' is still relevant as a rallying cry against racism? How can liberal democracy prove itself on the international stage when nations that champion the rule of international law set themselves above the law? What reforms may be needed to global institutions to ensure not just China but also all other member states to be responsible players? Should Western states with 12% of the world population begin to think about sharing power with the rest of the world?

There is an implicit assumption in western liberal democracies that given a free choice people will naturally choose a system of elected representative government. But what happens when people feel that democracy is not working for them, when liberal democracies failed to provide the basic needs of food and security? Tunisia, where the Arab Spring started in 2011 is a case in point. "We had tremendous progress on the freedom front and the political front despite all the crises," said Fadhel Kaboub, an associate professor of economics at Denison University in Ohio. "But what you have kept almost intact is the exact same economic development model that produced inequality, that produced the debt crisis, that produced the social economic exclusion, that the population rebelled against."[17]

So, what now? If past efforts at constructive engagement with China are deemed as not fruitful and cold war 2.0 risks real war, misery and chaos, what can we do?

Is it possible to integrate China's state capitalism with free market capitalism as advocated by the West? When do we compete and when should we collaborate? Although the Covid-19 pandemic has raised the importance of having supply security in critical areas, should we continue to develop co-dependent supply chains or will we divide into two competing spheres, not just in advanced technology but also in the way we support the development of poorer nations?

Keeping a rising China away from sharing power in the international order has resulted in unintended consequences. For example, the control of the World Bank, International Monetary Fund and Asian Development Bank by western powers has led to China establishing its own Asian Infrastructure Investment Bank. Preventing China from participating in the International Space Station has resulted in China creating a space station of its own. Stopping China from buying advanced silicon chips and photolithography tools is driving China to develop their own capacity.

Certainly, we need to engage with China, not just over trade, but more importantly how to integrate a superpower with distinct history, culture and values into the international order which up to now is primarily Western-centric. Is China a systemic challenge to transatlantic security as claimed by NATO? Is the threat and fear of China's pre-eminence as perceived by the West real? Are the trade and military strategies to contain China justified? What is the impact of sanctions and the tit for tat measures? Do they continue and escalate?

Bringing China into the international order is not about replacing the West with the East, nor about absorbing the East into the West. In the early years when China was developing, it was right that the West gave China a helping hand. However, now that China is a superpower, China has responsibilities to help build a more diverse, fair and representative international order. Freezing out China and decoupling the world into two warring blocs should not be the way forward. True, the engagement must be reciprocal but not in a transactional win or lose way. If each can learn from the other, transformational change can happen that enables the world (locally and globally) to better deal with the social and economic disruptions of pandemics, climate change and technology advancement.

During the Age of Enlightenment, China was a source of inspiration for debates on poverty, meritocracy, absolutism and political economy. Jesuit missionaries described China as a country more peaceful than Europe, which had just undergone decades of war. One major difference was the way the ruler governed. In Europe, the inherited nobility collected taxes, whereas in China an educated class was trained and appointed based on passing examinations. They were then "sent to China's various regions to collect taxes – and also to fight poverty and ensure the people had enough food. In Europe, fighting poverty was not a task for the nobility or king, but mainly for priests, nuns and the church."[18] The idea of a meritorious civil service was picked up and promoted by Voltaire.

Liberal Democracy
The rise of China does pose challenges to liberal democracy. But, it need not be a zero sum struggle, whereby if China triumphs, liberal democracy loses. Instead, we ought to enrich our understanding of liberal democracy by taking in non-Western perspectives. We have to acknowledge our own hubris. Why? Because the ideas, values and practice of liberal democracy as we know it today grew out of a specific set of conditions in Europe about 300 years ago during the Enlightenment. Nobody

would quibble over the fundamental principles of liberal democracy such as reason, liberty, equality, openness and rule of law. However, the ways these principles have been understood and applied are coloured by Western eyes, values, culture and religious beliefs.

We need to practise what we preach. The shenanigan over Huawei is a case in point. Huawei was not a threat to national security until the US decided it was based on the possibility that the Chinese government may demand access. Then Huawei was accused of violating sanctions against Iran (unilaterally imposed with extraterritorial enforcement powers that override international rules). When the decisions regarding Huawei are political rather than commercial, when the UK (for example) ignored the ruling of the International Court of Justice over the Chagos islands, our credibility is diminished and our insistence that others follow the rules are hypocritical.

Liberal democracy in the West is almost like the air we breathe. We are so used to it, take it so much for granted that we assume Western understanding and functioning of liberal democracy is exceptional and universal. We forget that there are other people from other parts of the world, from the developing South or from the East; each with their own history, cultures and philosophies, who see some things and value some things differently from the West.

The 21ˢᵗ Century no longer belongs only to the West. Not just because of the reawakening of China who succeeded in lifting itself out of poverty and becoming a superpower in a short period of time based on values and beliefs that appear alien to Western eyes. There are also India, Japan, Latin America and Africa, all jostling for their place on the world stage. Hence, for liberal democracy to go forward and accommodate a multi polar world it will need to adapt to new realities, accept other viewpoints and be willing to share power.

The late Lord Paddy Ashdown often described liberal democracy as Liberty, Fairness and Tolerance. It is imperative that all 3 words are understood and applied together. Perhaps the functioning of liberal democracy in recent years has over emphasised liberty and individual freedom; but not enough on fairness and tolerance. We need to work out again how liberal democracy can enable fairer and more equitable societies. We need to pay more attention to tolerance, even go beyond tolerating others to be open to discourse from other cultures, philosophies and value systems.

If we can better see ourselves through the eyes of others, perhaps we can transcend current understanding of liberal democracy to create new thinking, ideas and paradigms to solve the challenges of the 21ˢᵗ Century. We must learn, despite our differences, to develop a shared humanity that co-exists with each other and with our planet.

Chapter 3

The Chinese Economy – Why It Matters
Sir Vince Cable

Much of the current discussion of China in the West is focused on the things that the West doesn't like and in particular a system of governance which is alien and does not conform to Western ideas of 'liberal democracy'. As long as China was seen as poor, weak and marginal, these things didn't seem to matter much. Now that China is an economic superpower and a serious economic competitor in many fields, they do seem to matter. As President Clinton is supposed to have observed, 'it's the economy stupid'.

The China's economy matters above all to China itself. Progress in lifting hundreds of millions out of poverty is the defining achievement of the regime. Continued economic success underpins the legitimacy of the regime which has set rising living standards and full employment as the main metrics of its performance in office and prerequisites for political stability. Economic size and success also determine China's standing in the world: its 'hard' and 'soft' power and its ability to influence the rules of the international economic order.

China's economy matters enormously for the rest of the world too. Chinese demand represents, now, a sizeable share of global demand, driving commodity markets and the growth of other countries. Global economic recovery in the earlier part of the last decade was heavily indebted to China. The Chinese model of state capitalism represents uncomfortable competition for Western companies as did that of Korea and Japan, earlier, but the benefits to the world economy of Chinese manufacturing competition and integration into global supply chains have far outweighed the costs. There are also the externalities from China's growth in the form of greenhouse gases which makes Chinese contribution to global environmental agreements essential.

But there are basic questions about the Chinese economy which remain controversial:

1. How big is the Chinese economy? Can we trust the numbers and growth figures? Is China a genuine economic superpower or a new USSR?
2. How securely based is Chinese growth and development? Does it face a looming 'middle income trap' as some argue and a serious 'debt' problem?
3. How business friendly is Chinese capitalism? And specifically foreign business?
4. Is it possible to have sustained innovation in an authoritarian system?
5. Is Chinese economic success good for the world?
6. How can China be accommodated within global rules for trade and finance?

A brief reference to the history is necessary before seeking to answer these questions. The Chinese economy has seen remarkable economic growth over the last 40 years or so since the process of economic reform was initiated under Deng Xiao Ping. The China inherited by Mao's successors was a very poor country and the China inherited by the Communists even poorer. But neither were drawing on a blank sheet of paper. Despite the chaotic conditions of the Cultural Revolution under Mao and before that the devastating famine induced by the Great Leap Forward, there was development taking place and at the beginning of the reform era, China enjoyed significantly higher levels of life expectancy, literacy, access to sanitation and measures of industrial and agricultural development than countries like – say – India. And even in the pre-revolutionary period, when there was a long period of war and civil war, there was substantial modernisation with an estimated near doubling of output between 1885 and the revolution. Nevertheless, China's economy in the late 1970's accounted for only around 6.5% of the global total although China had 20% of the total population; by contrast China had around 30% of the world economy produced by 35% of the world population at the beginning of the 19th century.[1]

The Deng reforms had an immediate and spectacular effect. Growth doubled to 9 or 10% (albeit with a health warning about the numbers). The reforms involved the liberalisation of markets, the deregulation of prices and ownership – initially involving quasi-property rights for farmers – and the opening up of the economy to trade and investment. There was a deeper, political revolution in the form of decentralised decision making and the elevation of competence as a standard for party officials.[2] The first fruits of reform were the big increases in agricultural production, lifting farm incomes and lifting millions out of poverty and improvements in the quantity and variety of food. Agricultural productivity improvements freed up labour for the rapidly growing industries and exporting enterprises. The success of export-based activities can be seen from the fact that China accounted for 1% of world trade in 1978 and is now over 12%, by some way the world's largest.

For over a decade, however, there has been growing awareness that China's growth has been seriously unbalanced, storing up trouble for the future.[3] China has developed through extraordinary levels of saving and investment. The ratio of savings to GDP rose from 30% at the launching of reforms to 50% by the time of the global financial crisis, the largest in the world by some way. These savings have financed large-scale investment, mainly in infrastructure and industry. Whilst this investment has driven the economy forward and modernised the country it has become progressively less efficient and has created a legacy of debt in Chinese enterprises and bad loans for the banks and 'shadow banks'. Another effect of the large savings rate is that not all the savings could be absorbed domestically but were exported in the form of current account surpluses. This reached extreme levels – of around 9% of GDP- in 2007- at the time of the financial crisis but has since fallen sharply to around 3% of GDP. There is a recognition in China that future growth must be based more on consumption (public and private) than investment.

A key turning point was the global financial crisis after which China embarked upon a massive investment programme which sustained growth in China and lifted the world economy helping the global economy to recover. But the continued imbalance in the economy and the slow progress in improving the efficiency of state enterprise and public investment have slowed the trend growth to a (Chinese) estimated 6%. That in turn has been affected by the pandemic though China has been one of the first countries to recover, though the structural problems identified above will resurface. Despite these problems China has now grown to a point where it appears to match, in scale at least, the USA. China is now an economic superpower.

China as an Economic Superpower.
It might seem odd to be arguing about such basic facts as the size of China's economy since there is a vast amount of internationally recognised economic data and the Chinese economy is closely scrutinised by the IMF, the World Bank and China's wide array of overseas investors. But there is a wide range of estimates of GDP data and different interpretations of its meaning. At current exchange rates Chinese GDP is worth $15.7 trillion as against $21.4 trillion for the USA. (2020). But Chinese price levels are somewhat lower. If correction is made for the larger purchasing power of the Chinese cur-

rency than its official rate, then, according to the IMF, the Chinese economy is probably worth around $23.5 making it now larger than the USA. But in living standards it is still a middle income country with an average per capita income of around $16,500 (PPP) about a quarter of the USA; comparable to Thailand, Mexico or Serbia; and over twice the level of India.

There is more uncertainty about trend growth which was officially around 6% pa in the five years running up to the pandemic as against around 2.5% pa in the USA. But Chinese figures are calculated in a different way from in market economies and is based on expected figures according to the planning system. There are all kind of upward and downward biases resulting from the way officials respond to targets. On balance the numbers are probably overstated but not by much. China is not like Communist Romania or the GDR which produced phoney and basically meaningless estimates of performance. The more serious question is whether China is grinding to a halt because of mounting challenges.

Is China running out of steam?
There are China bulls and China bears: optimists and pessimists. The pessimists say that China is potentially caught in a 'middle income trap' beset by a series of problems. First, China's population is peaking thanks to the One (now Two) Child Family policy and the labour force is declining. In fact, China's labour market has been highly controlled through the 'hukou' system of managing rural migration to the cities and liberalisation of that system will alleviate labour supply issues.

Second, there are doubts about how well China can move from growth driven by state-inspired and inefficient investment to growth based on higher productivity and consumption rather than investment, which requires innovation, efficiently functioning markets. The pessimists say that innovation can't happen in a society where freedom of thought and speech is constrained. And efficient markets can't happen where the Communist party state machine over-rides the judgement of entrepreneurs and consumers.[4] The more optimistic view is that China is already demonstrating high levels of capacity for technological innovation as manifested in its tech companies and the sophistication of the Chinese internet platforms.

There is also plenty of evidence of China's progress in developing a competitive market economy. The World Bank survey of the Ease of Doing Business in 2019 has China improving rapidly in such areas as intellectual property protection, transparency of capital markets and access of foreign companies to financial markets. China ranks around 20th, way ahead of other emerging markets and comparable to France or Japan. It is certainly the case that Chinese billionaires, like Jack Ma, are having their wings clipped. This may be a genuine wish by the authorities to curb monopoly power and to ensure that financial innovation does not destabilise the system. But there is probably also a political motivation to ensure that the billionaire class do not become a competing centre of political power.

The critics argue that there is a basic flaw in the economic model. China needs to grow to achieve the rising living standards that are necessary for political stability. But the one reliable method of achieving growth is to promote investment which is heavily dependent on debt finance. China's commercial debt leverage is already high by international standards and will in due course lead to a debt 'crisis' either through a disorderly collapse of banks and 'shadow banks' or a period of Japanese-style stagnation as companies stop investing in order to shore up their balance sheets. As in Japan, a lot of finance has gone into property which, in the cities, has been developing speculative, inflationary bubbles.

The optimists point out that the Chinese bubble doesn't burst because it is under control: the corporate debt can be converted to government debt which is at healthy levels; corporate bond markets are beginning to work; the authorities are tightening up on lending and borrowing practices; and ultimately the Chinese state has such a degree of regulatory control that it can, in an emergency, intervene to prevent a Lehman–style collapse. So far the optimists have been right.[5]

So, China hasn't run out of steam yet. It led the world out of the pandemic recession and Western estimates are of around 8.5% growth following the slow-down to 2% in 2020. In the United States expectations are of around 6.5% growth in 2021 after a fall of 3.5% in 2020. These are short-term estimates but they demonstrate that faced with a unique and uniquely difficult shock, the Chinese system, with its harsh but effective lockdowns, provided it with a 'relatively' high resilience. How China progresses from here will depend in part on the dynamism of its private sector and on the country's capacity to innovate.

How Capitalist is Chinese State Capitalism?
The Chinese economy is described as 'socialist' but has a large private sector which, in theory, accounts for around 60% of GDP and 90% of employment. But there is a difference between the millions of family farms, SMEs and community enterprises many of which operate in a highly competitive, unregulated, 'Wild East' environment and larger companies which are subject to close political control and also operate in controlled credit and other markets.[6] The strong action taken to rein in Jack Ma, the founder of Ali Baba and Alipay, in 2021 was a strong reminder to other billionaires and other business leaders that they must not become an alternative power centre. Many 'private' companies are also offshoots of state enterprises; and, more generally, state enterprises are being required to operate on commercial lines and are subjected to market forces. One commentator suggests a 50:50 private/public split is realistic (in terms of GDP).[7]

Chinese leaders from Deng to Xi have made a distinction between political liberalisation which is anathema and economic liberalisation which is necessary and desirable. Even though President Xi has moved towards a more authoritarian political system, firmly under the control of the Communist Party, economic liberalisation has continued apace.[8] There are more bankruptcies allowed; there are more transparent capital markets; intellectual property is better protected; the financial sector has opened to foreign firms. But there remain in place strong exchange controls, restrictions on freedom of movement (the 'hukou' system) and some key prices are controlled. Nonetheless the World Bank judges China to be one of the better countries to do business in ahead of France, Japan and Italy and way ahead of other emerging market countries like India and Brazil (because of efficient infrastructure; speed of decision making; low and transparent taxation; relative open-ness).

Can China Innovate?
China's future economic progress and also its ability to compete with the other superpower will depend on its ability to innovate rather than, as in the past, simply use its vast supply of savings to invest at scale, but inefficiently. The China sceptics question whether the Chinese system will allow this to happen. They make two basic points. First, China has followed in the footsteps of Japan and Korea (and the United States in the 19th century) by acquiring and adapting foreign technology with a regime of weak intellectual property protection, pressure on investors to transfer technology or outright theft. As an emerging economy develops the emphasis shifts to the protection of IP and encouragement of innovation. China, like Japan and Korea before it, is seeking to make that transition. IP protection has been strengthened through intellectual property courts which are now prosecuting

more vigorously, including findings for foreign investors.

But sceptics doubt that China will be able to complete this transition since the authoritarian political system prevents the free exchange of ideas on which an innovative ecosystem depends. The Chinese 'firewall', which blocks access to politically unacceptable material on the Internet also has the effect of restricting access to scientific journals. The motivation of innovators is, arguably, blunted by controls on what they can say. And the collaborative projects with Western scientists are now being cut back in the hostile environment of 'the new cold war'. And there is a certain amount of detailed industry-level research which has exposed the failings of Chinese firms, especially bureaucratic state owned firms, to innovate in key areas like semi-conductors unless they have benefited from the know-how of the Chinese diaspora.[9]

The China optimists point out that China has already become a technology leader in some areas: 5G where Huawei is some way ahead of the field as reflected in its portfolio of patents; certain aspects of AI; fintech and, in particular, payments systems linked to ecommerce; drones; high-speed trains; some satellite applications. Furthermore China has both the resources and the political will to develop its technological capacity: the vast number of research scientists often with business and overseas research experience; a big venture capital sector, second only to the USA, able to finance promising start-ups and next-stage expansion; and a very large supply of raw material – data - for data-based innovation and without the privacy and commercial restrictions which apply to data collection and use in the West. Some see China's technological advance leading to conflict.

The Chinese authorities are well aware that technological competition is the new battleground. They will throw the resources of the state at the problem through subsidising R&D, government procurement and targeting new areas of priority like quantum computing. It remains to be seen whether this is ultimately more successful than the more open and commercial model of Silicon Valley.[10]

Is China's Economic Success Good for the World?

We should regard it as a positive for humanity that extreme poverty has virtually disappeared in China and hundreds of millions have been lifted out of poverty to middle income standards of living. But is it a positive for the rest of us?

China is now a big and rapidly growing market which provides a source of demand for commodity exporters (the leading consumer of iron, copper, aluminium, oil and gas, coal, soya and a key driver of the market for cotton, wheat, rice, seafood). It provides profitable business for many Western exporters and investors in China (the leading car companies including JLR; the leading pharmaceutical companies like Astra-Zeneca and GSK; energy companies like Shell and BP; the main consumer and luxury brands). After the financial crisis China was the main source of demand pulling the world economy out of recession and in the last decade China accounted for around a third of world growth.

China's emergence as the world's largest manufacturing exporter intensified competition and drove down prices of manufactured goods to the benefit of Western consumers and their economies overall. The pattern of trade has however changed considerably from the times when China imported raw materials and exported low cost consumer goods. Around half of China's trade is now 'intra-industry': part of complex global supply chains in sophisticated products like Apple computers and iPhones. Basic economics tells us that such trade is beneficial overall.

The idea that trade with China has negative impacts owes a lot to President Trump whose protectionist approach to trade, focusing on bilateral deficits, goes against basic economic logic but had considerable political appeal.[11] He did highlight also the impact on workers in import competing industries and there is academic evidence of the labour displacing effects of Chinese imports to the USA especially in some industries[12] though the same analysis suggests overall benefit to the US economy and that technological change was a bigger factor in the loss of jobs in those industries. Nonetheless, trade warfare has fuelled a wider sense of conflict.[13]

The current 'cold war' environment has caused both Western economies and China to think in terms of strategic vulnerability. For many years there was anxiety that the Chinese current account deficit was financed by the accumulation of US government bonds which, had they been sold massively and suddenly, would have driven down the dollar. But had the Chinese done so they would have devalued their own asset and understanding this they never sought to; the 'balance of financial terror' was maintained. More recently, anxiety has been expressed by Western dependence on supply chains involving key Chinese components; but, by the same token, the Chinese are also dependent on these interlocking trade networks themselves and have no incentive to disrupt them.

There are some specific areas of vulnerability – as with some rare earths – where China may have monopoly power over key supplies which it would be wise to hedge against. But, overall, there is currently a costly retreat into 'self-sufficiency' which is in no-one's interest.

China: Inside or Outside the Rules-Based System?
A key step in China's integration into the world economy has been its admission to the WTO, the World Bank and other multilateral organisations as well as its participation in regional trading groups and informal groups like the G20. As China becomes an even bigger player, its participation becomes even more important in the management of what are called international public goods[14]: shared environmental problems like climate change; nuclear non-proliferation; rules governing space and cyber-space; pandemic control. Central amongst these are the rules governing global economic governance: trade and investment; economic coordination and exchange rates; financial stability and regulation.

China presents two main challenges to the current arrangements. First, the rules and institutions were devised by Western countries, especially the USA, after the second World War and China now expects to play a bigger role commensurate with its importance. It has already demonstrated, by creating the AIIB – the Asian Infrastructure Investment Bank – that it is not willing to play a junior role in institutions dominated by others (in this case the US-dominated World Bank and the Japan dominated Asian Developed Bank).

Second, China has, it is alleged, often not been willing to follow the rules which it has signed up to. The World Trade Organisation is a case in point. Western businesses complain about 'unfair' competition from Chinese state enterprises which can enjoy subsidisation and preferential credit or other favours from the Chinese authorities, not available to firms in market economies. There are complaints too about attempts to coerce joint venture partners to hand over technological information and lack of protection for intellectual property rights. However these complaints are not unique to China; other emerging market economies like India or Brazil behave in a similar fashion. Japan and Korea also presented similar problems and, actually, China has a more open economy than they had or have. And when the USA disengages from the WTO and seeks to undermine it, as it did under Trump, it can hardly complain that China isn't fully compliant with its obligations.

It will be a challenge to assimilate China's state capitalism into a set of agreed multilateral rules and to make sure that they are observed.[15] But the alternative is anarchy and conflict. And the sense that conflict is inevitable is current proving a powerful factor making it more likely.[16] Getting China engaged in serious negotiations which lock it into world trade rules is a key step in heading off that conflict.

Chapter 4

China's Politicised Development Under President Xi

Laurence Vandewalle

Since 2012, when the General Secretary took up his new functions after the 18th Party Congress, China has undergone drastic changes. In 2021, the country is self-isolated and celebrates the 100th anniversary of the Party in a nationalist mood. The rebirth of the Chinese nation is to be complete by the anniversary of the country in 2049.

As soon as he rose to power, Xi Jinping had unveiled a robust programme for both the Party and the country. Some of the buzzwords used included the 'China Dream', 'rejuvenation' of the nation as well as poverty alleviation. Xi Jinping also unveiled a calendar with two Centennial goals, the first to be achieved by 2021 (to 'build a moderately prosperous society') and the second by 2049 (to 'build a modern socialist country that is prosperous, strong, democratic, culturally advanced and harmonious'). More recently, in autumn of 2020, the Party added two more Centennial goals: 'building a modern army military' by 2027 and 'building a modern socialist power' by 2035 respectively.[1] Though none of these concepts were new, their rise to prominence was an innovation. The vigour with which the Party apparatus implemented Xi's political agenda astonished many observers, as did the tone of the propaganda, closely reminiscent of Chairman Mao's days. The international dimension of Xi's tenure has surprised many countries and a number of them have gradually come to consider China as a systemic rival if not a threat.

Xi's reign has also been characterised by renewed Party control and a strong anti-corruption drive, amidst a decelerating economic growth and mounting nationalism. The Party's propaganda department has designed an image of Xi close to a 'big data Mao' who taps into Mao era vocabulary and methods, while relying on the newest technologies.

Since the outbreak of the Covid-19 pandemic in January 2020, the characteristics of the Xi Jinping style of governance have exacerbated: the Party seems to be fully united behind his persona and his goals while any internal tensions are less visible than previously. Since the country closed its borders on 28 March 2020, the Chinese people's exposure to the outside world has drastically decreased; the propaganda department has launched a political education campaign on the Party's version of history, culminating with the 100th anniversary of the foundation of the Party on 1 July 2021. Xi Jinping and his affiliates have grabbed most of the positions of power inside the Party, instilling a conservative atmosphere tainted with nationalism. For the moment there is little reason to believe that a policy shift could take place. At least not before the Party's 20th Congress in 2022, where Xi Jinping despite the practice of keeping two terms for the General Secretary instituted by Deng Xiaoping is widely expected to continue at the helm of the Party.

Sources of legitimacy

The leadership of the Party, in particular its 'ideology czar' Wang Huning, has long been obsessed with the fall of the USSR and of European Communist regimes after 1989, as well as the ensuing prominence of liberal democracies. It is probably true that nobody has studied the reasons behind the fall of the Soviet Union more than the leadership of the Communist Party of China (CPC). Similar to the Soviet Union, 1989 was a traumatic year for China, with massive pro-democracy demonstrations taking place on Tian An Men square, followed by a bloody crackdown by the Party's military, the PLA.

Thirteen years after the end of the Cultural Revolution and ten years after the beginning of the Reform and Opening Up Policy, the Party was faced with the need to rethink its social contract or lose power. The Party thus promised to the people that the country would be able to become wealthier, while cautioning that the leadership of the Party could not be put in question. Comprehensive propaganda and nationalist education campaigns followed, but all in a context of rapid economic growth.

Today, the Party claims that it 'serves the people', pointing out that it has drastically improved the quality of peoples' lives. A large part of the Party's legitimacy thus comes from the alleviation of poverty. Under Xi, the poverty alleviation campaign has been the most important policy objective of rural cadres. It was completed, as planned, in 2021. China sets the line for extreme rural poverty to a per capita income of less than 4 000 RMB, almost 11 RMB a day. This is quite similar to the World Bank's own definition, which establishes extreme poverty at 1.90 USD or 12.28 RMB a day. Beyond the numbers, reliable or not, it is obvious that since Deng Xiaoping launched the Reform and Opening up Policy, economic growth has penetrated even the most remote places of the country.

It is also obvious that a significant wealth gap exists, astonishing for a country that calls itself 'socialist'.[2] China's middle class remains rather modest in proportion to the size of the population while significant parts of the population lag behind and are likely to continue to do so due to an unequal education system and rudimentary social and medical insurance schemes. However, Premier Li Keqiang, to the surprise of many observers, did highlight this challenge during his address to the press that he gave at the end of the annual legislative assembly held in May 2020. An official ceremony announcing an end to rural poverty was held in February 2021. There the official media claimed that thanks to Xi's leadership nearly 100 million people had been lifted out of poverty. With the 100th anniversary celebrations of the Party in July 2021 and the completion of the first centennial objective, absolute poverty is now supposed to have been extinguished in China. The Party claims that this success was a result of a 'Chinese model', which has been declared 'superior' since the fourth plenum of the 19th Central Committee in 2019.

The Belt and Road: a domestic game changer that enables self-reliance
It is important to have a closer look at the Belt and Road Initiative (BRI), unveiled to the world in 2013. If European observers have largely focussed on its impact on Europe and the African continent, they have often underestimated its domestic impact.

Until recently, large segments of the rural population lived de facto outside of the monetarised economy. The main achievement of the tenure of Xi Jinping has been connecting almost all of the Chinese population through roads, high-speed trains, and the internet, in a very Marxist vision of society. In this, Xi has probably succeeded where all previous leaders of China had so far failed. One may, for example, remember the Great Western Development Strategy launched in 1999 under then General Secretary Jiang Zemin. Today, it is a reality that the most remote places in the most remote regions of China are equipped with roads and with a 4G connection. According to official Chinese sources, more than 100 billion USD has been invested in transportation and financing in the past five years. If the intense road construction has disfigured landscapes, it has also meant local populations have been gradually integrated into the economy and contribute to the national GDP. Nowadays, those living in rural areas can sell their products to city-dwellers, and flurries of WeChat groups permit farmers to sell their products to urban inhabitants. Likewise, rural populations are able to purchase goods online. The popularisation of mobile payments has been rapid – less than twenty years after Alipay first arrived on the scene, the overwhelming majority of Chinese people use mobile payment methods.

The hilly province of Guizhou, one of the poorest in China, offers an interesting case study. It was the first province able to connect all of its counties through highways. This achievement was realised under the leadership of Sun Zhigang, the governor and the later Party Secretary of Guizhou.[3] The importance of the poverty alleviation drive is evidenced by the fact that high-level cadres are often 'tested' in Guizhou before embarking on a nation-wide career (such as current NPC chair Li Zhanshu).

With the Western provinces of China better connected, the country can be less reliable on external trade. The resurgence of the concept of 'self-reliance' is another remarkable political feature of recent Chinese governance. This wording, which Mao coined during the 'Anti-Japanese War', was first used by Xi Jinping on the occasion of his inspection tour to the province of Heilongjiang in September 2018, as the relations with the United States were deteriorating. Since then, Xi has used this loaded term mostly in relation with the importance of boosting national innovation.[4]

A little more than a year later, in May 2020, the leadership came up with the concept of dual circulation. It builds upon the idea of self-reliance – a strategy of internal economic circulation next to a smaller external one. The two circles complement each other and allow China to avoid overreliance on exports. China intends to tap into its domestic forces to unlock the reservoir for growth, mostly made up of the poorer populations inside the country. The strategies of BRI, self-reliance and dual circulation also came as responses to the increasingly complex relationships between Western countries and China.

Political context
The decreasing dependence on the external world has enabled the Party to promote its system vocally, to speak of a 'China model' and to voice more nationalism. Xi Jinping and his followers have reintroduced the Party as the centre of the Chinese society, with Xi, in turn, at the core of the Party.

One of Xi's main contenders for the top leadership job of the Party was the mayor of Chongqing, Bo Xilai. Bo was arrested just after the annual parliamentary session of 2012. As soon as Xi was in charge, he launched a much-awaited anti-corruption campaign. However, it was quickly revealed that this was to be a Party-only campaign, while citizens that were denouncing corruption outside of the Party framework became a target of a crackdown.[5] This campaign turned out to have an intra-Party-political objectives with the aim of the new General Secretary being to neutralise those who could threaten his new power position. Such "anti-corruption with Chinese characteristics" should be understood in the broad sense of the word, as the Party's Central Commission for Discipline Inspection (CCDI) has a mandate not only on investigating the financial circuits, but also the working style and/or the working efficiency of the investigated. Its margin of manoeuvre is enormous.

After Xi Jinping rose to the top, Zhou Yongkang quickly followed - in December 2014, the former minister of public security and secretary of the powerful Central Political and Legal Affairs Commission was arrested, despite being considered 'untouchable' due to his very high party rank. Bo and Zhou were accused of having formed a clique, and all their supposed allies were arrested. The purge continued, with the indictment orders of corrupt officials regularly mentioning the phrasing 'double face'. This was for example the case of the former Vice Minister of Public Security Meng Hongwei, appointed the President of Interpol in 2016, but suddenly arrested in 2018.

It is clear that the motives behind Xi's anti-corruption drive were political in nature, since he largely tapped into the populist and neo-conservative political style of Bo and Zhou, with the aim of taking full control of the Party. Under the previous administration, it had been obvious that Zhou Yongkang enjoyed considerable personal influence, and that Bo Xilai's style of management of Chongqing was amply discussed. More so, the more reformist Wang Yang's rule in Guangdong was praised. Such Party factions were much too visible for General Secretary Xi, who did not tolerate alternatives to his thinking, and could make him look weak. There was place for one boss only and that was to be him.

Xi and his affiliates used many strategies and did not spare any effort to accumulate power within the Party. In 2016, he received the title of the 'core' of the Party's Central Committee' which elevated his position. As the centre of the Party, he launched ideological campaigns. The amount of fear in the Chinese system has been peaking again, with local cadres dismissed as soon as problems arose in their field of responsibility. In March 2018, the Party's anti-corruption body was reinforced by the addition of a parallel state body, the National Supervision Commission (NSC).

The Party's increased capacity to force the cadres into compliance has also driven the anti-poverty campaign. Local cadres and poverty alleviation offices keep precise tables with all the families whose poverty situation must be alleviated. Poor villagers have been lifted out of poverty literally one by one, with cadres helping the families out of their free time, afraid that they would otherwise not be able to complete the task by the end of 2020. The cadres have found many innovative ways for poor farmers to earn supplementary incomes, for example, beekeeping, harvesting of goji berries and mushrooms, or raising ducks and rabbits. Personal involvement from cadres to achieve the poverty alleviation target has been so immense that it is difficult to believe in its sustainability.

Xi Jinping's other signature campaign to 'Rule the country according to law' is another crucial element for improving governance and hence the credibility of the Party. It has nothing to do with the Western 'Rule of law', and can best be translated as 'Rule by law'. Numerous administrative reforms have taken place and public services can be delivered through apps, making them easier to check. Technological innovations enable the monitoring and control the population, as has become evident with the tracking devices put in place soon after the pandemic outbreak. Facial recognition, first deployed in the region of Xinjiang, is gradually being used to monitor access to compounds across the country.

Civil servants and cadres are urged to adopt exemplary behaviour, as the propaganda department resorts again to the use of heroic figures, in particular that of Lei Feng (1940-1962). Barely mentioned ten years ago, he is now everywhere. The iconic hero is yet another link between Xi and Mao, as it is the latter that launched a campaign to 'Follow the example of Lei Feng' in 1963, but the 'Annual day of remembering Lei Feng' dates only back to 2012, on the 50th anniversary of his death, the year where Xi was selected as General Secretary. Xi has regularly used heroic models to show the way to the population, but also to praise the exemplary behaviour of Party members, for example in his speech to the youth on the anniversary of the May Fourth movement in 2019, or during the ceremonies to award medals that Xi seems to love.

A China model
The nationalist China of 2021 claims to be a model of governance. Xi's long and powerful speech to the 19th Party Congress in October 2017 contained the major ideas of his Thought, the 'Socialism with Chinese characteristics of the New Era'. That speech showed that the Party challenges the West and its system of governance, as China is 'standing tall and firm in the East', offering a 'flourishing economic model of socialism with Chinese characteristics' as a 'new choice' for the developing world. Xi, in the same speech, also stated that China 'wants to be back to the centre of the world stage'

and suggested that China's development could be a model for other 'nations that want to speed up their development while preserving their independence'. Under Xi, the concept of a China model has become more prominent, but also more credible; in 2020 China was the only G20 country that achieved economic growth and it is one of the rare countries that has succeeded to bring Covid-19 under control.

The attitude of the Party regarding the 'China model' remains ambiguous: diplomats claim that there is no such model and quote the policy of non-interference. The nationalist tone of the propaganda, whether it be the 'Wolf warrior diplomats', and many of Xi's speeches point to what the EU has defined its 2019 Strategic Outlook on China as "systemic rivalry". Xi himself does not use that word, but rather the word 'struggle'. His 2013 speech entitled 'A few issues on upholding and developing socialism with Chinese characteristics' is a must-read. Released to the public only in 2019, it clearly speaks of the necessary struggle between communism and capitalism.

Thanks to the Party, China will win that struggle: its model of governance is superior. The text of the fourth plenum of the 19th Party Congress states that since the start of the Reform and Opening up policy, the Party has 'crossed the river by touching the stones' but under Xi, the leadership has 'arrived on the other side of the river.' The Deng era is over. China enjoys opportunities 'unseen in centuries' (as Wang Qishan has often said). That feeling of superiority goes along with nationalism, at times tainted with xenophobia, especially as many Chinese believe that the virus came from the outside world, brought in by foreigners.[6]

What's next?
The pandemic serves as a convenient pretext to self-isolate China. While China's netizens have already been cut off from the internet for years, it is now also difficult for the Chinese people to travel abroad! In addition, very few foreigners are allowed to enter China. Exposure to foreign ideas has thus drastically decreased. Propaganda campaigns have penetrated the lives not only of the 95 million members of the party but also that of the people. The fight against the pandemic has justified tight control mechanism over the people, called 'grid management', by means of apps and local resident committees. If a majority of Chinese are relieved to have escaped the pandemic 'thanks to the Party', the sustainability of such an authoritarian model is doubtful in the long run.

Crucial questions remain, to mention only three:

- Poverty alleviation. As long as the social challenges at the root of poverty are not addressed, the poverty issue cannot be resolved. Those who were poor can fall back into poverty after the campaign is over and attention is directed elsewhere. The leadership is aware of this problem and this is also probably the reason why the campaign following poverty alleviation is the 'Rural revitalisation' campaign, unveiled in the communique of the Fifth plenum of the 19th Party Congress in October 2020, and is an important element of the 14th Five Year Plan. As many 'ex-poor' are resident in urban areas, the leadership will have to face a growing mass of urban poors. However, urbanites are easier to control than peasants are, as they live in urban centres where neighbourhood committees can keep a close eye on them.

- Relations between the Han and the other ethnic groups. Centralisation has enabled a strong sinification or 'Hanisation' of non-Han inhabitants of the country. The Sinification of the Uighurs, Kirgiz and Kazakhs in the autonomous region of Xinjiang has taken an extreme turn and is increasingly recognised, while it is also true that the sinification of all minorities is real and has been done with the help of the anti-poverty campaign (as the inhabitants were strongly encouraged to move to small towns in valleys and to give up their land).

· Over-politicisation of the country, and its growing isolation: how much and for how long are ordinary Chinese people willing to endure the weight of the Party, the omnipresence of the Party cells, the surveillance of neighbourhood committees and the return of traditional values ...? The Orwellian society that they are slowly drifting towards? And how much is this a sign of internal weakness and fear rather than strength and unity?

Conclusion

The Chinese regime has drastically changed under Xi Jinping even if his main concepts had been coined by Wang Huning before 2012. Maoist in its rhetoric and terminology, it is much more organised and managed than Mao ever was or even wanted to be. The anti-corruption campaign, the enhancement of rule by law, the crackdowns on dissent, as well as pervasive censorship, have consolidated the Party's control over the people. Nationalism is on the rise, often with a distinct anti-western narrative, interwoven with anti-democracy arguments.

In 2020 the leadership closed the country and focused on making the Chinese people more Chinese, more nationalist, closer to the Party. The unity between the Holy Trinity – the Party, the people, and the country – can no longer be questioned.

The regime's relationship with the outside world has changed too. Propaganda increasingly targets foreign audiences and the international order: the regime seems to be challenging liberal democracies in many aspects. It suggests that the diaspora should be involved in the rebirth of the Chinese nation. It directly questions the credibility of liberal democracies and seeks to reshape international relations in its own model. In 2021, China is self-isolating and seems insecure about its place in the world.

Chapter 5

China's Belt and Road Initiative – Battle For The Narrative
Merlene Toh Emerson MBE

Introduction

China's Belt and Road Initiative (BRI), formerly called One Belt One Road, was first announced in September 2013 by President Xi JinPing on an official visit to the Nazabayev University in Astana, the glitzy capital of neighbouring oil-rich Kazakhstan.

This landmark speech was entitled "Promote People-to-People Friendship and Create a Better Future" and was aimed primarily at reviving the ancient trade routes through the countries of Central Asia to create a new economic belt westwards from China. In addition to improving transport infrastructure and connectivity, President Xi spoke of jointly tackling the "3 evil forces" of terrorism, extremism and separatism" in this region.

The initial policy announcement was followed by another official visit in October that year to Jakarta in Indonesia, the most populous developing country in South East Asia. This marked a two-pronged approach: in addition to the overland route across Central Asia to Europe, there was also the Maritime Silk Road linking China to ports around the world.

History relating to the ancient Silk Roads, from the Han Dynasty (206 BC- 229 AD) through to the rule of the Mongols (1271-1368), has not generally been taught in our schools, nor have the languages outside of the main European languages. Nevertheless, historians such as Peter Frankopan, author of "The Silk Roads - A New History of the World" (2016) and "The New Silk Roads - The Present and Future of the World" (2019) believed that UK could be well placed to play the role of narrator and interpreter of the changing world. In understanding the causes and stress points that the world system is now undergoing (whether from terrorism or displacement of populations due to climate change or war), we would be better equipped to find viable solutions.

BRI is clearly Xi JinPing's signature policy and part of his Chinese Dream of making China prosperous and a great nation again. Though there is no formal definition of what project is part of BRI, it appears to have expanded in geography, covering not 70 but over 130 countries, as far north as the Arctic, south through Africa and west or is it east, to the Americas. New terms such as Green BRI and digital BRI have been coined to widen its scope.

As Jonathan Hillman, another acclaimed author on this topic, wrote in his book "The Emperor's New Road - China and the Project of the Century" (2020), BRI is more than a policy, it is a brand. There are over 100 Chinese think tanks studying its implementation and roll out, there are summits, festivals and art exhibitions themed on BRI. There are numerous Chinese banks, both state-owned and commercial, which have been called to arms and encouraged to finance the companies involved in BRI projects.

It may be easier to understand the extent of the initiative by looking at a map of the countries involved in the grand scheme, with the 6 so-called economic corridors along the overland 'belt' and of the numerous port cities along the maritime 'road'.

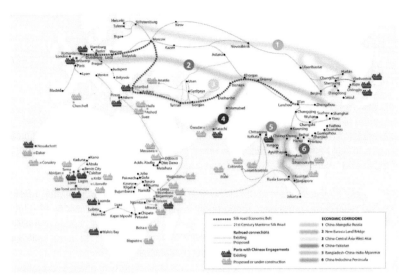

Source: OECD research from multiple sources, including: HKTDC, MERICS, Belt and Road Center, Foreign Policy, The Diplomat, Silk Routes, State Council Information Office of the People's Republic of China, WWF Hong Kong (China)[1] There is also an official Chinese website.[2]

The BRI has been presented as an open arrangement in which all countries are welcome to participate. However, there is no official list of participating countries or rather that it is changing all the time. The World Bank has identified countries associated with BRI by way of its geographical location with respect to the six overland corridors of the Silk Road Economic Belt and the 21st Century Maritime Silk Road (BRI corridors) as defined by China. There are in addition to these countries that are BRI signatories with China following bilateral arrangements or MOUs. The two approaches lead to different lists.

It has been said that as in the parable of the blind men and the elephant, BRI means different things to different people and countries. Observers have struggled to describe the BRI because they have grasped onto different parts of the animal. Before drawing any conclusions on the subject, we should see the whole picture, examine the evidence of the impact of the BRI on recipient countries, the environment, the macro-economy and on the new balance in the geo-political order.

In this chapter I will look at the China's rationale for BRI, where it has succeeded or failed in delivering on its promises, and suggest how the UK can work with other countries and global institutions to monitor these BRI projects and provide alternative development strategies to secure fairer and more liberal outcomes.

BRI from China's Perspective
By strengthening the old trade routes and opening new ones, China can have access to much needed resources and be able to integrate commodities-rich countries more closely into the Chinese economy. At the same time, it aims to tap into new markets and export its surplus industrial capacity such as in coal, steel and cement production.

The development of land routes across the less developed western region of China is an extension of the Go West policy first developed under Premier Jiang Zemin, part of the domestic policy of alleviating poverty and raising the standards of China's rural population. This policy covered provinces of Gansu,

Guizhou, Qinghai, Shaanxi and Sichuan. This region represents over 71% of mainland China but houses less than 30% of the population. Deng Xiaoping's modernization policies had been successful but led to great inequalities between the richer coastal cities of the East with the rest of China, something which later leaders have sought to redress.

The BRI could also expand the international use of the Chinese currency, the renminbi, and China's role as the major lender to the developing world. The Asian Development Bank has estimated that the region faces a yearly infrastructure financing shortfall of nearly $800 billion. In addition to physical infrastructure, China plans to build fifty special economic zones, modelled after the Shenzhen Special Economic Zone launched in 1980 during its economic reforms under Deng.

The BRI fulfils the aim of development of China's western region rich in natural resources and shift some of the wealth and reliance from the east. Importantly it will also open new routes to maritime ports to the south and west such as Gwadar port in Pakistan, European ports such as Piraeus and to Turkey, Iran and the Middle East. This could ensure that should there be any blockade of the naval sea routes at key choke points, such as in the Persian Gulf or the Straits of Malacca, China would have alternative routes and access to the 'string of pearls' in the Indo Pacific region and to ports in Africa and Europe.

Also related to China's fears of a maritime blockade is a fear of a blockade of oil supplies; BRI will help build oil supply routes and pipelines to Russia, Mongolia-Gobi, Caucasus, Horn of Africa, Myanmar and the Middle East. Hence along with the economic, pragmatic and diplomatic reasons for developing these economic corridors and commercial ports, China aims to secure and protect its borders, control the restive Western region and have access to and develop smart cities, digital highways and deep-water ports with capacity for militarization.

Interestingly, China chose for its first overseas naval base Djibouti in the Horn of Africa, located just six miles from the United States' Camp Lemmonier military base. Chinese officials have repeatedly sought to downplay the strategic implications of their new "support facility," emphasizing its support for China's U.N. peacekeepers and anti-piracy efforts. But this was as much a race in military expansion as in economic development. China was in fact late in setting up a base in 2017. US had sent troops there in 2002 as response to 9/11 and Japan has had a presence since 2009.

However, what is even more important in the modern version of the scramble for Africa is in the digital race. Djibouti has a geostrategic location and the country is a regional hub for data and telecommunications, with massive submarine fibre optic cables running through from Asia, Europe and across East Africa. The digital and telecommunications infrastructure and global connectivity would power the expansion of China's tech giants, such as Huawei, as well as bring markets closer to China through e-commerce and fintech.

BRI from the perspective of the Developing World
Some may say it was inevitable that China would have to step in where the West has failed, whether through international aid or trade, to provide for greater infrastructural investments in the developing world. According to the OECD in its 2018 report, there is a deficit in infrastructural development in the world today in the sectors of transportation, energy, water and telecommunications. These investment needs, if to be quantified, range from US$2.9 trillion to US$6.3 trillion. But should we take into consideration the Sustainable Development Goals, it would be as high as US$14.9 trillion till 2040.

The figures must be conservative and out-of-date, as in Asia alone, the Asian Development Bank in their 2020 report point to investment needs of US$26 trillion by 2030.

There is on the flip side tremendous potential for growth. The World Bank has estimated that trade in the BRI corridor economies is 30% below its potential and Foreign Direct Investment figures 70% below. BRI corridors can lower travel times and increase trade and investment. However they are inherently risky and work best with open procurement systems. There is also a need to meet local and regional needs, with spade work done which adheres to high social and environmental standards. These points were in fact highlighted in the second BRI Forum held in April 2019 in Beijing attended by representatives from over 150 countries; by which time as many as 22 European countries had signed up to the initiative including Hungary (the first to sign up) and Italy.

Refinitiv (an LSEG company) which is currently tracking $4 trillion worth of BRI projects with Chinese involvement, reported that a total of 184 projects valued at $137.43 billion, were announced in the first quarter of 2020 despite Covid 19. In terms of value, transportation accounted for 47 percent of all Belt and Road projects, or $1.88 trillion, followed by the power and water sector at 23 percent, or $926 billion.

Funding is of course key to the delivery of BRI, something much welcomed by the recipient developing countries. China founded the Asian Infrastructure Investment Bank (AIIB) in 2014 to rival the World Bank and the IMF. It was focused on developing Asia but with members from all over the world. There are currently over a hundred members and UK was one of the first signatories from Europe. This decision was taken despite displeasing the Americans and was a pragmatic move with economic benefits for the UK and one that was greatly welcomed by China.

There is also the Silk Road Fund which is a Chinese state-owned investment fund dedicated to fostering increased investment in countries participating in BRI. The Chinese government pledged US$40 billion for the creation of the investment fund when it was established circa 2014.

The China Development Bank has so far supported over 400 projects in 37 economies worth $110 billion. The Industrial and Commercial Bank of China (ICBC) was involved in 212 projects worth $67 billion, and is expected to arrive at around $159 billion. But not only Chinese banks are drawn to BRI opportunities. It has been reported that HSBC has arranged US$525bn of cross-border financing involving China between the start of 2017 and September 2019.

Even other governments have joined the fray. Turkey's sovereign wealth fund signed a US$5bn agreement with Sinosure to promote bilateral trade and investment as part of the BRI, while Etihad Credit Insurance (ECI), the UAE's export credit agency, partnered with three Chinese financial institutions to boost non-oil trade and investment between the UAE and China in 2019.

Criticism levelled at the BRI
BRI from the international development point of view could serve to promote and sustain growth in participating economies which make up half of the world's population and over a third of global GDP. BRI, Beijing posits, could also create more balanced regional development, contribute to food security, and promote more outward investments in developing economies that have been neglected by the developed world.

However as observed by analysts and critics, there are costs and serious risks involved in these large infrastructural projects.

One of the main criticisms of BRI is that it has led to debt traps and unhealthy and unsustainable dependency on China by recipient countries. The Centre for Global Development in their 2018 report found that BRI heightened debt risks in eight countries (including Djibouti, Pakistan, Mongolia and Kyrgyzstan) and called for better lending practices.

There is also a lack in transparency in the procurement and finance structures especially in earlier deals involving only Chinese banks and Chinese contractors without open tenders. Infrastructural projects continue to be prone to corruption at local levels as identified by Transparency International due to the complexity of the construction projects, the vast amounts of money involved and the layers of bureaucracy and approvals to deliver the projects.

Where politically driven, they could be skewed in China's interests rather than those of the third party recipient countries. Shifting China's excess capacity in less environmentally friendly energy sources, such as coal, to other countries could also yield little net gain from a global perspective.

Author and activist Rebecca Tinsley has worked in 9 African countries and founded "Waging Peace," an NGO in Sudan and "Network for Africa," a charity working with survivors of genocide. According to Tinsley, from Angola to Zambia, China's billion-dollar investments often went into vanity projects lining the pockets of the corrupt elites. Infrastructural projects were also opportunities for graft to be paid out of oil and other valuable resources, leaving the beneficiary countries with expensive debt and bridges and toll booths leading nowhere.

McKinsey between November 2016 and March 2017 conducted a survey of 8 African countries which found that 396 Chinese firms in Kenya, created 50,000 jobs and provided some 67,000 with local training. Another report from Chatham House attempted to debunk the myth of "debt trap" diplomacy, the luring of poor developing countries into agreeing unsustainable loans. It found that evidence for this was limited, China's international development financing was more piecemeal and the result of bilateral interactions, and with outcomes which were determined by interests and agendas on both sides.[3]

Some high-profile BRI scandals came to light where there had been a change in the Government of the recipient country and the unbalanced terms and corrupt practices were then exposed by opposition politicians.

An example was the development by Prime Minister Rajapaksa, well known friend of China, of the Hambatota port in Sri Lanka, strategically located in the Indian Ocean along the traditional east-west shipping route. However, due to massive cost overruns and delays, the port performed badly when in operation incurring huge losses. In Dec 2017 under Prime Minister Wickremesinghe, the Sri Lanka Ports Authority (SLPA) agreed with the China Merchant Port Holdings for an injection of US$ 1.1billion in exchange for an 85 per cent stake and 99-year lease of the port. This included an additional 15 acres for the industrial zone and land for the Navy. Needless to say, the acquisition of the port by China raised alarm bells in India.

Another example was the high-speed rail project in Malaysia negotiated with the Chinese during the premiership of kleptocrat Najib Razak, erstwhile Prime Minister and Chairman of the Barisan National coalition which had ruled Malaysia for the last 6 decades. He was sadly embroiled in the 1 Malaysia Development Berhad (1MDB) scandal involving alleged pilfering of the sovereign fund. After he was defeated by the 92 year-old veteran Mahathir in historic 2018 elections, Prime Minister Mahathir revisited the terms of the contract with China and managed to reduce the bill by a third from RM$66.7bn to RM$44bn.

The US has come to view China's BRI as a threat to its pre-eminent position as the world's super power. The recent Council for Foreign Relations (CFR) Task Force Report authored by Jennifer Hillman and David Sacks[4] postulated that BRI undermined global macro-economic stability as China funded economically questionable projects in heavily indebted countries. BRI also allowed China to introduce its technology and standards and lock these into the eco-system of third-party countries. It also found a lack of rigorous environmental and social impact assessments in BRI projects which ignored project management best practices and tolerated corruption.

The Council on Foreign Relations (CFR) has a useful tool, CFR's Belt and Road Tracker[5], which aids analysis of BRI in 67 countries and focuses on 3 BRI indicators: imports from China, FDI from China and external debt to China. The tracker shows overall debt to China has soared since 2013, surpassing 20 percent of GDP in some countries. We will need to continue monitoring the situation and the potential debt trap facing these countries.

Are there alternatives to BRI?
Despite the US enjoying a leading role in the World Bank, it has shunned the new AIIB and not joined in regional trade and investment agreements such as the Transatlantic Trade and Investment Partnership (TTIP) and the Regional Comprehensive Economic Partnership (RCEP) that would have enhanced ties in the Asia Pacific region.

The CFR task force recommended that the US should look to improving their own competitiveness, work with allies, partners and multilateral organisations and to protecting their interests in BRI countries.

So, what are these alliances, multi-development banks and institutions that UK and Europe could tap into to provide alternatives to China's BRI?

As announced at the G7 Summit in Cornwall in June 2021, President Biden launched B3W (Build Back Better World) Partnership as a new western version of the BRI. There are however no commitments yet relating to the funding of this project. Not so long ago in 2018, US Congress had passed the BUILD Act which which consolidated development finance activities into a new agency USDFC (Development Finance Corporation). The BUILD Act promised $60bn in funding for USIDFC. As for the EU, the Comprehensive Agreement on Investment (CAI) which was due to be ratified between the EU and China this year, has been put on hold following the sanctions imposed by China on European human rights advocates.

In Eurasia, there is the CAREC programme which since 1997 has succeeded in cutting transport costs and travel time across 6 corridors developed through a collaborative multi-country process overseen by the Asian Development Bank. This is apparently well benchmarked and evaluated. There is also the Eurasian Economic Union and the Shanghai Co-operation Organisation involving China, the Central Asian countries as well as India and Pakistan.

One might also mention the Blue Dot Network established by the US bringing together governments in

OECD countries to foster quality infrastructure investment through a certification scheme. This is intended to assist investments that maximise the positive economic, social, environmental and development impact of infrastructure.

The US views BRI as a threat of rising authoritarianism against western democracies. One can understand the qualms: due to the economies of scale of the mega constructions, China would build its systems and standards into the projects. Their technical standards will then become the "global defaults" in a number of fields. Examples include the ultrahigh voltage (UHV) power lines, along with smart electricity grids, transport logistics and smart buildings. Might there also be import of surveillance systems and facial recognition software to dictatorial regimes? What is happening in Xinjiang with the State-backed sinicisation of the Muslim Uighurs comes to mind.

In July 2019, 22 countries (including Australia, France, Germany and the UK) wrote to the UN Human Rights Council raising concerns over "credible reports of arbitrary detention" of the Uighurs. This was then swiftly followed by another letter sent by 37 nations including many Muslim countries in defense of China's policies and against the politicizing of human rights. More notable perhaps are the countries that have stayed visibly silent on this, including most of the central and eastern European countries,[6] How do we mitigate against the impact of the growing influence of China on the rest of the world then? A spokesperson for Siemens when interviewed by Bloomberg said that ignoring the BRI would be a greater risk to European companies than not getting on board. Duisburg at the confluence of the Rhine and Ruhr rivers in Germany is the largest inland port in the world. German companies stand to benefit from the BRI links where it takes less than 2 weeks for freight trains from ChongQing to arrive in Duisburg travelling through Kazakhstan, Belarus and Poland.

Piraeus port is another example of China's success in public relations. Having stepped in via COSCO Shipping to rescue Greece from its financial crisis in 2009, Greek Prime Ministers Papandreou and Tsipras have become avid supporters of the BRI. However, the EU lawmakers and officials will need more convincing. According to the EU Commission, the BRI projects have to be economically and environmentally sustainable, the procurement process has to be transparent, open and inclusive; and the values and practices of Chinese companies and banks have to conform to international best practices. Where there are BRI disputes, there must be mechanisms in place for recourse to independent mediation, tribunals or courts.

Currently, Chinese companies still lag behind on ESG (environment, social and governance) reporting and standards. There is a movement towards more ethical and responsible investments and there are even indices compiled on asset managers and their performance on ESG that include human rights considerations such as that pioneered by Share Action. More and more countries will be introducing FDI (Foreign Direct Investment) restrictions on investments in their key industries. Trade and investments along the BRI have to be mutually beneficial in reality and not merely in aspiration.

In Conclusion
Revival by China of the old Silk Roads and its expansion via the maritime 'road' should come as no great surprise. China had been trading with its neighbours under the formalised 'tribute system" involving giving of gifts to the Emperor up till the last Qing Dynasty. The impetus for BRI has much to do with China's need to develop its western provinces to secure energy and mineral resources in order to sustain its growing population and drive its economy. Since Oct 2017, BRI has been embedded in China's Constitution ensuring that it remains a core principle and the project has a theoretical completion in 2049, on the 100th anniversary of the PRC.

Under President Xi we have also witnessed China's ambitions to play a larger role on the world stage. Covid 19 has given China the opportunity for Covid19 diplomacy with donations of PPE and vaccines. China has even offered to mediate between Israel and Palestine when it had traditionally (officially) shunned interference in the internal affairs of other countries.

Meanwhile the trade war with the US, which had begun as Trump's election strategy, has moved on to new tensions even under Biden. Australia and China have been embroiled in some tit for tat measures with adverse impact on Australian farmers. At the same time, the EU has suspended the ratification of the Comprehensive Agreement on Investments due to the breaches of human rights in Hong Kong and Xinjiang. This has resulted in China sanctioning 10 European scholars and four European institutions under a new "scold" war.

All these, in my view, point to a new battle for the narrative. Who owns China's story and can pronounce on the success or failure of the BRI? We understand that China is advancing its "dual circulation" economy is especially important since the onset of the Covid 19 pandemic and containment by the US. BRI is intended to boost international trade and its foreign credentials. China has therefore stressed its pursuit of the principles of communication, co-operation, and the "promotion of people-to-people bonds" whilst down-playing aspects of geopolitical and military influence through BRI.

The Western narrative and perception of China, on the other hand, is that of China as a strategic rival and competitor, whose values and interests are incompatible with those of Western democracies. Whilst the Chinese Communist Party uphold societal stability and control above all else, the US and Europeans value open societies, transparency, inclusion and the protection of civil and political rights.

Could there be an alternative narrative? For all practical purposes, the EU and the international community should have an interest in the success of BRI too. The projects are so large and extensive that, should any fail through overstretch or macroeconomic constraints, it could have a negative impact on the world economy. An example was the case of the rescue of the CPEC (China Pakistan Economic Corridor) project which involved a bailout by IMF of US$6 billion in 2019. As money is fungible, any bailout of a developing economy could be seen as coming to the aid of the Chinese banks instead.

In brief remarks to nearly 40 world leaders and other high-ranking officials at China's second Belt and Road summit in Beijing in April 2019, Christine Lagarde (former IMF Director and current President of the European Central Bank) observed that the BRI program to build ports, railroads and other trade-enhancing infrastructure had a positive impact in certain countries but needed to be managed carefully. She therefore called for a revamped "Belt and Road 2.0"[7] to include increased transparency, an open procurement process with competitive bidding and better risk assessment in project selection. The answer must be for BRI to evolve into a multi-polar project adopting international best standards.

To borrow a quote by the scholar Eric McGlinchey about the global games which were played in Central Asia: "China is playing the game of Monopoly, Russia is playing Risk, the United States is playing Solitaire. For policymakers in Beijing, the game is business. For policy makers in Moscow, the game is existential. For policy makers in Washington, the game is an afterthought."[8]

What games will UK and the EU play as against China?

Chapter 6

China And The West: A Contest Neither Can Win
Dr Phil Bennion

When Jamil Anderlini claimed in the Financial Times recently that the Chinese Communist Party (CCP) is no longer socialist, but reactionary and conservative and committed to preserving the power of the elite, a predictably robust response appeared a few days later in the letters page from the Chinese Embassy. Anderlini went on to say that Chinese society is extremely unequal and that most members of the CCP are now white-collar workers. Xi's vision involves expansion of the military, assertive foreign policy and suppression of dissent at home, driven by fear of disintegration and popular revolt. The process is now undermining the economic liberalisation of Deng Xiaoping and is likely to weaken the economic growth that has cemented public support. If Anderlini is right similar contradictions are now inherent in the Chinese system that led, in the end, to the collapse of the Soviet regime in Moscow. Yet the power of the regime in China has never looked more secure. This very security seems to have emboldened Xi Jinping in his ambitions to project Chinese power. I will try to assess in the following pages whether this is likely to lead to a new cold war, or whether a new unwritten compact will see China and the West park their differences in order to address global problems in which they have a common interest.

Assumptions of western decline

Some commentators speculate that China's change of approach in asserting itself on the world stage is due to an assumption that the west is in permanent decline and that the next century will belong to China. The inevitable outcome is Chinese global dominance as it takes over from the US as the world's economic and military superpower. In my view Xi has underestimated the capacity of the West to re-cover its sense of collective purpose. The rise of Trump and Brexit, along with some lesser expressions of populist nationalism in Hungary, Poland and Brazil may have led him to his conclusion. He has also probably judged that trade with China was now so important to the US and EU that business lobbies in the US and German mercantilism in the EU would overcome any squeamishness over China's human rights record. The West would not have the stomach to make economic sacrifices in the name of human rights so China would continue to grow rich on this trade.

China used not to take on the bigger powers, but recently sanctions on UK, EU and Canadian politicians, including MEPs Kyuchyuk and Butikofer (see below) suggest a bolder approach. However, the European Parliament probably surprised China when it quickly hit back with the refusal to give assent to the Comprehensive Investment Agreement. My own experience of European Parliament solidarity led me to predict such a response. When I was banned from Cambodia by Hun Sen the EU External Action Service leapt into action in Phnom Penh and the partial suspension of Everything But Arms privileges became a formality for the European Parliament. From the western viewpoint China is making a strategic mistake and losing goodwill because of its newly assertive approach.

NATO has expressed worries about Chinese use of disinformation, its military build-up (including an expansion of its stock of nuclear weapons) and its cooperation with Russia. A Nato summit statement refers to China's "stated ambitions and assertive behaviour", which it goes on to say pose "systemic challenges to the rules-based international order". When I was invited to tea by the Chinese Embassy in London for the purpose of requesting me to withdraw the nomination of Ilham Tohti for the Sakharov

Prize in late 2019, there was no sign of "Wolf Warrior" tactics and we held a wide discussion on relations between China and the West. Trump was of course still in power in the US so I suggested that China would do well to become the mainstay of the international rules-based order in the absence of US leadership. Curiously in June 2021 I heard explicit support for the rules-based international system from the head of the Chinese delegation in his statement to the Inter-Parliamentary Union (IPU). China's actions conversely suggest that their ambition is to remake the international rules-based system in a manner more favourable to authoritarian regimes rather than democracies. Recent evidence suggests that the West is beginning the process of mounting a resistance to such changes and to Chinese assertiveness. The very fact that the rich democracies are not a monolithic block may have led China to misread their lack of unity as a lack of resolve. Unity is likely to be restored by the perception of China as a common competitor for global influence, or even domination.

Biden

President Biden is trying to make up lost time in assembling an alliance to take on the Chinese challenge. He is conscious that Xi Jinping has moved opportunistically during the Trump Presidency, when the West lacked leadership. Biden will attempt to peel off Russia from any alliance with China, hence his recent summit with Putin. It is unlikely that Biden's approach to China will take the form of a club of democracies uniting in purpose. I would expect a less ideological and more pragmatic approach. He will have to persuade mercantilist European allies like Germany that a robust approach to international norms is necessary. Not only do some Europeans fear that China could blow cold on joint economic projects, but they also fear being isolated if the US elects another tea-party president in 2024.

Internally China has convinced its citizens that their rise in prosperity is linked to their authoritarian one party, state-capitalist system. The problem with this approach is firstly that any hiccup in economic growth can cast doubt on the main premise. Xi Jinping sees danger coming mainly from minorities and so doubles down on the majoritarian approach of the regime.

China's breaking of international law regarding its claims on the South China Sea are a symptom of the assumption of western decline. Despite being a signatory of the United Nations Convention on the Law of the Sea (UNCLOS) and receiving a verdict that its activities contravene the law, China has continued to lay claim to this large maritime area and to increase militarisation therein. The area claimed enclosed by the so-called Nine Dash Line includes most of the sea area between China, Vietnam, Malaysia and the Philippines and is considered as international waters under the rules of UNCLOS. This action is causing potential flash points as other nations, including the US and UK, have felt obliged to sail into the area to visibly uphold their navigation rights, often with military vessels. It is difficult to see that China gains much from this, other than demonstrating its strength to other world powers.

In recent weeks the US has been running joint operations with Japan as an exercise in repelling any Chinese attempted invasion of Taiwan. I would expect Biden to move forward by strengthening US ties with ASEAN to build a strong bulwark against prospective Chinese aggression. Further west, Biden has already been pressing Modi in India on human rights in Kashmir. India is traditionally obsessed with the threat of China and would be a natural ally in any alliance, but the Modi regime's behaviour bears a reputational problem for Biden if he embraces them too closely.

Xinjiang and human rights

News about the camps in Xinjiang reached us in Liberal International early in 2017. It provoked my MEP colleague Ilhan Kyuchyuk to nominate imprisoned Uyghur activist Ilham Tohti for the Liberal International Prize for Freedom. At the award ceremony we spoke to Tohti's daughter Jewher by video link from the US. Enver Can of the World Uyghur Congress received the award on behalf of Tohti and over the next two years we were supplied with eyewitness reports at various meetings, which supported the theory that the numbers being interned were expanding into the hundreds of thousands. By the summer of 2019 reports of the camps were widespread and I suggested to Ilhan Kyuchyuk that we have another try at nominating Tohti for the Sakharov Prize. It was always going to be a nomination against the odds as the two larger political groups were likely to stick with their own candidates. However, with the help of Reinhard Butikofer MEP of the Greens (Chair of the EP China Delegation) we prevailed.

Tohti, of course, won the prize and his daughter travelled to Strasbourg to receive it on his behalf. As of this week (24th June 2021) Jewher suspects that her father has no knowledge of the award. As far as we know, he has not been allowed visitors since 2017, either from his family or lawyers, despite such rights being explicitly written into China's constitution. The successful campaign was one of my last acts as an MEP before Brexit and I was only able to see it through because of the extension. The groundwork in persuading MEPs to back the award was undertaken by my superb assistant Sophie Sohm and Lucia Parrucci of Unrepresented Nations and Peoples Organisation (UNPO), who do great work on the interests of Uyghurs and other peoples worldwide. In the meantime, we have taken the campaign to release Ilham Tohti to the Geneva Summit for Human Rights and Democracy where Jewher was a powerful advocate for her father's freedom last year.

The most recent development is the campaign headed by Rodney Dixon QC to take Chinese individuals to the International Criminal Court (ICC) and bring charges related to rendition of Uyghur activists from the territory of Tajikistan. Although China is not a signatory to the ICC, his case is that these particular crimes began in Tajikistan, which is a signatory, and so they do fall within its jurisdiction.

The labelling of China's human rights violations in Xinjiang as genocide by the US, UK and Canadian governments has provoked arguments as to whether this is either appropriate or useful. I have been assured by my Liberal International Human Rights Committee colleague Irwin Cotler that the Chinese actions satisfy the ICC definition of genocide as set out in Article 6 of the Statute of Rome, itself based on the UN Genocide Convention. I have expressed my own doubts on whether this definition is useful. The term genocide in popular parlance has been reserved for mass slaughter on ethnic or religious grounds, such as the holocaust or the Rwanda genocide. My question is, if a broader definition is to be used, the term genocide in the context of the horrific events of the holocaust and Rwanda is devalued. It may also lead to the mistaken view by the public that similar extermination policies are taking place in China. Several of my colleagues, including Vince Cable, have expressed similar misgivings. However, we are not going to change the definition, so we must accept it.

The more pragmatic question is whether using the term genocide helps or hinders achieving the goals of disbanding the internment camps and gaining freedom of religion for the Uyghur population, alongside a backing off from China in their authoritarian efforts of forced assimilation. Accusing them of genocide may make engagement so difficult that China simply ignores all western criticism and continues its egregious human rights abuses. On the other hand, the reputational damage could shock China into a change of direction. If the latter were to be the case, it certainly would never be announced. We will only be able to judge by China's actions in the next few years whether this approach by the western governments has been a success or counterproductive. My own view is that whatever terms we use, we should never shrink from calling out China, or anyone else, for abuses of human rights. A flexible approach to human rights would simply demonstrate to China that the West's principles can be bought.

The current Uyghur Tribunal under the chairmanship of Sir Geoffrey Nice took testimonies in June 2021 and a further session is due in September. The verdict, even if unofficial, will give a strong indication of the legal basis of using the term. In the 2019 China tribunal into allegations of organ harvesting from imprisoned Falun Gong followers, also led by Sir Geoffrey, the verdict of a Crime Against Humanity was clear, although the tribunal was undecided on the charge of genocide. The verdict expressly proposed that any government, company or individual dealing with the PRC should do so in the knowledge that they are dealing with a criminal regime. Of course, a Peoples Tribunal can only recommend that the UN or other legal authorities investigate, but the verdict was unequivocal.

The spat over cotton from Xinjiang brought the Uyghur issue back to the fore as accusations of forced labour emerged, causing boycotts of major clothing brands which manufacture in China. When the firms responded by cleaning up their supply chains, retaliation was evident in the Chinese market for their products, such as store lease termination. The message seemed to be that the companies would have to choose between ethical standards and access to China's growing market. These measures were apparently in retaliation to western Magnitsky sanctions on individuals involved in the human rights violations in Xinjiang. The EU, US, UK, Canada and others have moved to ban products which may have used forced labour in Xinjiang and more may follow. My guess is that the companies will follow the western line despite Chinese awkwardness and that they will need to demonstrate their supply chains. This pressure does have the potential to move China's policies, but we should not expect any explicit change.

China's record on human rights does not begin and end with Xinjiang, where I have been assured by Canadian colleagues that the threshold set by the internationally recognised definition of genocide has indeed been crossed. Other minorities have suffered too, most notoriously the Tibetans from the 1950s to the present day. China has also settled minority areas with Han people to alter the demographic. Other minorities include Mongolians, Manchu and Koreans.

China also has a poor record on property rights when villagers get in the way of projects. The policy of delivering greater prosperity for the majority through building industrial zones and dams has been delivered with scant regard for those displaced. Rural migrants moving to the cities for work also find that they have few or no rights away from their original home village.

Hong Kong

The situation in Hong Kong cannot go without mention, as China has clearly broken the terms of the Sino-British Joint Declaration which has treaty status at the UN and guaranteed Hong Kong a high degree of autonomy under the principle of "one country – two systems" until 2047. Opposition members of the Legislative Council have been stripped of their positions and a number have been imprisoned, along with elder statesman Martin Lee, who was a member of the Basic Law Drafting Committee. Lee was given a suspended prison sentence in April 2021. The election law was changed in March to marginalise the opposition even further by reducing the share of directly elected legislators by 60%. The use of primaries to avoid several opposition candidates splitting the vote was labelled "subversive" and some have been arrested for nothing more. The crushing of all dissent in Hong Kong began with the attempted imposition of a new extradition law and the abduction of some opponents to China proper.

Student leaders have been gaoled and others escaped to exile. The new national security law of 2020 reinterpreted the agreement with the UK which deemed that Hong Kong could remain capitalist, but it must be governed by Chinese patriots. Deng had made assurances that this meant patriotic allegiance to China and not necessarily its socialist system or the pivotal role of the Chinese Communist Party. President Xi now seems to regard adherence to China's authoritarian system as a necessary aspect of patriotism. The assault on Hong Kong's traditional freedoms has continued with the arrest of media owner Jimmy Lai, and the closure of his popular newspaper Apple Daily in June 2021. President Xi seems now to presume that China has outgrown the need to respect international law. When one very large and powerful state rejects the need to follow international law, it leaves law abiding states no choice but to coordinate their responses. The G7 and others would not be planning such a coordinated response regarding China if China were adhering to international rules.

As yet, the business community seems content to go along with China's suppression in Hong Kong. This could be short-sighted as China seems to be trying to force Hong Kong to turn into just another Chinese city. Some Hong Kong residents have managed to emigrate and the UK has offered BNO passport holders the chance of residency. The Liberal Democrats have called for that facility to be extended to all Hong Kong residents, who may now find leaving less than straightforward following further clampdowns.

Prosperity
China will claim firstly that their record on human rights is not the business of anyone but themselves. Secondly, they will point out that they have delivered outstanding levels of economic growth in recent years that has taken the population out of poverty. This has improved the lot of the Chinese people to such an extent that it dwarfs the negative factors brought by a lack of personal freedom. This claim must be taken seriously. It should also be welcomed by all that the Chinese people have so benefited from the economic growth in recent years that their material needs are now being largely met. There is little doubt that the economic policies of Chinese governments from the opening under Deng Xiaoping onwards are largely responsible.

However, more recently under Xi Jinping many of Deng's reforms have been reversed. Some entrepreneurs have been gaoled or are no longer looked on by the CCP or the public as the heroes they once were. There have been hints of a return to a more command-based economy, which if continued, will most likely have a negative effect on future economic growth. The question of whether the rapid growth which has taken China out of poverty to a middle-income status can be continued under such a return to hard-line authoritarianism is still to be answered. I would doubt that recent levels of growth can be sustained for more than a handful of years in these circumstances. At what point will a stalling in the growth of prosperity negatively affect the popularity of the regime? Are Xi's policies undermining the foundations of the continued rise of China?

Climate Change
China's approach to tackling climate change has been one where its engagement at international level has been largely positive. Some initial reluctance based on the need for economic growth was understandable, as was the commitment to reduce its emissions relative to GDP over several years. Of course, with economic growth hovering around 8% per annum, this has still meant a gross increase in emissions. However, that is now starting to turn around and China is targeting carbon neutrality by 2060, despite some coal fired power stations still being built. The US under Trump was the bigger problem. With Biden now in charge and John Kerry taking the portfolio, there is a real prospect of the

US and China, the world's biggest emitters, working together on bringing emissions down. Xie Zenhua has been appointed as climate envoy by the Chinese government and he has worked well with Kerry before. China has made some veiled threats of being awkward, based on criticisms of its human rights record, but self-interest points towards cooperation. China has made great strides in raising incomes but still suffers terrible air quality. The government sees benefits in tying actions on climate change to those which can deliver a cleaner environment. It also sees an opportunity to improve its reputation, which has taken a battering on human rights.

My overall assessment is that the global battle against climate change is a huge opportunity for positive engagement with China. It should not be too difficult to continue progress, even with the backdrop of bitter disagreement over human rights.

Belt and Road Initiative (BRI) and the Western Response

The BRI has been a mixed blessing for the recipients of loans and other infrastructure projects. For many developing nations China has become an important source of funding for roads, ports, railways and other big projects that they hope will present a route out of poverty. However, many of the projects have been of poor value, the loan terms have often been onerous and even much of the work went to Chinese contractors and workers. There is also now a sense that China is using the loans as a means of developing a caucus at the UN so that it has the votes to block criticism in the General Assembly and Human Rights Council. Developing countries have turned to China, often because of the lack of alternatives. MEP Reinhard Butikofer thinks there is now serious intent in the West to address this failure. "The Chinese made inroads because they had something to offer that we did not". He thinks we have an opportunity to be better partners to these developing nations than the Chinese. Projects backed by western lenders such as the European Investment Bank can counter BRI in terms of getting support from developing world governments. There is still no strategic plan like BRI, but plenty of individual EU-backed projects. There is an urgent need to prevent developing countries becoming over-dependent on China. The US is still lagging behind and some say the EU and US are too late, but others that onerous BRI terms present an opportunity for the west to step in. A joined-up approach is hampered by different attitudes of different governments to an alliance to counter Chinese influence.

Megan Greene of Harvard Kennedy School (writing in the FT) suggests that the proposal from the G7 for such a fund to rival BRI indicates a clear intent to use western economic power to counter Chinese influence in the developing world. Current Chinese loan conditions for BRI projects can leave the recipients worse off. On a positive note, China has now signed up to the G20 Debt Service Suspension Initiative (DSSI) that helps debtor nations restructure their loans in times of crisis. This has helped assure other lenders that their loans will not simply be used to pay off China, but Chinese loans are beset by confidentiality clauses, which mean that other lenders cannot assess a country's balance sheet and thereby assess the risk, before making their own loan. There are also clauses allowing for immediate recall of debt if a country changes policy. These factors make BRI debtors bad risks for other lenders as well as giving China direct leverage over the debtor country's foreign policy. However, so far there is no strong evidence of China exerting pressure on debtors that it might use such leverage.

The Response to the Geopolitical Challenge

There has been much talk of a western alliance, or an alliance of advanced democracies, to counter the geopolitical push of China. This kicked off in earnest when China imposed sanctions on some Australian products because of Australian criticism of China and its human rights record. The 2021 G7 summit saw the intention made official by the Biden team, although little detail emerged. The statement was of course condemned by China as western plotting. It is my view that a loose alliance is necessary, if only to stop China picking off individual countries through a divide and rule strategy. However, such an alliance should not be built around the idea of isolating China, which would be counterproductive. It should stick to the theme of a rules-based narrative to prevent countries breaking ranks for pure economic gain. It is also difficult to see such a loose alliance extending much beyond the US, EU, Canada, Japan, Australia and New Zealand. A potential positive response would be the provision of loans and investment grants for the developing world, so that impoverished nations have an alternative source of finance. The G7 might be the right vehicle for such an initiative, which would give China some competition as well as helping the developing world to level up.

The danger of an alliance that shuns engagement with China, is too quick to impose trade restrictions or starts to look like a military threat to Beijing risks descent into another Cold War. There is already a military aspect to the West's response, with the US urging Nato to become more active in countering China's ambitions, as well as the Quad, an alliance involving the US, Australia, Japan and India. Chinese incursions into Taiwanese airspace have continued to escalate and experts are divided on the likelihood of a full-scale invasion. Most believe that China does not have the wherewithal to mount such an invasion, even if it harbours ambitions. Whether or not Xi Jinping tries to invade Taiwan will depend on whether he thinks the US is able to stop him. At the moment he still suspects that it might. It would only take a major incident to freeze relations for the medium term. As neither China nor the US is looking for such a scenario, it should still be seen as unlikely, but accidents and miscalculations do happen.

The role of Russia in the possible scenarios of either increasing tension or a limited backing off by China should not be underestimated. To date Vladimir Putin has been something of a cheerleader for the problems China poses for the West. However, Putin may conclude that Russian bread is better buttered by a closer relationship with the EU and US. This was borne out by the summit between Biden and Putin and the proposals from France and Germany to "reset" EU relations with Russia. In my view Putin's cosying up to China is skin deep. He is probably getting some pleasure from EU and US discomfort. However, his deeper motives will be entirely transactional and selling gas to Germany and other economic gains will probably lead him westwards. The snag will be political and in the shape of Ukraine. A "reset" would mean drawing a line under the Crimea annexation, one way or another. This might be too much for some EU member states as they believe that allowing Putin his ill-gotten gains would be a hostage to fortune. It would show Putin that his adventures are likely to be rewarded in due course, even if he must spend some time in purdah. This drama has only just starting to play out and the outcome is far from certain, but my guess is that Russia will make some accommodation with the EU, possibly under pressure from the US, and will not become a long-term ally of China's global ambitions.

New Cold War or Uneasy Cooperation
It would be logical to conclude by looking at what the future might bring, but I am not making predictions with any degree of certainty. Change often happens suddenly and unpredictably so I would not be surprised to be wrong in my predictions.

To continue the rise in prosperity it has seen in recent years China will still need to trade and engage with the West. The reputational damage brought by their human rights record will hamper China's trading relations, but sanctions will continue to be highly targeted and will not expand into general sanctions or a trade war. China does need to make a transformation from a predominantly export oriented economy to one based more on home consumption, but that transformation cannot take place nearly quickly enough to alter dependence on international trade.

China's approach to human rights is unlikely to alter very much whilst Xi Jinping is in power. He clearly believes that chaos would result from relaxing the suppression of dissent. In my view it is probable that specific identifiable assaults on human rights will be abandoned, but there will be no return to the opening up seen under previous leaders. China will try and lessen the reputational damage that it has seen from its repression of Uyghur identity, but any change in policy will be strenuously denied. Pressure on companies to ignore human rights will founder as they choose continued operation in western markets as a priority. Unfortunately, this will still see prominent prisoners such as Ilham Tohti remaining incarcerated for some time to come. It will also mean that the crushing of democracy in Hong Kong will become a fait accompli, certainly for the duration of President Xi's tenure.

The West, with renewed leadership from the US and the EU less cautious about paying an economic price for upholding its values, will work together through the G7 and beyond, to hold the line on standards for human rights and to shore up its dominant geopolitical reach. Russia will try to ride both horses but will not side with China in any way that would threaten its economy.

Miscalculation on either side could precipitate a military conflagration or a new cold war, but it is neither in the interests of China, nor collectively of the powers of a western alliance. Xi Jinping wants to reunite Taiwan with China but he will probably conclude that the US is preparing a defence. I hope that he will consider such an adventure far too risky. This manageable scenario could also be upset by a return to power of Trumpite Republicans in the US. I believe that by 2024 the US electorate will see the Trump years as an aberration, but I do not rule out a Republican move back to the centre to gain power, although there has been little sign so far.

As long as the Democrats retain the White House, the battle against climate change will develop with tripartite leadership from the US, EU and China. This will provide an anchor should difficulties arise in other areas, reducing the chance of a broad breakdown in global relationships.

The West's decline is not absolute as poor and middle-income countries are inevitably closing the gap. This has made the task of foreign policy makers more complicated and the diversity incumbent in the West makes arriving at unity a slow process. This should not be confused with weakness or decline. The West can stick together to stand firm on human rights, and China will fail to divide and rule. Chinese economic growth will falter towards the end of the decade due to the partial return to a command economy, eventually bringing forward a new, more open-minded leadership. My bet is on the continuation of uneasy cooperation with trade sanctions and bans on individuals playing only a limited role. Chinese rhetoric may continue in "wall of steel" terms, but ultimately they will not want to descend into a new cold war. The rise of China is a geopolitical fact and will not be reversed, but neither will China become the single superpower in a unipolar world, even if that needs a more unified approach from the G7 and their allies.

Chapter 7

One Country Two Systems Revisited

Andrew Leung

A remarkably successful product of the East and West

When Hong Kong Island was ceded to Britain following the First Opium War (1839-42), Lord Palmerston famously belittled it as a "barren rock with hardly a house upon it".

Since reversion of sovereignty to China in 1997 under 'One Country Two Systems', Hong Kong has grown into a unique international metropolis with close connections to Mainland China, driven by a population of some 7.5 million citizens, a vibrant international financial centre, 1,500 regional headquarters of multinational corporations and a favourite international tourist destination with over 65 million visitors in a single year (2018).

Even after the riotous social disorder in 2019-20, it remains one of the richest cities on the planet with half a million citizens each possessing over $10 million Hong Kong dollars (US$1.3 million) in total assets, according to a Citibank Report of May, 2020.[1]

Hong Kong is a unique place where the East mixes with the West, in more ways than one. Its rule of law based on English common law with an independent judiciary has remained highly respected. Up to 2019, Hong Kong had been rated the freest economy in the world continually for 25 years by the Heritage Foundation based in Washington D.C. It fell only to second place in 2020, after Singapore.

From separation to integration

Since 1997, Hong Kong has been under the sovereignty of China ruled by the Chinese Communist Party (CCP) with One Country Two Systems. By 2020, the accolade of the freest economy in the world had been earned for 23 consecutive years.

During the first decade after Hong Kong's reversion to China, Beijing had kept Hong Kong at arm's length.

As the top civilian administrator of Hong Kong's Police Force before 1997, I remember how easy it was to organize a friendly football match between the respective police forces across the border. However, during the first few years after the handover, any direct contact between officials on both sides, even for a friendly sporting match, had to be referred upwards to Beijing for approval for fear of perceived interference with Hong Kong. This arms-length separation has soon proved impracticable.

Hong Kong has long been integrating economically with the Mainland. One of my former posts was Deputy Director-General of Industry (1987-91) when I oversaw the rapid migration of Hong Kong's diminishing manufacturing industries across the border to "the factory of the world". At the same time, as a free and open international city with a high standard of the rule of law, Hong Kong has been welcoming a rising tide of trade and investments with Mainland China and the rest of the world.

A decade or so after the handover, the old mantra of "not mixing river waters with well water" has proved hollow. The two-way flow of goods, capital, tourists, family relatives, and business and other contacts accelerated, creating a closely-knit economy between Hong Kong, the Pearl River Delta and further inland.

Growth of anti-Beijing sentiments

155 years of British rule resulted in generations of Hong Kong people brought up in a Western education system with scant affinity to China's history and developments. Few have a deep sense of Chinese nationhood. This has been exacerbated by a deepening sense of mutual mistrust between Hong Kong people and Mainland China after the 1997 handover (except during a brief spell during the 2008 Beijing Olympics and its afterglow).

In 2012, an attempt was made to amend the school curriculum to include topics on China's history, culture and national identity. This was vehemently opposed as brainwashing, leading to massive protests resulting in the attempt's abortion.

After 1997, accelerated socio-economic integration with the Mainland has brought about a massive influx of Mainland products, businesses, capital, as well as Chinese visitors and tourists. This has been subtly changing Hong Kong's cityscape and identity. Whole streets in some busy locations have turned into gold or jewellery shops or high-end department stores parading top-of-the-league branded merchandise beyond the reach of ordinary Hong Kong citizens. One may run the risk of being given the polite cold shoulder by shop assistants if one's Putonghua (Mandarin) proficiency reveals one's native Hong Kong identity.

What is more, earlier Mainlander tourists have long graduated to European or American destinations. Many recent arrivals came from remote inner provinces, visiting Hong Kong as their first trip abroad. Cases soon surfaced of some tourists from villages allowing their babies or small kids to answer the call of nature in public places or corners. There were reports of other ugly behaviours, including queue jumping etc., until more recent arrivals have been forewarned by Mainland authorities.

It's no surprise that many Hong Kong people harbour the feeling that Mainland influences are eroding Hong Kong's cityscape and identity. The perception that the government is beholden to Mainland interests adds to a feeling of animosity towards Beijing.

Brought up in an environment of negative impressions of China and a general lack of a sense of nationhood, many Hong Kong people, particularly the younger generations, identify themselves as "Hongkongers" first and foremost.

According to a University of Hong Kong survey of public opinions released on 27 June, 2019 [2], 53 per cent of interviewees considered themselves "Hongkongers" while only 11 per cent regarded themselves as Chinese. 12 per cent identified themselves as "Chinese in Hong Kong", and 23 per cent as "Hongkongers in China". When asked if they were proud of being a national citizen of China, 71 per cent said "no"; only 27 per cent said "yes." 90 per cent in the age group 18-29 answered "no."

Bubbling protests

With more freedoms allowed under One Country Two Systems, Hong Kong has become a city of regular organized protests. The following are milestone examples.

In 2003, half a million people took to the streets against the implementation of Article 23 of the Basic Law, Hong Kong's mini-constitution, which prohibits treason, secession, sedition and subversion against the Chinese government. Article 23 has failed to be enacted to this day.

The 2012 protests (mentioned earlier) against a proposal to amend school curricula were led by then 15-year-old Joshua Wong, (now a Hong Kong protest icon), who formed a group called Scholarism to oppose the proposal.

2014 saw the launch of the "Umbrella Movement", resulting in massive protests occupying Hong Kong's major urban thoroughfare for 79 consecutive days to oppose the package of government proposals for universal suffrage (one-man-one-vote) to select Hong Kong's top leader (Chief Executive) but with pre-screening of candidates.

In 2016, thousands of people protested outside Hong Kong government's headquarters calling for Hong Kong's independence from China. The protests were sparked when the electoral commission banned six pro-independence candidates from running in elections for the city's legislature.

2019-20 was marked by monumental protest marches participated by what some estimated at 2 million citizens against the introduction of an extradition bill to allow criminal fugitives in Hong Kong, on a case-by-case basis, to be extradited to jurisdictions with which the territory lacks a formal extradition treaty, including mainland China. Even after the bill was eventually withdrawn, the protests continued apace to press home their "five demands", including the resignation of the current Chief Executive Carrie Lam and the implementation of "real" universal suffrage for electing the Chief Executive and all members of the legislature.

A significant number of protesters eventually turned radical or violent with use of petrol bombs and sharp instruments, including occupation of Hong Kong's international airport, storming of the Legislative Council Chambers, surrounding the headquarters of the Hong Kong police, doxing of police officers and their close relatives, defacing of national emblems on the front of Central Government's representative organs, trashing "Beijing-friendly" shops, restaurants and banks, in general, holding the city's law and order to ransom. Many protesters were inflamed by reports of perceived "police brutality".

During this period of almost weekly violence-infested protests, ordinary citizens found themselves in the middle of a horror movie. They had to avoid going near hotspots picked by protesters. Most of the violent protests were staged after dark. People had to be psychologically prepared for evening social engagements to be abruptly cancelled if journeys happened to cross the protesters' chosen paths. For those preferring the security of their homes, the television screen offered a nonstop real-life drama of familiar routine – road-blocking by black-clad rioters' many wearing face and high-grade gas-masks, provocative flags with pro-independence slogans, throwing of petrol bombs, protective umbrellas used for shielding rioters, vandalism of road guardrails, traffic lights, and mass transit installations, stand-off against cordons of riot police, etc.

On one occasion, a cache of TATP, a highly volatile ingredient preferred by terrorist bomb makers world-wide, was found by the Police.

The saga of violent protests came to a head with the siege of the Chinese University of Hong Kong campus. This was followed by a much larger and more entrenched 12-day standoff at the Polytechnic University. Following a police blockade, the latter siege ended with hundreds of protesters arrested. A massive cache of hand-made petrol bombs and military-grade bows and arrows was found in the university campus.

An open plot for legislative paralysis and "mutual destruction"
The anti-extradition-bill protests coincided with local district council elections, where the pan-democratic camp, which has been backing the demands of the protesters, took a clean sweep of council seats. The camp has gained absolute majority in both votes and electoral seats in all but one of the 18 District Councils, tripling their seats from 124 to 388.

Benny Tai, a university academic-cum-political-activist, who helped to launch the earlier "Occupy Central" tactic leading to the "Umbrella Movement" in 2014, came up with a detailed "35+" plot, "10 steps to real mutual destruction", in a Chinese-language Hong Kong newspaper article on April 28, 2020.[3] His stated objective is to coerce Beijing into accepting the protesters' demands. His plan was embraced by the pan-democrats.

As outlined[4] by Henry Litton, a retired Hong Kong Court of Final Appeal judge of many years standing, the Benny Lai plot is first to capitalize on the pan-democrats' domination in district council elections by expanding their 35-plus legislative seats into dominance in the 70-seat legislature. The objective is to use this domination to form a united front to thoroughly paralyze the legislature, including the annual budget, in order to force the resignation of the Chief Executive in accordance with Article 52(3) of the Basic Law. According to the plot's calculations, Beijing would have to intervene, in turn resulting in "strong" protests in the streets with bloody repressions to follow. Western countries would then respond with political and economic sanctions on China in a downward spiral of "mutual destruction".

Even if this somewhat fanciful Armageddon may not come to pass, dominance of the legislature and the district councils by anti-Beijing pan-democrats will translate into king-maker influence in Hong Kong's Election Committee, responsible for electing Hong Kong's top leader (the Chief Executive).

A divided society with deep-rooted socio-economic and political challenges
Even before the Benny Tai plot, Hong Kong's legislature had already been in a state of gridlock with opposing pan-democrats obstructing government proposals at every turn. Even the election of a House Committee chairperson took 17 meetings over six months. Many critical proposals including housing and land development grind to a halt.

The series of massive protests has revealed deep-seated divisions in the society, between the pan-democrats and pro-establishment camp and between the haves and have-nots.

Hong Kong's Gini coefficient – in which zero represents maximum equality and one represents maximum inequality – now stands at 0.539, its highest level in 45 years. By comparison, the highest Gini coefficient among the major developed economies is 0.411 (in the US). The economy is dominated by an oligarchy of big businesses enjoying unrivalled positions in many sectors. The economic base is also extremely narrow, skewed towards property and finance. Upward mobility is seriously eroded.

The tip of the iceberg of the economic divide is housing. Hong Kong's housing property is fiendishly expensive. The median price of a small apartment of a few hundred square feet in an ordinary neighbourhood is more than 20 times the annual median household income. "Nano" apartments of 200 square feet or less are getting more common. Subdivided units in old tenement buildings are everywhere. As rents, let alone purchase prices, are sky high, many young people, even with a college education, have to work as many as twelve hours a day, six days a week, to make ends meet.

As the New York Times points out, tiny apartments and punishing work hours are the economic roots of Hong Kong's protests.[5]

National Security Law and Electoral Reform

During the prolonged violence-infested protests from June 2019, leading protesters and activists were given audience with top Western leaders, including former American Vice President Mike Pence. During overseas visits and appearances at international forums, they made repeated calls for foreign governments to sanction Beijing and Hong Kong. This coincided with a rising tide of Western pushback against China across the board.

Additionally, evidence emerged that some protesters had been trained in advance at the Oslo Freedom Forum as early two years before the Umbrella Movement.[6] Jimmy Lai, the founder and proprietor of the Apple Daily (a leading anti-Beijing tabloid in Hong Kong), and the most prominent local champion of the protest movement, has long been viewed by Beijing as having connections with the CIA (Central Intelligence Agency), a charge Lai denied for lack of concrete evidence.[7] At the time of writing, he and a number of Apple Daily's top executives have been arrested under the National Security Law. Certain funds connected to his company and related entities have been frozen, pending trial. Meanwhile, Jimmy Lai was awarded the Truman-Reagan Medal of Freedom by America's anti-communist organization Victims of Communism Memorial Foundation.

One Country Two Systems is implemented under the Basic Law, a national law of the People's Republic of China.[8] Article 23 of the Basic Law states:

"The Hong Kong Special Administrative Region shall enact laws on its own to prohibit any act of treason, secession, sedition, subversion against the Central People's Government, or theft of state secrets, to prohibit foreign political organizations or bodies from conducting political activities in the Region, and to prohibit political organizations or bodies of the Region from establishing ties with foreign political organizations or bodies."

The failure to enact Article 23 of the Basic Law in 2003 due to protests has revealed a gaping loophole in the eyes of Beijing against subversives, both local and foreign, trying to turn Hong Kong into a base to undermine China's stability under the CCP. The escalation of apparently well-funded and well-organized riotous protests with growing calls for Hong Kong's separatism or independence, the shadow of foreign backing, if not infiltration, the serious breakdown of law and order, the legislative gridlock and the lack of a strong governance system to tackle Hong Kong's deep-seated socio-economic divide all concentrated Beijing's mind. The outcome was the rapid introduction of the National Security Law.

The National Security Law [9] took effect in Hong Kong on 30 June 2020. Following a hasty process of the Standing Committee of the National People's Congress (SCNPC), the law was incorporated in Annex III of the Basic Law, Hong Kong's mini-constitution, bypassing Hong Kong's own legislature.

The same national security imperatives drove home Hong Kong's Improving Electoral System (Consolidated Amendments) Bill, using a similar quickened legislative process through the SCNPC.[10] The "electoral reform" is calculated to drastically dilute the influence of directly-elected legislators, increasing the proportion of Beijing loyalists and creating a powerful political vetting system for Legislative Council and District Council candidates. The stated aim is to ensure that only "patriots" can take part in Hong Kong's governance.

Whys and wherefores

The violence-infested protests openly trampling on China's redlines has been a shattering wakeup call. In the eyes of Beijing, many people both in and outside Hong Kong seem to have forgotten the role of the One Country under the Two Systems. There is a lack of appreciation that Hong Kong is a Special Administrative Region of China, where the Chief Executive must be trusted by, work with and accountable to Beijing.

Hong Kong's aspirations for more freedom and democracy are well understood by Beijing. The city has been enjoying unprecedented freedoms compared with its former status as a colony. It's no small feat for Hong Kong, under the sovereignty of the CCP, to be voted the freest economy in the world for well over two decades.

Let's not forget that one man, one vote to elect the Chief Executive, or universal suffrage, is NOT included in the Joint Declaration with Britain. It was, however, on Beijing's initiative to include such provisions in the Basic Law, Hong Kong's mini-constitution, subject to certain safeguards in Article 45:

"The method for selecting the Chief Executive shall be specified in the light of the actual situation in the Hong Kong Special Administrative Region and in accordance with the principle of gradual and orderly progress. The ultimate aim is the selection of the Chief Executive by universal suffrage upon nomination by a broadly representative nominating committee in accordance with democratic procedures".

There are two important safeguards for Beijing: (a) the gradual process is not a straight line. It may be adjusted in the light of the actual situation and under the principle of gradual and orderly progress. (b) The ultimate aim is selection of the Chief Executive by universal suffrage but the candidates are to be pre-screened by a nominating committee in accordance with democratic principles.

One may argue that the provision of a screening committee is not "democratic". But that was the deal under the unique One Country Two Systems. It is better than having no vote at all to elect the city's leader in colonial times.

That explains why Beijing has become so disillusioned when Hong Kong's universal suffrage package under Article 45 was formally rejected by the pan-democrats on 18 June, 2015. This fanned the Umbrella Movement and continuing demands for "real universal suffrage" in the Anti-Extradition Bill violent protests.

In the eyes of Beijing, there is no one-size-fit-all democracy. Singapore's model is different from the United Kingdom's, while the latter's is also different from the United States'. In any case, Hong Kong's One Country Two Systems is unique. Its constitutional safeguards must be respected. Another wakeup call for Beijing is that many Hong Kong people, particularly the younger generation, lack a strong sense of nationhood and have an ingrained distrust of the Communist Party. This phenomenon seems to permeate different sectors of the society, including education, legal, medical, labour and welfare. Many anti-Beijing legislators, activists and professional union leaders fall into this category.

Most recently, Beijing is alive to the risks of Hong Kong's One Country Two Systems being a pawn in the intensifying Great Power rivalry with the United States. Hence, the extension of China's "Anti-Foreign-Sanctions Law" to be implemented in Hong Kong subject to local legislation.

CCP legitimacy

The main reason for negative views of the CCP, not only in Hong Kong but throughout the West, is that the Party is authoritarian and a One Party state is illegitimate.

However, according to the Harvard Kennedy School Ash Center research report of July 2020 [11], the CCP tops many governments in terms of people' support, multiple ranks above the United States.

Under the CCP's tutelage, the lives, self-respect, and national confidence of the Chinese people have improved miraculously. According to the World Bank, China has brought more than 800 million people out of poverty since economic reforms in the 1970s. Its extreme poverty rate fell from 66.3% in 1990 to just 0.3% in 2018 – accounting for over 60% of global poverty reduction, according to the Centre for Strategic and International Studies.

Following redoubled efforts, China now claims to have lifted all of its people out of extreme poverty, using the poverty line of US$2.30 a day – slightly above the World Bank's lowest threshold of US$1.90. Nearly everyone completes compulsory schooling, matching the average level in high-income countries. There is almost universal access to electricity and safe drinking water. Child mortality rate has plummeted, according to the United Nations.

If democracy is to deliver better lives for the vast majority of people, then China doesn't have to stick to America's one-taste-for-all Coca-Cola formula, as China's Foreign Minister Wang Yi recently quipped.

In the 1950's, China used to be poorer than India, the world's largest democracy. Now, China's GDP is 4.78 times larger than India in nominal terms. This by no means proves that China's One Party state is superior. But at least, people should reflect before casting aspersions on the CCP's legitimacy in the eyes of the Chinese people.

Impact of the National Security Law and Electoral Reform

Beijing doesn't lack foresight of the massive international backlash resulting from draconian changes to Hong Kong's legislature and governance. Twenty-four years of ups and downs in One Country Two Systems have taught Beijing that total political laissez faire only backfires in Hong Kong's socio-political ecology.

In the final analysis, without political and social stability, Hong Kong would be stuck in a rut, unable to amass the capabilities to tackle its deep-seated socio-economic challenges. This would greatly reduce the usefulness of One Country Two Systems to Beijing. As a last resort, the threatening unrests pushed Beijing to opt for major surgery, at the cost of some pain.

According to the American Chamber of Commerce in Hong Kong in May 2021, 42% of respondents are considering or planning to leave Hong Kong, with 62.3% citing their discomfort with the controversial national security law imposed by Beijing. Those intending to remain cited factors such as a good quality of life and excellent business environment.

Similarly, a number of Hong Kong people are choosing to emigrate to the United Kingdom, Canada, Australia or the United States, following special immigration and settlement concessions introduced by these countries in response to what is perceived as Beijing's crackdown on Hong Kong.

Such unease, doubts and mistrust amongst Hong Kong citizens are reminiscent of what happened before the handover in 1997. Hong Kong's subsequent performance under One Country Two Systems had proved them misguided. For example, as many as 300,000 Hong Kong citizens returned to live in Hong Kong permanently after acquiring their Canadian passports. In Beijing's calculations, in due course, doubters would be proved wrong once more.

Usefulness to Beijing of One Country Two Systems
In the summer of 1990, I was invited in my private capacity by the U.S. State Department to visit the United States as a sponsored "International Visitor". The object was to brief America's top corporate leaders, including Steve Forbes (at his Fifth Avenue office), on what I expected China to become beyond Tiananmen Square. That was before China's admission to the World Trade Organization (WTO). I pointed out that Hong Kong represented some 20% of China's then GDP. Beijing had to rely on Hong Kong for a substantial proportion of foreign currency earnings to maintain regime stability. Moreover, China wanted to embark on a road of reform and opening up, expecting to join the international community.

In 2003, I was invited to HRH Prince Andrew's Buckingham Place private office to brief him personally on China for his newly-acquired role as Special Representative of UK Trade and Investment. By then, Hong Kong's economy size relative to China had fallen to some 8%.[12] But China was on the rise, and continued to press ahead with opening up to the world, supported by Hong Kong's One Country Two Systems.

Although Hong Kong is now equivalent to only some 2% of China's GDP, under China's Five Year Plan (2021-25), One Country Two Systems is expected to turbo-charge the internationalization of the Guang-dong-Hong Kong-Macau Greater Bay Area.[13] This has a combined population of some 70 million people and an economy 12th largest in the world. Additionally, as a world-class financial centre, Hong Kong could help accelerate the internationalization of the Renminbi (RMB), the Chinese yuan, and China's budding digital sovereign currency. Likewise, Hong Kong is expected to play a pivotal role as a fund-raising international financial centre and a regional arbitration centre for China's global Belt and Road Initiative.[14] In the final analysis, absent One Country Two Systems, what is the point if Hong Kong becomes just a smaller Shanghai?

Part of a rising, more powerful China
According to the Centre for Economics and Business Research, thanks to being first to recover economically from the Covid-19 pandemics, China is now expected to overtake the United States as the largest economy in the world by 2028, five years sooner than expected.[15] China is the world's largest manufacturer, trader, and centre of the global supply and value chain. Seven of the world's ten largest and busiest container ports are in China including Hong Kong. 124 countries have China as the largest trading partner, compared to 56 for the United States. With Hong Kong, China is the central trade and logistics hub for the Regional Comprehensive Economic Partnership (RCEP), the world's largest trading bloc, comprising all the ASEAN countries and their main trading partners. RCEP has a combined population of 2.2 billion people, representing a third of the world's GDP and half of the world's manufacture. It's also home to the largest cohort of middle-class consumers the world has ever seen, according to Paraq Khanna in his eponymous book, "The Future is Asian"[16].

According to the Organization for Economic Cooperation and Development (OECD), the developing economies, of which China is the largest, are expected to represent 60% of global GDP by 2030.[17] The days when the so-called G7 advanced countries called all the shots are long gone.

As China has four times the population of the United States, provided its productivity is more than a quarter of the latter, it will become the world's largest economy. This looming reality cannot be wished away by denialism or decoupling. Nor is it realistic to expect that China can be coerced into reversing its development trajectory.

The challenge is how to engage a rising, more powerful, more confident, and yet "problematic" China constructively to the benefit of both sides and the rest of the world.

Way forward

There is no doubt that China wants One Country Two Systems to succeed, but not at the cost of compromising national sovereignty and security. Now that law and order and relative political calm have been restored, it's time to ponder how liberal ideas and democracy could be further advanced in Hong Kong and how the United Kingdom and other foreign countries should deal with China and the One Country Two Systems as re-defined. Under One Country Two Systems, Hong Kong is well placed to play a dynamic role in engaging with China involving foreign stakeholders and businesses. However, Beijing's safeguards in the Basic Law, Hong Kong's constitution, must be respected. As they say, when in Rome, do as the Romans do.

The following perspectives may offer some food for thought.

How the West deals with a rising China translates into how Hong Kong is treated by Beijing and by the West. While pressing China to reform perceived problematic behaviour and practices, the West should abandon ideas, if any, of triggering regime change with or without involving Hong Kong. Instead of obsessing with demonizing China, what is likely to be more constructive are wide-ranging trust-building exchanges and partnerships, including academia, think-tanks, environmental NGOs, familiarization visits by Parliamentary groups, legal reform studies, Belt and Road infrastructural projects, green energy joint ventures, offshore conduits for renminbi internationalization, pandemics collaboration, scientific research, space exploration, as well as arts, culture, cinema production, and sports.

Trade and investment opportunities should also be explored, taking advantage of Hong Kong's position in the Greater Bay Area, its role in China's Five Year Plan 2021-25, and its linkages with the RCEP, including consumer products and services, technology development, and smart city management.

Shortly before the "umbrella movement", a Democratic Party leader was surrounded by over 100 university students on campus who berated her for her party's ineffectiveness in not daring to take to the streets. I later asked some of the students if they wanted a revolution. Shocked to hear them reply in the affirmative, I asked how it would succeed. They said they didn't care: that was the spirit that overthrew the Qing dynasty.

This defiance, now subdued or repressed, is unlikely to disappear, only waiting for the next flashpoint.[18] While Hong Kong's education system is being "reformed" to introduce a sense of nationhood, there need to be meaningful political outlets to channel aspirations to constructive ends.

Even with the newly-introduced "electoral reform", there is room for a new-styled "democratic" or "liberal" party in Hong Kong, working within the confines of the Basic Law and National Security Law. The government must be held to account on livelihood issues such as housing, upward mobility, socio-economic divide, integration with the Greater Bay Area, development as a smart city, and Hong Kong's long-term development.

Given a successful track record of trust-building with Beijing and greater popular support by the Hong Kong people, there is every chance that such a party could be invited to share power in Hong Kong's governance at some point in time. To young activists, instead of tilting at windmills, this could be a rightful channel to achieve self-fulfilment with meaningful change in Hong Kong's political ecology.

Hong Kong is expected to play a pivotal role in China's long-term initiatives such as the Greater Bay Area development and the Belt and Road Initiative. As China grows in size and international presence, so will Hong Kong's relative importance to the nation's strategy. With Beijing's national security worries now resolved, there is every likelihood that One Country Two Systems may well be renewed beyond 2047, its supposed expiry date. If so, like the Joint Declaration on Hong Kong's handover in 1997 which entered into force on 27 May 1985, a decision to renew One Country Two Systems would have to be taken by 2035 at the latest, if business and citizens' confidence is to be maintained.

Regardless of the introduction of National Security Law and "electoral reform", and unfazed by what seem "astronomical" prices by international comparisons, the city's new housing property developments at both ends of the market continue to be snapped up by investors and the public at large, a vote of confidence in the city's long-term future. To paraphrase Mark Twain, report of Hong Kong's death seems over-exaggerated.

Chapter 8

Taiwan and its Relationship with the People's Republic of China
Past, Present and Future
Dr Juli F. Minoves

Imperial China was the most powerful nation in the world until its decline in the 18th and 19th centuries. The shame of unequal treaties imposed by western powers in gunboat diplomacy framed the nationalist and sometimes xenophobic rhetoric that both Nationalists and Communists would use in the 20th century to reclaim control over historical borders and their perceived rightful place in the international arena. The Kuomintang Nationalists ended up in Taiwan controlling their own brand of authoritarian regime until the late eighties, and asserting their representation of all China which was undermined by the loss of China's seat at the United Nations in 1971. The establishment of the People's Republic of China in 1949 allowed "the world's most populous nation" to "achieve sufficient sovereignty and unity throughout its vast domain to enjoy a monopoly of full control over foreign relations in the central government".[1]

Since 1949 the rise of China has been spectacular both in economic terms and as an actor in international relations. Mao Zedong created the conditions for an effective control over the territory and presided over the consolidation of an increasingly powerful army with access to nuclear weapons. Deng Xiaoping, a more pragmatic leader who did not care what color the cat was as long as the cat would catch the mouse, cemented the foundations of China's economic rise.[2] Subsequent leaders, while not being able to claim the generational legitimacy granted by the communist victory in the Civil War, have been mindful of the old "mandate of heaven" that made each imperial dynasty legitimate in the eyes of the people: attaining benefits for the Chinese population[3]. Linz and Stepan have recognized that some nondemocratic regimes "have to their credit considerable achievements in one or another realm of societal life", notwithstanding the obvious negative dimensions of the regime.[4] They referred, among other polities, to Taiwan before democratisation but their thinking could be extended to China under present circumstances. And thus lies the crux of the present and future relationship between the PRC and the ROC: the PRC is a nondemocratic regime, no matter how many achievements it can claim in the economic sphere while Taiwan is a consolidated and well-functioning democracy. Who rules and who decides who rules has become intertwined with the issue of history, nationalism and sovereignty and the IR dimensions of the US-China rivalry.

---

1 Allen S. Whiting, "Foreign Policy of China" in Roy C. Macridis, ed. Foreign Policy in World Politics, States and Regions (Englewood Cliffs NJ: Prentice Hall, 1989), 252
2 See Eugenio Bregolat, The Second Chinese Revolution (New York: Palgrave MacMillan, 2015) p. 14 Digital edition: "The quintessence of all these is Deng Xiaoping's most famous saying: 'it doesn't matter if the cat is black or white, what matters is that it catches mice". According to Deng himself, this is a traditional Sichuan saying [...] Pragmatism, opposed to Mao's egalitarian Utopia: the priority is to create a strong and wealthy country ..."
3 See W.M. Spellman, Monarchies 1000-2000 (London: Reaktion Books, 2001/2012) loc. 4461 Digital Printing: "In the estimate of one recent observer, the success and consolidation of the 1949 revolution could not have been achieved 'without conscious direction from a state inheriting all the mysterious prestige of the traditional bearers of the Mandate of Heaven' "
4 See Juan J. Linz and Alfred Stepan, Problems of Democratic Transition and Consolidation, Southern Europe, South America and Post-Communist Europe (Baltimore: The Johns Hopkins University press, 1996), p. 145

Historical Situation

As of June 2021 Taiwan's population was 23,487,509.[5] The indigenous people of proto-Malayan or Austronesian origins are only 575, 967 (Oct. 2020).[6] The vast majority are Han Chinese, arrived in early migrations of the Hakka, and later of the Hoklo, and after 1949 mainlanders flowing with the nationalists of the Kuomintang (KMT).

Taiwan is also known as Formosa or "Ilha Formosa" (Beautiful Island) a Portuguese name originating in the 16th century.[7] The Dutch East India Company which had been in Taiwan since 1623 was driven out by Koxinga, a Chinese merchant-pirate and able administrator loyal to the Ming dynasty after its defeat by the Manchus.[8] A succession of early deaths in the Koxinga dynasty ultimately resulted in the end of their realm in 1683. The administration of Taiwan was then placed under Qing rule through the governor of Fujian. Taiwan was governed with neglect for two hundred years until 1887 when, mindful of interest from Japan and western powers, Beijing decided to separate Taiwan from Fujian and make it a proper province of China. One could say that this was a bit too little too late. On 17 April 1895 with the signing of the Treaty of Shimonoseki at the end of the first Sino-Japanese War, China ceded in perpetuity the sovereignty of Taiwan and the Pescadores Islands to Japan.

The Japanese Colonial period is one of contrasts. On the one hand Japan wanted to make Taiwan a showcase for its advancement and modernity as an imperialist world power. It created a predictable and rational governance, developed railroads and communications, schools and higher learning, and endeavoured to eradicate tropical diseases. The economy flourished. On the other hand, it kept the Taiwanese population separate from the colonial masters until later in the 1930s when a policy of Japanization was deemed necessary. One just needs to visit Beitou, an area of Taipei with hot springs baths from the Japanese colonial period, or the National Taiwan University Campus, formerly of Taihoku Imperial University, the seventh of the Japanese Imperial Universities founded in 1928, to realize that the Japanese were planting long-term roots in the island. They left a mixed bag of good and bad: racial colonial attitudes difficult to stomach by the Taiwanese yet important social and economic progress.

---

5 Source: Statistical Bureau (National Statistics, Republic of China) at https://eng.stat.gov.tw/point.asp?index=9
6 Source: Department of Household Registration Affairs, MOL, ROC at https://ws.moi.gov.tw/001/Upload/OldFile/site_stuff/321/1/month/month en.html
7 Jonathan Manthorpe, Forbidden Nation: A History of Taiwan (New York: St. Martin's Griffin, 2009) p. 22
8 Margery Wolf, Women and the Family in Rural Taiwan (Stanford: Stanford University Press, 1972) p. 2 See also Manthorpe, op. cit.,84: "In Beijing's eyes Koxinga was also the man who firmly and irrefutably made the island of Taiwan an inaliable part of China. Before Koxinga, the mainland made no claim to own Taiwan".

Photo 1: Chiang Kai-shek, FDR and Winston Churchill at the Cairo Conference in Egypt. 25 XI 1943.[9]

The 1943 Cairo Declaration prefaced how the new post-world war II order would affect Formosa and the Pescadores. The islands would be brought back into the Chinese fold of the Republic of China (ROC).

The new Chinese Governor of Taiwan appointed by Chiang Kai-shek, General Chen Yi, arrived in the island in October 1945. His corrupt and brutal rule of detentions and arbitrary executions was going to create great disturbances in Taiwan and prove disastrous for the economy. In October 1949 the Communists achieved victory on the mainland. The ROC fled to Taiwan. "By the time Chiang formally moved the capital of the Republic of China to Taipei in December 1949 there were about two million mainlanders on the island, among them 600,000 surviving members of the Kuomintang army".[10] Two authoritarian and highly nationalistic state apparatuses on both sides of the Taiwan strait, the PRC and the ROC, were claiming to represent the totality of the Chinese people and its ancient culture.

The Korean War, and the cold war in general, would place Taiwan at the centre of a delicate balance of power in Asia and the Pacific ocean in which the United States of America would be a central player. While Chiang Kai-shek's priority, at least in the first years, was to envision how to conquer the mainland, the US strategy would be to maintain the status quo and make sure that Taiwan, and its geo-strategic position, would not be lost to the West. Meanwhile the government in Taiwan would be the recognized government of China and would control China's seat at the United Nations until 1971. On 25 October 1971 the UN General Assembly through resolution 2758 decided to recognize the representatives of the government of the PRC "as the only lawful representatives of China" and to expel "the representatives of Chiang Kai-shek".[11] The rapprochement between the United States

9 Source: National Archives Catalog Collection FDR-PHOCO: Franklin D. Roosevelt Library Public Domain Photographs, 1882 - 1962 at https://catalog. archives.gov/id/196609
10 Manthorpe, op. cit., 194
11 See A/RES/2758(XXVI) of 1971 in Resolutions adopted by the General Assembly during its 26th session, 21 September-22 December 1971. - A/8429. - 1972. - p. 2. - (GAOR, 26th sess., Suppl. no. 29) at https://digitallibrary.un.org/record/192054?ln=en

and Mao's China, an important piece of the Vietnam puzzle for President Nixon, would soon follow as the result of a number of secret meetings undertaken by then US National Security Advisor Henry Kissinger. Nixon visited China in a historical trip in 1972. A year later, Henry Kissinger, in conversations with Mao Zedong addressed the issue of Taiwan. Mao's approach was to try to separate the issue of Taiwan from the relations with the US, assert that in his view there would not be "a peaceful transition" but essentially to affirm that there were no time pressures for the issue: "I say that we can do without Taiwan for the time being, and let it come after one hundred years. Do not take matters of this world so rapidly. Why is there need to be in such great haste"?[12]

Photo 2: President Richard Nixon Shaking Hands with Chairman Mao Tse-tung, 2/21/1972.[13]

The US and the PRC normalized relations in 1979, during the Carter administration. The American Embassy was moved from Taipei to Beijing. Normalization was understandably badly received in Taiwan: the trip of Deputy Secretary of State Warren Christopher to Taiwan in December 1978 to chart the "post-normalization relationship" was greeted with "violent demonstrations".[14] The US Congress passed the Taiwan Relations Act in April of 1979 which, among other matters, states that:

"the United States decision to establish diplomatic relations with the People's Republic of China rests upon the expectation that the future of Taiwan will be determined by peaceful means and that any effort to determine the future of Taiwan by other than peaceful means, including by boycotts or embargoes is considered a threat to the peace and security of the Western Pacific area and of grave concern to the United States. [...] the United States shall provide Taiwan with arms of a defensive character and shall maintain the capacity of the United States to resist any resort to force or other forms of

12 Henry Kissinger, On China (New York: Penguin Books, 2012) p. 280
13 Source: National Archives Catalog Collection RN-WHPO White House Photo Office Collection (Nixon Administration), 1/20/1969 - 8/9/1974 at https://catalog.archives.gov/id/194759
14 Steven M. Goldstein, China and Taiwan (Cambridge: Polity Press, 2015) p. 55

coercion that would jeopardize the security, or social or economic system, of the people of Taiwan".[15]

Taiwan's Democratisation

Possibly the most significant event in Taiwan's political life of the recent decades is the transformation of the authoritarian KMT regime into a full-fledged democracy. After Chiang Kai-shek died in 1975 his son Chiang Ching-kuo took up the reins of government and was elected President by the National Assembly in 1978.[16] In 1987 he lifted martial law. He also allowed family visits to the PRC. As Larry Diamond writes "Taiwan is often viewed as a paradigmatic case of controlled political opening from above by a strong and self-confident ruling party" but "the social movements and protests of the 1980s 'translated long-suppressed popular discontent into ardent social forces that eroded the effectiveness of one-party rule and softened the resolve of the state elite to retain the authoritarian arrangements".[17] This democratisation from above with social pressure from the grassroots was also facilitated by high levels of economic progress and a broad consensus on economic policy which caused "the moderation of their party politics and the continuation of their economic growth".[18]

In 1996 Lee Teng-hui, the Kuomintang candidate, won the first direct democratic presidential elections. In 2000 Chen Shui-bian, leader of the Democratic Progressive Party (DPP), a party affiliated to Liberal International, the World Federation of Liberal Political Parties, was elected President of the ROC. He was reelected in 2004. His tenure was marked by clashes with the KMT, who controlled the legislative Yuan, on environmental issues (nuclear power), and was also significant in a reaffirmation of Taiwan's identity and a new focus on educational programmes. In foreign policy he clashed with the PRC, which started a campaign of reaching out to the Kuomintang. His tenure was marred by corruption allegations that ultimately sent him to jail.

Ma-Ying-jeou of the KMT was elected president of the ROC in 2008 and reelected in 2012. During his time in office an Economic Cooperation Framework Agreement (ECFA) – a preferential trade agreement- was signed between the ROC and the PRC.[19] Ma met personally with Xi Jinping in Singapore in 2015, a highly choreographed encounter and a historical first, marking Xi's desire to engage in political negotiations, an issue 'not to be passed on generation after generation'.[20] This new sense of urgency on China's part was cut short by the DPP's Tsai Ing-wen election shortly after the summit of the leaders of the ROC and the PRC, in 2016, and her reelection with over 57% of the vote in 2020. Tsai Ing-wen is the first female president of Taiwan.

---

15 See Conference report filed in House, 3/24/1979, H. Rept. 96-71, H.R.2479 - Taiwan Relations Act, 96th Congress (1979-1980) at https://www.congress.gov/bill/96th-congress/house-bill/2479
16 See Manthorpe, op. cit., p. 204 on Chinag Ching-kuo: "The younger Chiang is an elusive figure. He is adored beyond comprehension by some people and hated by others (...) He carries the ultimate responsibility for the deaths of tens of thousands of Taiwanese (...) At the same time it was the younger Chiang who finally saw that Taiwan's long-term security lay in political reform".
17 Larry Diamond, Developing Democracy Toward Consolidation (Baltimore: The Johns Hopkins University Press, 1999) p. 235 partially quoting Yun-han Chu, Crafting Democratisation in Taiwan (Taipei: Institute For National Policy Research, 1992), p. 99
18 Diamond, op. cit., 86
19 See Cross-Straits Economic Cooperation Framework Agreement 29 June 2010 at https://www.ecfa.org.tw/EcfaAttachment/ECFADoc/ECFA.pdf
20 See Kerry Brown and Kalley Wu Tzu-hui, The Trouble With Taiwan – History, the United States and a Rising China (London: Zed Books, 2019) pp. 119-120

Photo 3: President Tsai Ing-wen (left) with Taiwanese legislators at the Presidential Office Building in 2018. Bi-khim Hsiao (right) is now the Taipei Economic and Cultural Representative Office (TECRO) Representative in the United States.[21]

A tale of Two Regimes

Who rules and how they rule is a useful way to grasp both the present and the future relationship between China and Taiwan. The ROC and the PRC both have highly successful economies, with their own particular challenges. They are polities where the state is in charge and where policies determined by those who rule are carried out in orderly fashion. They both started after World War II as autocracies where a common nationalist view diverged over how to bring modernity to China. They both used terror, repression and control to impose their visions of modernity. Earlier than the mainland, Taiwan became a miracle economy, thanks in part to an agrarian reform carried out by the Kuomintang in the 1950s that freed land and capital for economic development. The PRC, animated by communist ideology, went through different stages of upheaval, until, after the death of Mao, Deng Xiaoping was able to place China into a path of pragmatism and market liberalization.[22] In 1999, the "theory of Deng Xiaoping" was added to the preamble of the Constitution of the PRC, together with the principles of "Marxism-Leninism" and the thinking of "Mao Zedong".[23]

Chinese communist leaders have rejected linking economic liberalisation with political liberalisation: they need an authoritarian state, they often argue, to safeguard national sovereignty, and speed up efficiency in decision making particularly for issues of economic development as well as to achieve social and political stability in a country with great inequalities.[24]

---

21 Photo Credit: Liberal International, Taipei 2018
22 Friedrich and Brzezinski in their classical work on regimes referred to Mao's China as a "totalitarian dictatorship" where the leaders had "retained, adapted and elaborated" techniques of personal agitation and the "mass line" for propagation of the party line. See Carl J. Friedrich and Zbigniew K. Brzezinski, Totalitarian Dictatorship & Autocracy (New York: Praeger, 1972) pp. 145-146
23 Eugenio Bregolat, La Segunda Revolución China (Barcelona: Destino, 2007) p. 284
24 See Bregolat, op. cit., pp. 262-264 He does a comparative analysis with the case of the Soviet Union where political liberalization preceded shock therapy, rather than gradual, economic liberalization. He argues that this historical example looms heavily on Chinese leaders.

The contrast between regimes in the PRC and the ROC is still more accentuated in the era of both Xi and Tsai. Whereas in Taiwan, a woman is President and she leads an administration that endeavours to take Taiwan into the levels of respect for human rights (for example the historical adoption of gay marriage) and the environment common to the most advanced democracies, in the PRC the rule of Xi Jinping backs away from more reform-minded policies of the first decade of the XXIst century and reinstalls vocabulary and methods of the past such as the mass line, leading to "ideological indoctrination" and "mild self-criticism sessions".[25]

The PRC and the ROC Taiwan in Perspective and Possibilities for the Future
To consider possible scenarios for the future of the intricate relationship between the PRC and the ROC Taiwan it might be useful to look comprehensively at the evolution of each polity so far in terms of regimes, world politics and nationalism, as in Table 1:

	PRC	ROC Taiwan
Regime Evolution 1950-2021	*Totalitarian *Post-Totalitarian *Nationalist Authoritarian with Post-Totalitarian Characteristics	*Nationalist Authoritarian *Democracy
World Politics Evolution 1950-2021	*Mao opening to West *US rapprochement to China to counter Soviet Union *Post-Tiananmen Tensions + Low International Profile and trying to develop soft power *Nationalist Assertive Period w/ Belt & Road Initiative	*Representing all China and holding UN seat at Security Council *Attributes of a State but no recognition beyond close US & Japan alliance and diplomatic relations with 15 States
Nationalism Evolution 1950-2021	*Affirmation of Sovereignty + Ideological Internationalism *Cultural Insularity vs. Cultural Cosmopolitanism *New Nationalism to buttress legitimacy for new generations of party cadres	*Official KMT nationalism of arriving mainlanders/chasm with old Han and indigenous population *Merging of identities in a new Taiwanese identity
Future of the relationship between the ROC and the PRC	*Scenario 1: Increasing (to extreme) pressure or War *Scenario 2: Traditional Chinese Long View: lowering tensions while asserting One China principle *Scenario 3: China democratises (unlikely but not impossible)	*Scenario 1: Maintains Status Quo *Scenario 2: Renewed dialogue with PRC, with or without reference to 1992 meetings *Scenario 3: Works towards unification under one country, two systems (highly unlikely especially after failed Hong Kong example) *Scenario 4: Taiwan distinct identity increases

Table 1: Evolution of the PRC and of the ROC Taiwan in Terms of Regimes, World Politics, and Nationalism and Scenarios for the Future Relationship Between the PRC and the ROC Taiwan.

---

25 Kerry Brown, China's Dream – The Culture of Chinese Communism and The Secret Sources of Its Power (Cambridge: Polity Press, 2018) p. 130

China after Mao could be considered a Post-Totalitarian regime, as a particular case of Authoritarian regimes.[26] We will qualify the China of today, decades after the death of Mao as a Nationalist Authoritarian Regime with Post-Totalitarian Characteristics. As we have seen before the ROC Taiwan transitioned to a democracy with a very active civil society.[27]

In terms of world politics and international relations the China of Xi Jinping is one with an ambitious foreign policy in contrast to the more soft-power oriented and lower profile preference of some of Xi's predecessors. The Belt and Road initiative, the expansive building in the islands of the South China Sea, a renewed urgency towards the issue of Taiwan vs. the long-term game of previous administrations conform to a new Chinese Nationalist Assertive Period.[28] The PRC enforces the one-China Policy dogmatically which has eroded the number of countries with whom the ROC entertains full diplomatic relations. Taiwan thus is a unique case in the world of a polity that enjoys many of the attributes of sovereign states, is highly developed, maintaining close economic relations with many nations, and yet is left out of the international world order. As an example, the recent Covid pandemic that Taiwan has tackled with good governance and transparency, and generosity with shipments of masks and other medical material that were in short supply overseas, has reminded the world of the ROC and its more than 20 million people's exclusion from the World Health Organization.

The rise of cultural nationalism in China is not new.[29] Nationalism has been a common component of the two parallel revolutionary movements of the 20th century dedicated to state building after the fall of the Imperial system, the Kuomintang and the Communists.[30] I have included in Table 1 three stages of nationalism in the PRC since 1950, but one could probably find more nuances in the evolution of Chinese nationalism since 1950. The first one is linked to the affirmation of the new state and its sovereignty controlled by the Communists after their victory over the Kuomintang in parallel with socialist ideological internationalism, a second one is the result of a tension between cultural cosmopolitism praising the West in Deng's China and cultural insularity promoted after Tiananmen Square, and the third stage would be the one we witness today, the result of a quest for legitimisation by the Chinese Communist Party (CCP) and the new leaders of China that cannot claim revolutionary legitimacy or civil war victory as the basis for their power. Dickson offers a nuanced portrait of agency regarding PRC nationalism: "What if the CCP is not the cause of Chinese nationalism but is captive to it?" he asks.[31] As the important chicken and egg question that probably finds its answer in the fact that the CCP needs nationalism to buttress its ruling legitimacy yet is also constrained by popular national sentiment and demonstrations into a tight hawkish jacket in some aspects of foreign policy. Meanwhile the ROC Taiwan has evolved from a public discourse dominated by the nationalist rhetoric of the arriving

---

26 Linz considered Post-Totalitarian regimes those Authoritarian regimes with a more or less recent totalitarian past and the fact that the dominant elites would preserve elements of the totalitarian utopia. See Juan J. Linz, Sistemi Totalitari e Regimi Autoritari – Un'Analisi Storico-Comparativa (Soveria Mannelli: Rubbettino, 2006) p. 75. Also, Hermet reaffirmed the totalitarian roots of the Chinese regime. See Guy Hermet, Totalitarismes (Paris: Economica, 1984) p. 184: Hermet explained that "a totalitarian regime is not only a regime that imposes terror: it is a regime that has the means to exclude any political occurrence, to pretend to dominate all society, and finally to consider as reversible the commitments it has undertaken with all or part of society".

27 The nationalist authoritarian regime that existed before had been responsible for the "White Terror" jailing and torturing tens of thousands of Taiwanese questioning the regime, advocating for reform or favoring independence. Many had been executed summarily.

28 Economy asserts that "on the security front, China's military expansionism in the South China Sea and claim to sovereignty over Taiwan pose a significant threat to peace and stability in the Asia Pacific region". See Elizabeth C. Economy, The Third Revolution – Xi Jinping and the New Chinese State (New York: Oxford University Press, 2018) p. 242

29 See Bruce Gilley, "Deng Xiaoping and His Successors (1976 to Present)" in William A. Joseph, ed. Politics in China, An Introduction (New York: Oxford University Press, 2010) p. 119: "Rising cultural nationalism in China, coupled with post-Cold War American global hegemony, created the conditions for rising tensions between China and the West, particularly the United States".

30 Domenico Fisichella, Totalitarismo – Un regime del nostro tempo (Roma: Carocci editore, 1987) p. 174

31 Bruce J. Dickson, The Party and the People – Chinese Politics in the 21st Century (Princeton: Princeton University Press, 2021) p. 217

KMT erasing the voice of the Taiwanese and the aboriginal people that were in the Island before the KMT's defeat in the civil war, towards the creation of a distinctive new identity for the islanders. Beyond the economic agency and identity that the PRC allows for Taiwan, Brown and Wu note the impact that democracy has had on Taiwanese identity: "Democracy has created a much more liquid notion of what it is to be Taiwanese. It has had an impact on people's identity and how they see themselves".[32] Also, polls in Taiwan show that "self-identification as Taiwanese has grown consistently throughout the democratic era" and that "significant numbers of respondents have moved from Chinese identity to dual and Taiwanese identification over a period of less than two decades".[33] The relative small size of Taiwan both in square miles and in population is also likely to have an effect on the identity of the islanders. Their identity will be less dependent on glorious ideas of history than larger countries and more in synch with collective achievements despite the odds.

Conclusion: scenarios for the future

The future scenarios envisaged in Table 1 are not mutually exclusive. They offer different avenues that might be taken, some less likely than others, in the political life of both the PRC and of the ROC Taiwan. Some of them might be possible only after changes at the political helm, something difficult to envisage in the PRC where Xi Jinping has solidified his grasp on power with the abolition of presidential term limits. Recent analyses of China's attitude towards Taiwan exacerbate what some in foreign affairs circles name "invasion panic". Esplin Odell and Heginbotham argue that if "regime security is the top priority for Chinese leaders, an invasion would risk everything on dim prospects for glory" and is unlikely.[34] Others, witnessing Hong Kong's protest movement and China's systematic repression and progressive legal decisions retiring to the dustbin of history the idea of "one country, two systems", wonder whether Taiwan is next.[35] The use of force to reunite Taiwan to China has always been a card on the table of the PRC's leadership. China, in scenario 1 could put extreme pressure on Taiwan, or even start a war, and that cannot be discarded. But despite important investments in the military of the PRC the outcome of a war to occupy Taiwan by force is more than uncertain and would come at huge costs. It is possibly a no less preoccupying saber-rattling in a high stakes confrontation with the US, to which the US is responding with arms sales to Taiwan. Beijing also wishes to deter Taipei from altering the status quo and what they call the "1992 consensus".[36] Above all it wants to make independence a non-viable road.

If Beijing, who most likely will never abandon the one-China principle, would take again the long view and kick the resolution of Taiwan's status into the future, and if that was met by some kind of dialogue by Taipei, matters would probably deescalate. But Taiwan is now a full-fledged democracy and policy is determined by an electorate and civil society that are vigilant yet do not shy away from asserting a distinct identity in elections or demonstrations, such as the ones during the Sunflower movement in 2014, and do not wish to be ruled from a mainland authoritarian regime. Dr. Tsai walks a fine line trying to address the needs of security of an unyielding Taiwan and to manage the situation with Beijing in non-provoking ways.

---

32 See Brown and Wu, op. cit., p. 97

33 See Dafyyd Fell, Government and Politics in Taiwan 2n. ed. (London: Routledge, 2018) p. 164

34 See Rachel Esplin Odell and Eric Heginbotham, "Don't Fall for the Invasion Panic", in Rachel Esplin Odell and Eric Heginbotham; Bonny Lin and David Sacks; Kharis Templeman; Oriana Skylar Mastro, "Strait of Emergency? Debating Beijing's Threat to Taiwan", Foreign Affairs Volume 100, 4 July/ August 2021 and September/October 2021 at https://www.foreignaffairs.com/articles/china/2021-08-09/strait-emergency

35 See Sarah A. Topol, "Is Taiwan Next?", The New York Times Magazine (August 4/5, 2021): "First Tibet, then Xinjiang, then Hong Kong – the edges of empire had been dutifully absorbed. Taiwan was the only one remaining".

36 In 1992 there were talks between the ROC's Straits Exchange Foundation (SEF) and the PRC's Association for Relations Across the Taiwan Strait (ARTS). Whether the two sides reached an agreement that both accept that there is one China but accept as well they have different interpretations of one China is a controversial question to this day in Taiwanese politics. See Fell, op. cit., p. 181

The most likely outcome for the near future of Beijing and Taipei's relationship, given the costs associated with direct conflagration, is the maintenance of the status quo. The ROC Taiwan will not unify willingly with the PRC even more so now that the "one country, two systems" is in shambles. It will not push for independence, aware that that would turn China's hand to the use of force. And the PRC will not let up putting pressure on Taiwan and its allies, aggressively asserting the one-China principle. There is always the possibility that China will itself transition to democracy. What seems impossible given the trend of the last few years might be something that new generations of the Chinese people might favour.[37] As Hermet notes, even in totalitarian settings history still works.[38] A coincidence of democratic regimes on both sides of the Taiwan strait might bring peaceful closure to the relationship between the PRC and the ROC Taiwan.[39]

---

37 See Kerry Brown, The World According to Xi (London: Tauris, 2018) p. 100. Brown entertains possible options of political reform in the PRC: "there are other options – along the lines, for instance, of what happened in Taiwan in the 1980s, where there was a relaxation of the rules, rather than the formal acceptance of more pluralism in politics, a decade or so before institutional change took place. Maybe a one-party system with competition within itself might be possible; indeed it is likely that this is the preferred option of the highly cautious leaders of the People's Republic".
38 Hermet, op. cit., p. 199
39 Bregolat concludes his analysis by considering democratisation possible yet, if it happens, long in time and without shortcuts. Bregolat (2007), op. cit., p. 416

Chapter 9

China And Its Neighbours
Humphrey Hawksley

I came face to face with a Chinese method of dealing with its neighbours in the northern Philippine village of Masinloc, a rugged coastal community whose fishermen have worked the same patch of sea for centuries.

Jurrick Oson, a big man, muscles bulging inside his purple sleeveless vest, had been raised to work around nets, fish, tides, and weather, his skin leathery from a lifetime on the water. His boat was moored at the end of a dirt track, with shacks and small stalls on one side and the gently lapping sea on the other.

It was a colourful, chaotic old vessel, painted in yellows, greens and blues, and she plied her trade as such boats had done for hundreds of years. Ropes and wires lashed different bits together around a narrow wooden hull, and bamboo stabilizers stretched out on each side like the wings of an albatross.

This was a place with echoes of America's rust-belt steel towns and the long-closed textile mills of Britain, a way of life that could not last.

The sea stretched westward, dappled with sunlight in a mix of bright tropical blues and murky greys towards Osun's fishing ground, Bajo de Masinloc, or Lower Masinloc, about a hundred miles away. Here it was named after the village but in the tense geopolitics of the Indo-Pacific takes the name of a colonial East India Company ship that ran around there in 1784. International law says Scarborough Shoal is inside Philippines waters. China says this is its sovereign territory and calls it Huangyan Island.

This is one of four contested flashpoints of the South China Sea which draws in many of Beijing's neighbours and is the theatre where American and Chinese militaries are increasingly testing each other's resolve.

In 2016, an internationally-recognised tribunal in the Hague found against China's claim to some ninety per cent of the South China Sea. The Philippines had taken the case to the Permanent Court of Arbitration whose ruling Beijing ignored. It went on to finish building and then militarising island bases which give it the capacity to control trade routes through sea lanes that handle a third of all global shipping.

The three other critical areas are the Paracel Islands in the north-west, which China claims against Vietnam; the Spratly Islands which it contests with the Brunei, Malaysia, the Philippines and Vietnam and the Pratas or Dongsha islands in the north which Taiwan controls.

The South China Sea is now the showdown theatre where China is challenging American power and the militaries of authoritarianism and democracy are being pitted head-to-head. The situation has raised questions as to where China's neighbours stand in this rivalry, not only the weaker governments of Southeast Asia, but also its long-standing allies such as Japan and South Korea.

After leaving Masinloc, we will move west to east from Pakistan to Japan discussing historical and current contexts. I will argue that liberal democracy will have to be less rigid in its thinking if it is to take root and succeed among China's neighbours. If it fails to grasp what for many readers may be an unpalatable reality, liberalism risks defeat. As President Joe Biden stated bluntly in the first press conference of his administration, 'Democracy must prove that it works'.

Jurrick Oson's story helps the context.
Oson was fishing Scarborough Shoal in 2014 when his ramshackle boat was buzzed by Chinese helicopters and he was threatened by armed men in speedboats and blasted with water cannon.

"This powerful jet of water smashed into my boat," he told me. "Then it hit me directly and I was thrown into the sea. I tried to scramble up and they hit me again. It was as if they really wanted to kill me." Oson managed to cling on and pull himself to safety. The Philippine fishing crews retreated and China occupied the reef, arguing that it lies within Chinese territorial waters.

"I am so angry," Oson's eyes flitted between his motorcycle and the sea. "If I had a gun, I would have fought them. If America supports us, we should go to war with them."

Despite having a defence treaty with the U.S., the Philippines was told that America would not go to war over a fishing reef, raising the question among Southeast Asians on what grounds exactly would the U.S. protect China's neighbours. This sentiment was strengthened during the unpredictable and isolationist era of the Trump administration and the American withdrawal from Afghanistan.

How things then unfolded for Oson may show how China plans to unseat America as the prevailing power in the Indo-Pacific.

Unable to fish Scarborough Shoal, Jurrick and others in the village had no income. They could not support their families. Jurrick's wife, Melinda, was forced to take a job as a domestic servant in Saudi Arabia. Other wives and mothers did the same. The community was gutted. Grandparents looked after children. His esteem shattered, Jurrick tried to earn money as a rickshaw driver. The village economy was ruined.

Knowing his country was outgunned, the populist Philippine President Rodrigo Duterte flew to Beijing to cut a deal: Chinese investment in exchange for his keeping quiet about Scarborough Shoal. Next, a Chinese official appeared in Masinloc itself, all smiles and handshakes, and invited members of the local fishing association to visit China, all expenses paid.

Once there, the Masinloc fishermen were shown around a marine research ship and a hi-tech fisheries centre. They took a bullet train to more meetings in Beijing where China put in an offer to buy all of Masinloc's fish at above market price, thus guaranteeing the villagers' income.

Then, Jurrick got word that it was safe to work again around Scarborough Shoal. The day I saw him he had just come back from a week's fishing there. He glanced affectionately across to his old, colourful boat, moored at the water's edge. He loved her, but it was a symbol of Masinloc's way of life that was no match for either Chinese fishing technology or its water cannon.

The Chinese coast guard kept watch while Jurrick fished Scarborough Shoal. He knew they could throw him out at any time. But that week's work earned him ten times more than ferrying passengers on his rickshaw. Fishing there again would give him enough money to bring Melinda back from Saudi Arabia to reunite with her children. The village could breathe again.

"I had lost all my confidence," he said, his lip quivering as he ended his story. "I am a fisherman. It is who I am. It is all I want to be."

There are millions like Jurrick Oson throughout the Indo-Pacific who, thirty years after the end of the Cold War, are getting caught up yet again in a clash between opposing ideologies. Most want nothing to do with. They simply want to get on with their lives. They know from family histories the cost of what politicians and think-tanks in the West glibly refer to as the Cold War. In Asia, with the Korean peninsula, Vietnam, Bangladesh, Indonesia and dozens of insurgencies, the Cold War was very hot indeed.

American attempts to bring liberal democracy to Asia, the type that delivers freedom of expression, strong impartial institutions and a higher standard of living, has succeeded in only three places: Japan, South Korea and Taiwan. Other governments are a mishmash, swinging from military regimes such as in Thailand and, now, Myanmar, communist ones in Vietnam and Laos, authoritarianism in Singapore, overt military influence in Pakistan, corrupt electoral democracy in India where poverty and human rights abuse remain endemic.

Indo-Pacific communities have a deep understanding of the non-ideological shades of grey needed to hold things together in a way that does not exist in the mindset of North America and much of Europe. Chinese repression in Xinjiang and Hong Kong are cases in point. Apart from a few low volume exceptions, the impetus of international outcry has originated from Western, not Asian capitals indicating that on issues of freedom and human rights there are vastly differing views between Asia and the West.

Although Taiwan is outside of the remit of this chapter, I will use it as a benchmark of how to move from dictatorship to democracy without conflict. What is needed is a gradual loosening up of authoritarian restrictions while impartial institutions are strengthened. Keep this benchmark in mind as we move through different countries in the region.

China regards Taiwan as a renegade province which in 1949 became sanctuary for national forces fleeing the communist advance. Until 1987, it was governed through martial law, some of it brutal, first as an impoverished, war-ravaged society and later creating institutions and infrastructure dealing with housing, transport, education, health and so on. It introduced property ownership, taxation and built trust between government and citizen. There was no political freedom.

In 1985, when the per capita Gross Domestic Product reached US$5,000, the government judged the society was cohesive enough to start loosening up. People were allowed to organize into civic groups. Next came a more open press, travel, freedom of speech, the start of opposition politics and the holding of government power to account. This led to establishing laws suitable for the more liberal society.

In 1996, under threats of a Chinese missile strike, Taiwan held its first free presidential election. There was no bloodshed. People went to work in the morning. Nothing changed, but everything changed. Overnight, Taiwan became a democratic society.

In early 2021, while in Washington D.C., I discussed Asian liberal democracy with Hsiao Bi-Khim, a former vice president of Liberal International and now Taiwanese representative in the U.S.

"Some people argue that democracy is not for Asians," she told me. "But Taiwan's existence as a modern, liberal society challenges any notions about democracy being applicable only to certain cultural heritages. We created a democracy that was not transplanted by a foreign regime. It was a process of domestic evolution with many fights and challenges."

Taiwan's 1985 $5,000 per capita level would be just under $13,000 now. Among China's neighbours only Japan, South Korea, Singapore and the oil-rich sultanate of Brunei have per capita incomes above $13,000. Russia is almost there at just under $12,000.

Most Indo-Pacific countries have a very long way to go. As a sample, according to the World Bank in 2019, India stands at $2,099; Pakistan $1,284; Sri Lanka $3,853; Myanmar $1,407; Thailand, $7806; Vietnam $2,715; Malaysia, $11,414 and Myanmar $1,407.

A decade ago, the British developmental economist, Dr Paul Collier, estimated that if democratic reform was attempted beneath a per capita of $2,700 societies become more prone to instability. If reform is not started when income levels exceed that then those same societies also risk unrest. By reform, Collier did not mean sudden Western-style elections as was attempted in Iraq and elsewhere with catastrophic results. Even by his benchmark which would be $3,300 today, Myanmar, Vietnam, Pakistan, and others would be categorized as too poor for democracy.

The economy is not everything. Geography and history also need to be taken into account. China's neighbours broadly separate into three sub-regions, South Asia, Southeast Asia and Northeast Asia which also takes in Russia.

In all, China's methods remain broadly in line with the experience of Jurrick Oson and the water cannon at Scarborough Shoal.

The strategy was first set out in the eleventh century BC by military analyst General T'ai Kung in what became known as the The Six Secret Teachings on the Way of Strategy. He argued that a bond needed to be developed between the victor and the conquered by using the "certainty of reward" and "inevitability of punishment". This was later followed by the more famous The Art of War by fifth century BC general Sun Tzu, who stated, "The supreme art of war is to subdue the enemy without fighting."

In short, China's philosophy of dealing with its neighbours is through a stick and carrot approach, while keeping its guns holstered.

South Asia, the world's most densely populated region of 1.9 billion people, is dominated by India and comprises Bangladesh, Bhutan, the Maldives, Nepal, Pakistan and Sri Lanka. It was once India's domain, but not anymore. India's relationship with its neighbours has been heavy-handed and fractious. China has exploited this weakness by spreading its influence with infrastructure building, military hardware, money and political muscle.

India and Pakistan became independent from Britain in 1947 in a hastily-arranged partition which has proved disastrous. The division into the two countries based on the Hindu and Muslim religions led, in the first instance, to some two million deaths, then three wars, numerous threats of war, two nuclear armed states and India abandoning its secular origins to embrace, like Pakistan, religion as a cornerstone of its politics.

Delhi's fractious relationship with Beijing was set in 1962 when India was militarily trounced during a brief Chinese incursion to 'punish' it for supporting Tibetan activists and giving sanctuary to the Dalai Lama. China still uses that same border to test India's resolve with lethal clashes there in recent years.

Pakistan, meanwhile, was setting itself up as the main instigator of South Asian instability. It fuelled Indian insurgency among Sikh separatists in the Punjab in the 1980s and among Islamic separatists in Kashmir after that. With Chinese help, it built a nuclear weapon and, through A Q Khan, the founding father of the bomb, it became the world's greatest proliferator of nuclear material, selling to whichever government was willing to buy, including North Korea. Khan's status as a national hero remains undiminished.

Pakistan has been a key exporter of terrorism both to India and Afghanistan in its support of the Taliban insurgency. It gave sanctuary to America's most wanted enemy, Osama bin Laden. It is also China's closest ally in the region.

The relationship with Pakistan dates back to the 1960s when Islamabad found itself in a unique position of being both an ally to Beijing which saw the country as a strategic balance against India and Washington which saw the Islamic Asian nation as a firewall against the spread of communism.

When President Richard Nixon came to power in 1969, Pakistan's military leader, Mohammed Ayub Khan, acted as an unofficial emissary with the Chinese leader Mao Tse-tung to test the waters on Sino-U.S. rapprochement. That initiative led to Nixon's famous visit in 1972.

From there came a flow of events which remain geopolitically relevant today.

When Nixon announced in 1971 that he would be visiting China, India forged an alliance with the Soviet Union which in turn prompted Washington to view democratic India as a Cold War hostile power. The trigger to Indo-U.S. hostility was Bangladesh's 1971 successful war of independence which India supported. The U.S. sided with Pakistan, sending warships to the Bay of Bengal to threaten the Indian navy. Delhi asked for Moscow's help, and the Soviet Union deployed its navy to face down the Americans. Britain's Royal Navy reinforced the Americans, creating a situation whereby the world's two leading democracies were taking military action against the world's most populated democracy that was protected by the most powerful communist dictatorship.

In South Asia, there was none of the Cold War clarity so talked up in recent years.

China's relationship with Pakistan continues to strengthen, and it is now a central pillar of its Belt and Road Initiative. Beijing has built the port of Gwadar near the mouth of the Persian Gulf from where the $50 billion China-Pakistan Economic Corridor will link South Asia to China and eventually carry eight per cent of Beijing's oil supplies, giving it a hedge against disruption to sea traffic. A similar project is underway from Myanmar into the southern province of Yunnan.

In a more faltering way, Beijing has moved into Sri Lanka. It bankrolled the government's brutal ending of the long civil war in 2009 which has been much condemned by human rights groups and within the U.N.. It is responsible for much of Sri Lanka's new infrastructure and has modernized and leased the strategic port of Hambantota. Bangladesh, Bhutan and Nepal are, in similar ways, falling under the sway of China.

One underlying, but little-reported cause of South Asia's weakness is its inability to reform society for the modern age. Unlike the U.S., Russia and China, India has never undergone a political revolution that forced new thinking. Instead, it more or less accepted the system bequeathed by the British and moulded it something that worked for the elite.

The result has been a failure to eradicate cultural practices that keep millions living in a semi-medieval state. These include forced marriages, the stoning to death of couples who fall in love because family honour is violated and the horrific Chhaupadi, when a menstruating girl or woman is banned from the home, from touching others, or from going to school.

Bonded labour, defined by the United Nations as slavery, is widespread in which the poorest live in conditions of unresolvable debt. The International Labour Organisation estimates that more than twenty million are in forced labour worldwide. Most are in India and South Asia. Laws have been passed banning it, but for the most part they are not implemented.

Populist democracy has diminished hope of change. Vote banks are increasingly based on ethnicity and religion. Members of parliament win at the ballot box despite facing serious charges such as corruption and murder. The judiciary is slow, cumbersome and politicised.

In 2017, more than seven hundred million Indians had no access to toilets. India's founding father Mahatma Gandhi referred to the situation as the 'violence of poverty'.

India's unreformed political structures encourage insurgencies that rack South Asia, whether under the banner of Islamist, Communist or straightforward separatism. China and Pakistan have been responsible for supporting and arming some of these campaigns.

India's record in delivering security, freedom and quality of life is not good. A new-born baby in India is more than three times likely to die in its first year than one in China and nine times more likely than one in Taiwan. Indians are more than twice as poor as Chinese and seven times worse off than Taiwanese.

So, what should India do now? It has fallen so far behind that it cannot compete either economically or militarily with China.

Either it does nothing and watches as influence continues to melt away; or it links up more closely with the U.S. in the alliance with Australia and Japan, known as the Quad. With that, it risks losing its fiercely-guarded independence and its economic relationship with China. Or it supports China's aspirations. To do that, it would have to concede that it is a junior partner on its own patch. Beijing would then see itself as creating a string of vassal states beholden to its power, with India as its biggest prize.

Further east, Southeast Asia comprises ten countries, Brunei, Cambodia, Indonesia, Laos, Malaysia, Myanmar, the Philippines Singapore, Thailand and Vietnam. Seven hundred million people live there with vastly different living standards.

No single political system has embedded itself with the sprawling archipelagos of Indonesia and the Philippines coming closest to what could be described as democracies. They are far away from delivering the highest standards of living. That prize goes to the authoritarian city state of Singapore.

Southeast Asia also has large ethnic Chinese communities which drive economies. The numbers vary from Singapore being 76 per cent Chinese to Malaysia's 34 per cent and Cambodia's four per cent. Chinese communities make up less than ten per cent of Southeast Asia's population, but are estimated to control two-thirds of the retail trade and own eighty per cent of all publicly listed companies.

"The idea of one China is deeply embedded in the minds of all Chinese people," writes former Singaporean cabinet minister George Yeo, explaining how Chinese culture focuses on family and respect for hierarchy. "The Confucianist idea of society being one big happy family is programmed into young minds. The political idea of one China is also a cultural idea. This distinguishes Chinese cultures from other ancient cultures."

Beijing, therefore, has a hold not only over Southeast Asia's trade but also its psychology, believing that, should the chips go down against the U.S., it can call on the loyalty of the Chinese business communities.

China has an added card when it comes to competing against Japan or Western powers. Like Southeast Asia, it, too, suffered from the brutalities of colonialism.

America's current plan to bring Southeast Asia into a loose alliance to balance Chinese influence is the latest in a string of initiatives that have not done well. After the Second World War, the United States attempted to forge a pro-Western defence alliance based on the new North Atlantic Treaty Organization, which was protecting Europe. The Southeast Asia Treaty Organization (SEATO) came about in 1955, but the region was too diverse, the governments too new, weak and corrupt to hold it together. In 1977 SEATO was officially dissolved. Instead, there is the Association of Southeast Asian Nations (ASEAN), which was created in 1961 and carries an ambitious slogan, "One Vision, One Identity and One Community."

This grouping has worked better, but mainly because it has kept its head below an ideological and military parapet with a rule that members should not interfere in individual internal issues or in other states.

If Southeast Asia has an intellectual heart it lies in Singapore and its outlook and policies forged by its founding father, the late Lee Kuan Yew.

"With few exceptions, democracy has not brought good government to new developing countries," he argued. "Asian values may not necessarily be what Americans or Europeans value. Westerners value the freedoms and liberties of the individual. As an Asian of Chinese cultural background, my values are for a government which is honest, effective and efficient."

Southeast Asia's colonial and post-colonial eras are mere slithers of a long and rich history which has forged outlook and culture. At one time, the region used to be known as Nusantaria, operating under a system of thalassocracy which requires sea and river routes to remain open for trade at all time.

One kingdom, Srivijaya in Sumatra, dominated trade between the Chinese and Indian arcs of influence and was open to all those who had anything to buy or sell. Srivijaya was such a globalized hub of international trade that a visiting tenth century Persian writer noted the parrots spoke many languages including Arabic, Persian and Greek.

For Southeast Asia, trade and cutting deals supersedes politics and ideology which is why there has been such a wall of silence in support of the Hong Kong democracy protests and the Xinjiang camps.

No Southeast Asian country has escaped the tumult of war and upheaval which is currently being exercised by China with its strategy of punishment and reward. Many have experienced the equivalent of the water cannon and economic loss that impacted so much the life of Jurrick Oson in the Philippines.

China's South China Sea claim has been tested against Vietnam where fishermen have been beaten and their boats wrecked. There have been incursions into Indonesian and Malaysian waters and continuing pressure on the Philippines.

U.S. criticism of Southeast Asian governments has also opened the door for increased Chinese influence. President Rodrigo Duterte made a point of courting China after complaints about his lethal extra-judicial campaign against drug traffickers. Thailand moves closer after condemnation of its 2014 military coup and ended up returning dissidents to China, including more than a hundred Uighur activists.

Weaker governments such as communist Laos and Cambodia, led by an authoritarian strong-man, are seen as little more than Chinese vassal states.

In the early 1990s, Cambodia was a U.N. test case of creating a liberal democracy out of war and genocide. Billions were poured in, together with thousands of peace-keeping troops. In that post-Cold War era, China and Russia had withdrawn and Vietnam, which had ended the 1970s genocide and occupied Cambodia, stepped back in order to end its U.S. sponsored international isolation.

It didn't work.

Hun Sen, Cambodia's Prime Minister, has been in power since 1985 and runs an autocratic and corrupt state that is now beholden to Beijing.

In 2017, for example, Cambodia cancelled routine U.S. joint exercises and held them with China instead. It also expelled a U.S. Navy unit that had been involved in delivering health care for nine years. In return, Beijing gave Cambodia a billion dollars for a sports stadium, a new airport, and other projects.

When reaching out to Southeast Asia, liberal democracies must be aware of China's many advantages, including its geographical location, the overseas Chinese communities and the region's prioritization of trade over politics.

Further north, however, liberal democracy has taken root to become a dominant system of government.

Northeast Asia comprises the extreme dictatorship and nuclear weapons state of North Korea, the superpower autocracies of Russia and China, together with the democracies of South Korea, Taiwan and Japan which the U.S. has successfully mentored into free-market capitalist economies.

In each of those three cases, democracy was achieved against the backdrop of war. For Japan, it came after defeat, occupation and a NATO-style security treaty which includes U.S. protection guarantees. Similar arrangements are in place with South Korea and Taiwan, both of which live under the threat from an autocratic neighbour. They were once governed by dictatorships guilty of widespread human rights abuse. It took more than forty years to ease each into a full democracy.

There had been hope that these democracies of Northeast Asia would take a lead throughout the region to build institutions along the lines of the European Union and NATO, that Japan and South Korea could become beacons others could follow.

That hasn't happened because of unresolved antagonism between Tokyo and Seoul which has allowed old wounds from Japan's infamous colonial history to fester. There is no substantive bilateral, let alone multilateral, security arrangement between Asian governments. With minor exceptions, each government's security operates through America and not Asia.

Northeast Asian fault lines manifesting themselves again in 2012 when both Chinese president Xi Jinping and the former Japanese prime minister Shinzo Abe came to power. Beijing began its South China Sea military building programme while simultaneously challenging Japan's claim to a chain of disputed islands, the Senkaku or Diaoyutai and encouraging anti-Japanese protests in China itself.

For his part, Abe bolstered the Japanese military, curtailed by its pacifist constitution, and opened the doors to a more nationalistic Japanese voice.

Further north, Japan is also in dispute with Russia over the Kurril Islands which it calls the Northern Territories, occupied by Moscow since the end of the Second World War. And above that, just beneath the Arctic circle, Russia and America share a border which, for the most part, remains quiet and rarely reported. The exact boundary line has yet to be ratified by the Russian parliament.

The Northeast Asian island disputes are holding back a flourishing of shared values and regional trade. It carries far more clarity in terms of politics and power. This is precisely where the aspirations of autocracy and democracy come head-to-head. There is little of the in between grey that we see in South and Southeast Asia.

Chinese analysts make no secret of wanting American troops out of South Korea by 2030, which would mean forging a bindable arrangement with the North Korean regime, and from Japan by 2049, the centenary of the Chinese Communist Party taking power.

But, to succeed, China would need the Indo-Pacific to feel far safer under its influence than it does now. Beating up Filipino and Vietnamese fishermen, starting lethal confrontations on the border with India and inciting nationalistic hostility against Japan may be a way of showing blunt power, but it does little to build trust and authority and have its power accepted by its neighbours.

China may, one day, dominate the Indo-Pacific but it is not yet ready, which is why Asians are, once again, looking toward America and its allies for protection.

What then is the role for Liberal Democrats and for Britain among China's neighbours
As Joe Biden said, "Democracy must prove it works... We have to defend it. Strengthen it. Renew it. We have to prove that our model isn't a relic of our history."

First, we must change our narrative and widen our understanding of how we can best contribute to building fair, free and open societies in far-away places. Our spotlight on human rights abuse and repression needs to go far beyond the headlines. Yes, we can argue for the rights of those in Hong Kong and Xinjiang, but we must also call out India for its appalling treatment of millions forced into illegal bonded labour.

We must be careful, too, about focusing on democracy and holding it up as a solution to all problems. Asians are very aware of the failure of the export of democracy in Iraq in 2003 and later with the Arab uprisings in 2011 and in Afghanistan. They also note the near-collapse of the Western-designed financial system in 2008. Asians know the impurity of America's ideology with older generations remembering the U.S. sponsored dictatorships in Indonesia, the Philippines and elsewhere.

The way to win Asian hearts is through trade and wealth creation. Beneath the headlines, skirmishes for Asian influence are being played out through two new regional trade initiatives.

They are clumsily called the Regional Comprehensive Economic Partnership (RCEP) of which China is a predominant player and the Comprehensive and Progressive Trans-Pacific Trade Partnership initiated by Japan and Australia.

RCEP includes the ten Southeast Asian countries plus China, Japan, South Korea, Australia and New Zealand, comprising nearly a third of the world's population and account for almost 30 per cent of the global economy.

The CPTPP, with tighter regulation, comprises eleven Pacific Rim nations: Australia, Brunei, Canada, Chile, Japan, Malaysia, Mexico, New Zealand, Peru, Singapore and Vietnam, with a population of around 500 million, accounting for thirteen percent of the global economy. This was originally an American initiative that ended with the Trump administration. If the U.S. joins, the CPTPP will become far bigger and more influential. Britain has applied for membership.

In, geopolitical terms, these are two embryonic and rival trade institutions, which share several members, and which reflect differing regional values. Depending how things unfold, they will compete, cooperate and, possibly, amalgamate. The RCEP will also give China an opportunity to show itself as a less bullying and more collegiate influence.

On a balmy Philippine evening, I sit with Jurrick Oson and others in the house of Leonardo Cuaresma, a slight, bespectacled man who had led the Masinloc's fishermen's visit to China."

On his paint-flaked wall are posters of the Empire State Building and Statue of Liberty. "Will you soon be putting up pictures of Shanghai and Beijing?" I ask.

Leonardo opens a drawer and pulled out Chinese ornaments and posters he had been given while on his all-expenses paid trip there. "I have them," he says. "But I won't show them in my home. I don't trust them."

Everyone laughs and nods. Their T-shirts show Hollywood characters and American sports teams. The baseball cap is still capturing imaginations over the Mao cap. If liberal democracy treads carefully, does not lecture and listens to China's neighbours, it still has everything to play for.

Chapter 10

The Changing Context Of EU China Relations
Professor Emil Kirchner

Introduction

Until recent years, EU-China relations – apart from the Tiananmen Square incident in 1989 – were generally stable and driven by extraordinary growth rates in trade and partly in investment flows, which in turn enabled the EU and China to become each other's biggest trade partner. Success in trade and investment inspired joint actions in related fields, such as on climate change, nuclear non-proliferation and the anti-piracy naval operations in the Gulf of Aden. It also motivated China to intervene financially in 2012-14 in efforts to stabilise the Euro crisis. However, EU-China relations also experienced noticeable challenges in fostering mutual understanding in the areas of human rights, cyber security, economic competition and global governance. What makes these challenges so pertinent today is the fact that they are growing in intensity and are burdened by new obstacles arising from the deteriorating treatment of the Uighur ethnic community, the hardening of political repression in Hong Kong and the handling of the Covid-19 pandemic. Such behaviour undermines mutual trust and strengthens the perception of EU policymakers and the general public that relations with China have moved from those of a benign trading partner to those of an economic competitor and strategic rival.

It is important therefore to understand the reasons and implications of the changing context for EU-China relations generally and for given policy areas specifically. As bilateral relations do not take place in a vacuum, attention also needs to be paid to the influence that external actors, such as the United States, have on the EU-China relationship. It is the aim of this chapter to explore in some detail: the differences which exist in given areas of EU-China relations, the measures the EU has introduced to overcome such differences and the areas where EU-China cooperation appears more or less likely in the future. First, let us take a closer look at areas where and why the EU and China have had diverging views, such as on human rights, economic competition and global governance.

Impediments in EU-China Relations

EU pressures for Chinese human rights and democratisation reforms have been long-standing, but represent a naïve EU belief that a China with open markets and a firm rule of law will be more likely to respect human rights and allow democratic freedom. While economic interactions have grown successively, no significant progress has been made with the EU-China Human Rights Dialogue that was established in 1995. Consequently, the EU has begun to separate more explicitly the economic aspect of the relationship from value-related issues and to press more forcefully for Chinese human rights and democracy reforms. However, this change in attitude applies more to the European Commission and the European Parliament than to individual member states, which give lip service to such needed reforms, but are often unwilling in practice to uphold demands for fear of compromising economic interests.

Prioritising economic interests over normative values has become particularly fashionable with EU states who either were negatively affected by the Euro crisis (Greece, Italy and Portugal) and are therefore in need of investments, or generally lack economic development such as Central European states. EU cohesion is further undermined by the link China has forged with mostly Central and Eastern European states, known as the 16+1 group; a mechanism that has been seen as a Chinese "divide and rule" tactic. Nonetheless, due to rising concerns over human rights violations in the Xinjiang region, the EU has been able to upgrade the level of collective action, as expressed in specific human rights provisions in the December 2020 EU-China Comprehensive Agreement on Investment (CAI), and the introduction of sanctions in March 2021, involving travel restrictions and asset freezing of a number of Chinese individuals who are responsible for the so-called re-education camps in Xinjiang. Canada, the UK and the United States have issued similar sanctions. In retaliation, China has issued even more aggressive sanctions against EU institutions, European parliamentarians and independent research institutions such as the Mercator Institute for China Studies (MERICS), Europe's leading think tank on China. Besides taking actions on human rights violations, the EU has also expressed great concern over China's imposition of a new security law in Hong Kong in May 2020, and the on-going crackdown against pro-democracy activists there. However, despite taking some more forceful action on these issues, it is also the case that the EU struggles to reconcile the conflicting objectives of doing business with a huge and vibrant economy, and protecting human rights and democratic principles. This conundrum also affects the US, but the Biden administration is renewing calls for the protection of human rights and democracy in China, which may create opportunities for joint EU-US efforts on these issues.

Although the EU has long had concerns about economic competition with China, the impact was diluted for a considerable period by perceived comparative advantages under which China would export low-level manufacturing goods into the EU and in return the EU would export high-technology goods to China; a quasi win-win situation. As China has moved steadily into the high-tech market, the EU has been losing its competitive edge.

Restrictive methods for EU goods and investments entering the Chinese market, such as forced technology transfers, have further sharpened the competitive element in the relationship. These discriminatory measures were eventually addressed to some extent in the December 2020 CAI. Another EU concern is the rapid increase of Chinese investments, mergers and acquisitions into sensitive sectors of EU economies and critical infrastructure projects, such as on 5G technologies, which might – according to a European Parliament report in 2020 – hinder European strategic interests, public security objectives, competitiveness and employment. In response, the EU introduced in 2019 a screening mechanism on foreign direct investment to protect the single market from unfair competition and from foreign presences that risk becoming a platform for subversive activities. On the downside, the screening mechanism, which is to be carried out by the European Commission, is not mandatory and some member states may decide not to use it. There is also concern that Chinese investments in Europe via its State Owned Enterprises (SOEs) might be gaining political leverage on the recipient EU states, particularly economically less developed member states.

In contrast to value-related and economic competition issues, concerns about China's global governance behaviour are of more recent origin and reflect the EU's perceptions of China as a rapidly growing, economic and technological power, endowed with the ability to bolster authoritarianism, to undermine democracies in many parts of the world and to challenge the liberal governance model with new rule-setting power. Examples of this global power drive are China's membership in the BRICS organisation and the establishment of the New Development Bank, and the pursuance of cyber sovereignty or digital nationalism, insisting that cyberspace should be governed primarily by states, which have the right to regulate its content. At the regional level, China already is the biggest economic partner for most Asian states, and this position will be further enhanced through the establishment of, for example, the Belt and Road Initiative (BRI), membership in the Regional Comprehensive Economic Partnership and the foundation of the Asian Infrastructure Investment Bank (AIIB). China combines the regional economic partnership principle with assertive/aggressive maritime behaviour in the East and South China Seas, where it claims 80 per cent of the territory. Moreover, China's record as a trusted and reliable governance stakeholder has also been questioned in the coronavirus outbreak, with respect to circumstances and associated record keeping on fatalities. Not only that, China has also been accused of spinning the pandemic to its advantage by giving the impression that it is more effective than the EU in combatting the pandemic and by spreading disinformation to EU publics to this effect. The March 2019 European Commission paper on EU-China strategic outlook represents the first attempt to take account of China's emerging geo-economic and political presence at the international level by not only designating it as a partner, but also as a competitor and rival, all at once.

Prospects for EU-China Cooperation
Whether or not the EU can overcome the climate of frictions and sanctions and/or enhance further cooperation with China will depend to a considerable extent on: (a) the success to which the CAI can be successfully implemented and/or elevated into a platform for further EU-China cooperation, (b) the extent to which a meaningful EU engagement with the BRI can be secured and (c) the extent to which joint multilateral principles can be promoted at the international level. In turn, the outcome of these attempts will be influenced by the degree to which the EU can act as a cohesive actor and the extent to which the EU can achieve a balanced approach in its dealings with China and the US. Whether or not the EU succeeds in these endeavours will be examined in the following, starting with the CAI.

The EU-China Comprehensive Agreement on Investment
After seven years of negotiation, the Agreement reached in December 2020 will make it easier for the EU and China to do business in each other's markets. It addresses many of the EU's concerns about a level playing field, forced technology transfers and other distortive practices; and establishes rules on Chinese SOEs. China is also making commitments for EU investments in various services sectors, such as cloud services, financial services, private healthcare, environmental services, international maritime transport and air transport-related services. In addition, China signed up to a number of commitments on sustainability (including to effectively implement the Paris Agreement on climate change), corporate social responsibility and to make continued and sustained efforts to ratify the International Labour Organisation's fundamental Conventions on forced labour. These conventions are meant to address the treatment of the Uighur minority in Xinjiang. The Agreement also creates a specific working group to follow the implementation of sustainable development related matters, including on climate.

However, opinions vary on the impact of the CAI. The Commission argues that binding commitments have been secured, and that the Agreement will rebalance the EU's economic relationship with China. This view is contested by the Bruegel think tank, who finds that the CAI amounts to little, is littered with vague pledges, and lacks methods of enforcement. Most damningly, it notes that even on market access, the agreement's primary focus, only a few concessions have been made bilaterally and all of them are limited. Complaints have also come from the Biden administration, which felt that a jointly worked out approach would have provided greater leverage on China and a more satisfactory outcome.

Clearly, the Agreement is not equivalent to a Free Trade Area, which carries more elaborate provisions, and will do little to reduce the role of the Chinese SOEs, whose commercial status is questioned, yet account for more than 70 per cent of Chinese government-backed investment in the EU. Given China's erratic record on international rule compliance, the binding implications of the CAI might also not find the required level of commitment. Moreover, there is fear that, as a consequence of economic slowdown, debt-ridden EU states will be susceptible to Chinese support or company acquisitions and therefore willing to make trade-offs between cash and political influence, or between cash and security concerns. This could weaken EU cohesion, if not stability, and could reinforce existing divisions between member states belonging to the 16+1 group and the rest of the EU.

The CAI will help to facilitate and promote trade and investment transactions between the EU and China, and as such will please the business community, especially those in manufacturing like the car industry of which Germany is a big exporter. But its impact on related aspects, such as enforced labour, environment and the role of the SOEs, appears limited, due in part to the lack of credible enforcement provisions. In any case, by April 2021 no approval from the European Council and the European Parliament had been forthcoming. Nonetheless the sheer economic importance of the Agreement will make approval highly likely, in which case the Agreement is bound to have an impact on how the EU seeks to approach and/or conduct its participation in the BRI.

The Belt and Road Initiative
The BRI represents economic opportunities but also challenges for the EU. Engagement with the BRI, if conducted as an equal partner, could increase EU trade and investment and could contribute to economic and political stability in Central Asia. On the other hand, the absence of equal partnership would imply a continued Chinese use of bilateral agreements with respective states, which are creating a dispersed, open-ended governance network under the umbrella of BRI to suit China's national interests by more easily coordinating economic integration and trade liberalisation, pillars of the existing liberal order, on its own terms. As such, this governance approach offers China the opportunity to pursue a larger geo-economic role throughout the Eurasian continent. It would create a direct competition of economic benefits, political influence and strategic importance in the EU's back yard and represent a direct threat to EU interests.

With these potential developments in mind, the EU has introduced some counteracting measures in the shape of the Central Asia Strategy of 2019 and the 2018 EU Connectivity Strategy to Asia. The latter covers all dimensions of connectivity including digital, transport, energy and people-to-people exchanges. It was extended to the 2019 EU-Japan Partnership on Sustainable Connectivity and Quality Infrastructure, and the EU-India Connectivity Strategy of 2021.

Despite promising statements in joint EU-China communiqués, the EU has so far made no formal commitment to participate in the BRI, citing concerns about the lack of transparency and the undermining of competitive and environmental standards in the proposed BRI rules of engagement. However, in breach of this collective stance, some member states, like Italy, have signed Memoranda of Understanding for participation in the BRI. A majority of members have also joined the Asian Infrastructure Investment Bank, which is the financial arm of the BRI.

EU participation in the AIIB and potentially the BRI has found disapproval from the United States, especially under the Trump administration. The United States seeks counteracting measures to the BRI in alliance with Asian Pacific states, such as India and Japan. The launch of the EU Strategy for Cooperation in the Indo-Pacific in April 2021 could be seen as a similar counteracting measure, but it is unclear to what extent this strategy will be linked with United States efforts and/or seek to provide a mediating role between China and the US. Decisions on these matters will also have a bearing on the EU's ability to promote multilateral and good governance principles.

Multilateralism and Global Governance

The practice of effective multilateralism and good governance is part of the EU's DNA. It seeks to spread these principles internationally and to attract partners with mutual interest. As the United States, during the Trump administration, disengaged from international accords and institutions, the EU and China moved closer on multilateral issues, such as on climate change, the Iranian nuclear deal of 2015, known as the Joint Comprehensive Plan for Action (JCPOA), and the World Health Organisation (WHO). The incoming Biden administration quickly sought to rectify this by, for example, re-engaging with the Paris Climate Accord and re-joining the WHO. While the EU has found China to be a partner on some issues like climate change, the Iranian nuclear deal and the anti-piracy naval operation in the Gulf of Aden, it is also wary of China's pick-and-mix approach on multilateral or global governance matters, which includes altering existing institutions or setting up alternative ones, such as the New Development Bank, or the AIIB. China has also refused to heed joint EU and US pressure to become a compliant member of the World Trade Organisation (WTO) and/or to accept reform efforts of that organisation, such as with respect to the role of SOEs. Of course, it is also important to recognise China's unresolved demands for obtaining the status of market access under WTO rules and for lifting the 1989 imposed EU arms embargo.

A real test of China's multilateral commitments will be on climate change, a policy area on which the EU has been the key international driver and agenda setter. China is currently the world's largest greenhouse gas emitter, responsible for nearly 30 per cent of global carbon dioxide emissions. China has indicated a target of net-zero emissions by 2060 and backing of broader international efforts to combat climate change. But this rhetorical posturing masks a very different reality: China remains addicted to coal, the dirtiest fossil fuel, and serious decarbonisation remains a distant prospect. On the other hand, China might be more willing to support any comprehensive international effort to curb greenhouse gas emissions, if it can extract leverage to advance Chinese interests in other areas primarily from the US, but potentially also from the EU.

Arguably, a joint EU-US initiative would have a greater impact on China's climate change policy. However, it is not clear whether the scars created by Trump's troublesome transatlantic policy have sufficiently healed to pursue such an undertaking with rigour.

Conclusion

With trade and investment factors dominating EU-China relations in the past, it is likely that this will continue in the future. However, there are a number of factors that could affect the pace of economic interactions. The coronavirus pandemic has exposed the problem of relying too much on one supplier, which was the case with medical equipment from China. The EU is therefore making an effort to diversify suppliers across a number of products, but also to strengthen internal production capacity with obvious implications for EU industrial and competition policy. On the other hand, with the Chinese economy poised to recover more swiftly than the European one, European recovery will depend in part on China's economic success, which is likely to result in greater Chinese investments in Europe, some of which might be in strategic infrastructure and/or might involve political influence on recipient states. It is also likely to result in greater European investment in China.

Much of the benefit from mutual investments will depend heavily on a successful implementation of the CAI, which seeks to address current asymmetries in market access and to ensure a level playing field. However, doubts have been raised whether the CAI has sufficient enforcement mechanisms to make that aim possible. Indirectly, the success of the CAI implementation is also linked with EU involvement in the Chinese BRI, which has the potential to become a pathway for greater EU-China co-operation on, for example, combatting terrorism, and energy security; areas in which EU-China cooperation has only made limited progress. So far the EU has not taken formal steps to engage with the BRI, but a number of individual member states have done so, which undermines the collective EU stance.

Aside from the strictly economic factor, considerable differences remain between the EU and China over values, such as on the concepts of democracy and sovereignty, and the issue of human rights. More specifically, the EU has great concerns over the treatment of ethnic Uighurs in north-western China, the tense situation in Hong Kong regarding the "one country two states" formula, China's military brinkmanship over Taiwan and aggressive maritime activities in the East and South China Seas. It is in respect of the abuses of the Uighurs that the EU, in April 2021, issued sanctions against China, which were met with even stronger Chinese counter sanctions, making the climate of EU-China relations more fractious.

There is also EU apprehension over China's growing challenge to liberal norms globally and its use of economic weight, internet strategy and soft power instruments for this purpose. Put differently, the crucial question for the EU will be what support China will provide in maintaining the multilateral system and the central role that institutions such as the UN, the WTO and the WHO, play in that system. The 2019 European Commission paper on China – which depicted China simultaneously as a partner, economic competitor and systemic rival – is a clear response to the perceived challenges. In this new conception, the emphasis of EU policy makers is less on China as a strategic partner, and more as a competitor with which the EU has profound differences, be it about their economic systems and managing globalisation, democracy and human rights, or on how to deal with third countries. In practice, this means that in policy areas where the EU has closely aligned objectives, as on climate change, health, civil protection, and the anti-piracy naval operation in the Gulf of Aden, China can be a cooperation partner. Collaboration on combatting the coronavirus pandemic, especially in Africa and Asia, could be another beneficial area. Yet closely aligned objectives are not the same as full commitment to them. For example, China, given its dependence on coal energy, might not be able to meet declared decarbonisation targets. It can be a negotiating partner with whom the EU needs to find a balance of interests, for example on the AIIB, the BRI and on non-proliferation matters, such as with regard to the Iranian nuclear development. The notion of economic competitor and even systemic rival against whom the EU needs to defend its interests and values applies primarily to human rights, cyber security and liberal governance rules.

The exchange of sanctions between the two actors in April 2021 is a clear indication of the extent to which EU-China relations are becoming more competitive. It will be interesting to see to what extent the CAI can help to keep excessive competition in check and/or instill a more cooperative spirit in EU-China relations. Adjusting to the more competitive, if not fractious, environment with China requires considerable internal cohesion as well as agreement on the extent to which cooperation with the US should be envisaged. Unlike China or the United States, the EU is not a single state and most of its foreign and security policy decisions are subject to agreement by its 27 member states. This drawback is aggravated by the arrangement China has found with a group of EU member states, known as the 16+1, which hampers EU cohesion. But in matters of internal market and external trade the EU has considerable leverage as a collective actor with regard to China or the United States.

How the EU will position itself between China and the United States has become an issue of lively debate. The EU shares similar values with the United States, unlike with China, and also still depends on

United States' protection. The EU has welcomed Mr Biden's reaffirmed United States' commitments to its European partners and NATO allies. On the other hand, the EU has recognised China as a systemic competitor, but it is still in search of the right approach given its close economic ties and multilateral cooperation with China.

A statement by the European External Action Service in 2020 warns that the EU should avoid becoming entrenched or entrapped between the United States and China, and instead should look at the world from its own point of view, defending its values and interests, and using the instruments of soft power available to it. In line with this strategy the EU decided not to succumb to pressure from the newly elected Biden administration to delay the introduction of the CAI that was signed in December 2020, in favour of a joint EU-United States approach with respect to China. There is, however, a warming of EU-United States relations evidenced by the coordinated introduction of sanctions against China over human rights violations of the Uighur minority and by the establishment of an EU-United States dialogue on China in April 2021.

Ideally, the EU would like to strike a balance in its relations with China and the United States and avoid having to take sides in the growing Sino-American rivalry. In practice, this would appear difficult to achieve. Instead, it is likely that the EU will take a multi-faceted approach by taking decisions on a case-by-case basis, such as to engage with China on the BRI, which the United States opposes, and to support United States efforts to defend an open and liberal international system, which China seeks to counteract.

There clearly are major challenges ahead for relations between the EU and China, and whether there can be a deepening of cooperation will depend not only on the strategic choices that either side is willing to make, but also on the changing external environment in which these relations develop, not least with regard to the policies of the United States.

Chapter 11

China and the West: military conflict, cold war or cordial rivals?
Paul Reynolds

Introduction – the importance of threat perceptions

Any assessment of the future of relations between China and the 'West' over the longer term should include the prospects for war. This is not because war is inevitable, but because it is not inevitable. The extent of inevitability depends upon perceptions of both sides.

If decision makers in the US believe that China is hell bent on world domination with economic prowess and its by-products of global trade and investment merely the advance guard of military global control, then war is more likely.

If decision makers in China believe that the US will never accept an economically dominant China with global reach; thus the current concept of 'disengagement' with China, and other such policies, looks like preparation for war, making war more likely.

This is not to say that the prospect of war is the most important factor in Western-Chinese relations. It is however, given the catastrophic consequences of such a war for the world as a whole, important to consider how such a war may arise, and the pursuable circumstances under which it would become much less likely.

Thus, potential war can be a prism through which much of the relationship can be better understood. Inevitability as an underlying assumption on one or both sides may be self-fulfilling, and thus there is value in exploring the nature of 'leadership perceptions' and how they have developed. Perceptions of the inevitability of war can spiral out of control very quickly, especially if de-escalation mechanisms have not yet developed.

Setting out the 'military versus economics' landscape of rivalry

What will the real relationship be between China and the rest of the world over the longer term, say, fifty years from now ?

This question looms large in academia and government ministries and volumes have been written on this and similar topics.

For most academic explorations this is a question of US relative economic decline and China's relative economic rise. The latter is perhaps more famed than the former; in the years after World War Two the USA represented more than 30% of world GDP, but today it is closer to 20%.

However, the military and security aspect of these relationships receives less attention than the economic aspect, but the two are inextricably linked and one cannot be well understood without the other. By contrast to the economic sphere, there has been no US relative decline in US military capability and 'reach', and this is an important part of the US-China relationship.

For example, the prospect of a blockade of Chinese imports features significantly in underlying Chinese economic and military planning, and manifests itself in Chinese investments in Myanmar,

Djibouti, Cambodia and elsewhere. It partially drives the 'Belt and Road Initiative' (BRI), the 'Maritime Silk Road' (MSR) and Xinjiang policies. A potential blockade, of course, features significantly in military strategy, including military development of islands in the South China Sea and military agreements which closely follow economic agreements with other countries.

China's response to a potential military blockade and indeed many other such problems, both military and economic.

Linked to military planning and the fear of blockade are the Chinese leadership's perceptions of what is sometimes called the US's 'China surround' policy. This is the perception that the US has arranged bases, military agreements and allies so as to surround China militarily.

Guam, Japan, Afghanistan, Singapore, Taiwan, Darwin, Diego Garcia and the Philippines featured in a flurry of popular news items of propaganda style in Western countries in 2016 and 2017, in which '400 US bases' surrounding China were frequently referred to.

This was exemplified by a December 2016 headline in the British popular tabloid, 'The Sun', which stated 'US readies for war with China with 400 bases of ships and nukes to create 'perfect noose' around superpower rival'.

Unsuspecting readers were directed to the John Pilger documentary 'The Coming War with China'. However the 'merry dance' of US-China rivalries, economic and military, extends to a complex web of subjects.

These include such diverse issues as US vulnerability over the prospect of China ending its pro-gramme of recycling dollar earnings into US dollar denominated government securities, the reliance on Chinese-made capital goods in US manufacturing and Chinese advances in further developing 'satellite-killer' and nuclear missiles.

Sober assessments reflect more holistically on the interplay of factors that bind the US and the West to China, and vice versa (largely economic), versus those factors that pull them apart (largely military). Setting aside theories of global hegemonic intent in China's economic expansion, it's a fair assessment that China sees its global role as largely economic-led, with a defensive military, but sees the US global role as military-led, with offensive intent.

A 'merry dance' the relationship may be, but it is hard to avoid the conclusion that each side is dancing to a very different tune.

How can a spiral of escalating military tensions, leading to war, be avoided ? This is something of a double bind problem. For example, if China believes that 'China hawks' in the US, in favour of a blockade threat for example, are getting the upper hand, then they may take measures to lessen the effectiveness of any blockade. This may then be taken as an aggressive stance, even a plan to attack US assets, which further strengthens the hand of China hawks in Washington supporting that blockade idea.

The reverse process can occur too, with anti-US military 'hawks' in Beijing. For China there is a converse argument. This line of thinking often expressed is that the US has 'total hegemony' as its central geopolitical aim which is threatened by China's potential economic dominance and the military strength that may follow.

Given US dependence on Chinese imports and purchasing of securities, the US will instead use military strength, and threats, selectively, to contain and disrupt the Chinese economy over the medium term, gaining leverage over the negotiation of containment measures. The suspicion in this scenario is that the US is trying to buy time to enable a reduction in economic dependence and pave the way for a wider conflict.

Thus, this line of logic implies that there is a limited time window for the US to 'contain' China.

Whilst the normal language of diplomacy in such circumstances typically proposes strategic military 'confidence building measures' to reverse the spiral, which in the case of Cold War One included arms limitation agreements, mutual inspection/verification and easier communication channels, there are reasons to believe that such an approach may not progress in US-China relations in the coming years.

Confidence building as a bilateral or multilateral process is obviously more problematic if representatives of one nation or group of nations participating in the process are insufficiently in control of the issues under discussion.

There are differences in this respect between China and the US in that in the former, the leadership has full knowledge of, and indeed participates in formulation of, underlying strategies, as well as public narratives.

This is at least in part embedded in Chinese communist thinking, in the sense that inculcating 'right thinking' among the population necessitates dualism in communicable narratives. The Chinese leadership is used to the idea that much energy must be invested in achieving sufficient consensus to be able to negotiate internationally (eg on military and economic matters), and that the related narratives for public consumption are separately determined later, by the leadership. This 'dualism' is certainly made easier in China by almost total media control by the party, with its vast apparatus.

In the US this is much less certain, despite its de jure democratic constitution and at least theoretical adherence to concepts of transparency and accountability. The Chinese perception of US decision-making related to international negotiations (including on any potential confidence-building in the military sphere) is that it is not only the case that the Head of State and surrounding executives have had limited influence over underlying strategies, but that they may not even be aware of some key components of it. It is sometimes hard to avoid the impression that the Chinese leadership believes that they have better knowledge of US underlying long-term strategies than elected US leaders do.

These dynamics provide opportunities for the Chinese government to take advantage of Xi Jinping's more unified, less 'collegiate', method of governance relative to his predecessor Hu Jintao, when they arise. Senior US military figures have conceded that Chinese military-economic decision-making in international affairs is more fleet of foot than US decision-making.

Thus, the prospects for war and related military rivalry do feature prominently in the US-China relationship. The extent to which there is the prospect of war between the West and China is best assessed through the prism of intertwined economic and military rivalry, usefully illustrated by the potential for a US maritime blockade of China.

The dynamics of the relationship, and mutual expectations, play an important part in the prospects for war, and determine the level of distrust and the scope for confidence building measures. The scope for confidence-building is limited due to mutual distrust, relative to that of the first Cold War between the Soviet Union and the West.

Will the prospect of a military conflict lead to a second Cold War between the West and China, and will this be the path to eventual confidence-building measures?

The race for allies in a new Cold War II?
In 2020 and 2021 parallels have been drawn between cooling Western-China relations and the post-Cold War between the West and the Soviet Union that dissipated between 1989 and 1991. In support of such a parallel, accelerated 'clustering' of pro-China and pro US countries is cited. But is a second China-West Cold War a realistic prospect?

In the 'clustering hypothesis', on one side is the US plus other Five Eyes countries, EU, Singapore, India and Middle Eastern allies such as Jordan, Israel, Saudi Arabia, Egypt and UAE. On the other side is China plus Russia, Iran, Syria, parts of Africa and some South American countries. The rest broadly are assumed to be 'non-aligned'. There are other factors supporting the Cold War hypothesis including the continuing US global campaign against Huawei, and both US-China and Australia-China trade disputes.

Whilst the recent 'clustering' is more apparent in mid-2021 than before, there are factors which make the relationship very different to the Soviet-West relationship in the first Cold War, suggesting a new Cold War in the mould is unlikely.

Many countries in the 'US camp' have close economic and military relations with China, including Israel and Egypt. Some have close interdependent economic relationships such as Australia, Canada and Singapore, and indeed many EU countries.

India, the world's second most populous nation, is a separate case. India-China trade is remarkably small, and Indian exports to China almost non-existent. The two countries have fought minor wars with each other and have disputed border demarcations.

US overtures to Indian PM Modi in 2020 and 2021 were based on mutual mistrust of China, plus US support for the BJP approach to Muslim issues.

However, India has a close economic and military relationship with Russia which goes back to the Soviet era. Russia is India's largest supplier of military hardware. There is even an Indo-Russian Inter-Governmental Commission (IRIGC), an institution that conducts affairs at the governmental level between both countries.

It is very unlikely that Russia will support too close an alliance between India and the US, and Russian influence extends to political parties in India in opposition to the BJP. In practice, PM Modi can do little more than pay lip service to the new Cold War concept, in order to obtain support from the US on some international political issues.

India has been an ally and aid provider to Afghanistan, and US policy there, in contrast to the close relationship between China and Pakistan. However even this is more shades-of-grey than black and white. India hasn't been able to prevent large scale Chinese investment in Afghanistan, such as over the Wakhan Corridor and large scale copper mining.

To complicate assessment of a new Cold War hypothesis, India has cordial relations with Iran, and while there are significant foreign policy differences, India is the largest external investor in the Iranian hydrocarbon sector, and Iran is India's second largest supplier of oil, despite sanctions. This relationship is likely to accelerate if there is a new nuclear agreement (JCPOA) between Iran and the so-called P5+1. Iran has close economic and military relations with China and Russia.

The first Cold War involved the Soviet Union and allies being much more militarily and economically separate from the US and its allies, and the ideological divide was more stark.

This ideological divide included Soviet attitudes to Western European and US colonialism, and the Soviet government supported post-colonial self-determination and self-reliance for former European colonies in Africa and elsewhere; from Angola and Mozambique to Vietnam and Cuba.

In the supposed prospective new Cold War between the West and China, there is no such clear-cut ideological divide, and apart from China-India relations, China is better economically integrated with the 'other side' of any new Cold War divisions than the Soviets were.

A new Cold War in the mode of the old one in practice appears unlikely.

Addressing Chinese perceived vulnerabilities
In assessing the prospects for a military confrontation further, the importance of the dynamics of the threat perceptions, especially among the respective leaderships, is paramount.

In practice this means assessing perceptions of 'tenacious vulnerabilities' over the longer term, and how well-rooted they are.

For example there are perceptions of vulnerabilities in China over military capacity, nuclear doctrine, the scope for a blockade, and other factors, which are broadly less well known than US perceptions of its own vulnerabilities.

Military capabilities
The military vulnerability of China perceived by its leaders extends not only to the US's far superior geographical reach and equipment. It also relates to the perceived slow pace of reform in the PLA.

The slow pace of military reform is seen in contrast to the speed Deng Xiao Ping's 'opening up policy' and related economic reforms over the last 40 years.

These military reforms have been seen as a precursor to better effectiveness organisationally, strategically and technically in defending China's mainland and periphery. The roots of this problem lie in the PLA's origins and the internal victories over the Kuomintang and warlordism, after World War Two. A legacy from these origins has been that the PLA has not been so outward looking as Western forces.

Up until the PLA reforms rather shakily started 40 years ago, the overall homeland defence doctrine involved enticing external forces into land incursions, then getting them bogged down in Chinese territory, as they were subject to guerrilla attacks. This doctrine put minimal focus on China's periphery, or on the economy.

After the 'opening up policy' and the economy began to improve, the need to protect economic infrastructure began to force a change in doctrine.

By the mid 1990s, wars were expected by the PLA to start with electromagnetic dominance, hence Chinese military focus on this. Multi-disciplinary rapid response forces were seen as superior to large conventional forces, traditionally in 'silos' and independent of each other. These reforms are still seen by Xi Jinping as moving too slowly, and indeed were a factor in Xi Jinping becoming leader and integrating military and economic strategy.

The significance of these changes in understanding US-China rivalries today is fundamental. The economics-led stealthy expansion of 'peaceful rise' also meant downplaying military reach & capability.

From the point of view of confidence building measures, this history is key to understanding the difference between defensive capability development in the Chinese military, and other measures, for example in creating military negotiation leverage (e.g counter-blockades).

The advantages of the Xi Jinping institutional approach were on public display in the case of: Djibouti, Ethiopia, Myanmar and Cambodia (see below) where economic-military integration and military flexibility created problems for US strategy and unusually revealed US weaknesses in decision-making.

Blockade-related examples
At the forefront of integrated military-economic thinking within the Chinese leadership for at least twenty years has been the prospect of a naval blockade to restrict supplies of oil and food to China, and this is usefully explored further.

In economic terms, the problem is the rapid rise of consumption and the exponential rise in the demand for oil, increasing fragility in keeping up with needs. This problem combines with geography to create the vulnerability.

The vast majority of oil imports into China pass through the narrow Malacca Straights, which are busy and close to pro-Western military assets.   The fall back passages are the narrow spaces at Sunda Straights. and passages at Nusa Tenggara. There is open sea between Timor and Darwin, but there are Australian assets at East Timor and the US has a 25 year Force Posture Agreement with Australia for 2500 troops in Darwin, Australia. The US is also constructing a large new naval base just north-east of the existing Darwin Port.

If hostilities broke out an oil blockade could be relatively easily applied. Whilst it would not halt all oil supplies to China, shortages in China would have serious consequences in a country where the leadership's legitimacy has been built on economic growth, peace and stability. Moreover, Chinese exports to much of the world could also be blockaded.

The threat of blockade contributes to other Chinese strategic positions.

The most important is the Belt and Road Initiative (BRI).

Overland export-import routes to the Middle East and Europe would mitigate against the maritime blockade risk. Similarly the Maritime Silk Road network of ports makes the host countries less vulnerable to US pressure.

A further factor is Xinjiang, key to BRI routes west. Xinjiang is also a region with significant oil reserves, although extracting and transporting oil from where it has been found present severe challenges.

The two oil & gas pipelines from Rakhine State in Myanmar into China provide a route for oil into China that avoids the Malacca Straits.

The (alleged) proposed Chinese naval facilities at Ream and Koh Kong under construction in Cambodia would shorten Chinese naval reaction time substantially.

The PLA has a new large facility in Obock in Djibouti, displacing US forces there. This at least in theory provides the scope for a retaliatory blockade of oil to Europe by China, since a third of all maritime oil to Europe passes through the 10m wide Straits of Bab-el-Mandeb on its way to the Suez Canal. The Chinese government maintain it is an anti-piracy base but the treaty with Djibouti allegedly allows staffing up to 10,000.

A potential obstacle to future confidence building measures is what has been seen as an emerging pattern of stealth and denial in the development of Chinese military reach across the world.

This view is supported by alleged Chinese stealthy approach to bases in Cambodia, at Koh Kong and Ream National Park near Kompong Saom. There are parallels with the way in which the Chinese military established a base in Djibouti.

Chinese state-linked companies first took over one of Djibouti's main ports at Doraleh, ousting DP World from the UAE, and the Chinese government led a funding programme to develop other ports. The Chinese government supported the building of a railway to landlocked Addis Ababa in Ethiopia, and are building an international pipeline which terminates in Djibouti. Many other Chinese investments followed.

There was a similar pattern in Ethiopia, where economic agreements and investment were followed by military agreements. Chinese government-linked institutions financed the Addis Metro and there are major Chinese oil exploration and production investments in the Ogaden desert, plus hydroelectric dam projects. A new military agreement was established in 2016.

If there is a pattern to be established in these cases, it is that it is a manifestation of the integration of economic and military strategy, with economic relations first, and with the military aspect following, with carefully controlled sequencing which requires unified decision-making.

Addressing US perceived vulnerabilities

In foreign policy academic discourse, the US is often presented as a hegemonic military & security power pulling the strings in every part of the world. However, there are weaknesses on the US side too.

Time is the enemy

As China's economic power grows, US policy appears to assume that military power follows close behind. Very broadly the US represents about a third of world defence spending, and China about a third of that, likely to approximate a half US spending from about five years from now.

However, Chinese equivalent costs are much lower than the US and the spending is focused more on 'home & periphery' territorial defence rather than a 'world policeman' role.

China, in developing its military capability, has less expensive historical baggage and more of an open landscape in choosing where it wishes to focus its spending; for example it makes large investments in drone swarms, space war and electronic counter-measures for air and underwater drones in line with the 'hi tech local wars' doctrine.

The US perception is thus that it may be only a matter of time before significant US military superiority in any conflict with China is lost. If it is lost then the likely consequences of a war for the US may be too difficult politically and economically. The chances of 'containing' Chinese economic and military expansion may soon be gone forever.

Economic vulnerability

A full economic separation would have a major impact on the world economy as well as the USA and thus will be hard to predict for policymakers.

If a decision was made in the US today to go to war with China, the implied economic separation would have to be factored in to military calculation. Better then at least in theory to take steps towards separation, and manage the consequences, before the kinetic phase of a conflict ensues.

This type of thinking has important consequences for leadership perceptions about conflict, on both sides, especially if a 'trade war' is seen by China as part of a plan for economic separation to limit the negative impact on war for the US.

If confidence-building measures are to be sought, then it probably follows that China must perceive trade disputes as genuinely about trade and not a campaign of creeping economic separation in preparation for a future war. This would be a laudable aim for the West, including Europe.

Debt, the dollar and securities

Does China's programme of recycling dollar earnings into US government securities, represent a Chinese vulnerability or a US vulnerability ?

A fall in oil prices and the manner of QE deployment have both helped the US avoid the inflationary consequences of monetary expansion and, for example, substantial annual increases in defence spending. However the key underlying reason why the US avoids inflationary consequences of monetary expansion is the US dollar as global reserve currency, backed by several major oil producers.

China, Russia and Iran have been moving away from a dollarised trading system, between and outside their 3-way trade. However steps in this direction to date have been cautious and limited. Renminbi-denominated oil trading is as yet embryonic. A more dramatic success would be devastating for the US economy.

Obviously, a way of widening the military time window for the US, is to for the US to spend substantially more money. Clearly if China is able to dent the US dollar's reserve currency role it could have the ultimate effect of limiting increases in US defence spending.

Fragmented decision-making

Does the Chinese shift to a more unified decision-making system under Xi Jinping create a vulnerability for the US ?

This question was posed at a number of US Congressional debates on the loss of the US base at Obock in Djibouti, in favour of Chinese forces, providing a rare glimpse into the issue.

In both US Congressional intelligence committees and in the US Emerging Threats and Capabilities Sub-Committee, representatives of the DoD and armed forces conceded that they were not sufficiently fleet-of-foot to deal with Chinese pursuit of aims in Djibouti and the wider region, despite the proximity of the US multi-agency base at Camp Lemonnier and its advanced support capability.

The multitude of US security and military institutions, plus foreign policy and intelligence institutions, it was starkly stated, make it difficult to combat the more unified and flexible decision-making which had developed under Xi Jinping, it was revealed.

Whilst there may be particular circumstances which relate to the Obock base, which do not apply elsewhere, the Chinese leadership clearly regards this as a global vulnerability for the US, which they are minded to exploit where possible.

A similar process has played out in coastal Cambodia, with US assets being removed.

The extent of this potential US vulnerability in decision-making may expand given the difficulties of making institutional changes in the US administrative and military system.

Importantly however, as discussed above, such decision-making and institutional issues on the US side make it more difficult for them to sustain and implement negotiated confidence building measures, and more difficult for the Chinese side to have confidence in US adherence to such measures that they have agreed to, referencing the JCPOA in Iran.

This factor and the way in which it could lead to conflict provides an important role for allies of China, but particularly so for allies of the US, especially the EU.

The UK and Europe
If there is a war between China and the US, the EU with its relatively open markets and globally integrated economies will suffer more than most. Oil shortages and added costs, and shortages of capital goods, would devastate the EU economy. A retaliatory blockage of the Straits of Mandeb, leading to the Suez Canal.

What's more whilst EU nations and 'European NATO' would be pressured to participate, probably only the UK and France would be involved kinetically, and probably only in peripheral ways.

EU countries and the UK have criticised China over alleged Chinese recklessness and lack of prudential management in the way that BRI-related and other 'investments' are made. Certainly in Africa, notably Kenya, Djibouti and Tanzania, and in Asia, for example in Sri Lanka, financing terms for projects have proven disadvantageous for recipients, according to the IMF and IBRD.

However, whilst EU narratives suggest these investment issues provide the scope for the EU to use such problems to its advantage, the question remains as to whether the EU has the unity and administrative capacity to lessen the negative impact of a Cold War II on Africa, South America and South Asia and supplant Chinese investment.

In South Sudan, South East Ethiopia and Somalia, Chinese officials and state-run companies have largely been out of the 'realpolitik' loop. In Djibouti however, combined Chinese economic and military interests have been deployed more effectively. These geographic areas have become stages on which any potential further development of Cold War II between the US and allies, and China and allies, will play out.

European countries, however, with a focus on post-colonial political as well as economic development, have better experience in grappling with complexities and promoting stability in economic development. Today, the EU is seen as less driven by global agendas.

These factors serve to remind us that the rise of China has had some less visible consequences, such as the scope for the EU to play a more important international role economically, politically and militarily, in a new, more multipolar world. How the EU organises itself, and how it adjusts its relations with the USA, will determine whether it remains in 'scope' only or whether the EU actually furthers a future multipolar approach.

Conclusions

There are a number of important issues in the subject area not addressed in this article. These include the balance of nuclear defence and counter-measures capabilities, the economic interdependencies in detail by sector, the nature of Chinese military capability technically among others.

However with respect to the key themes of leadership perceptions and the prospects for war, there are a number of tentative conclusions that might be drawn.

One is that China has made strenuous efforts to modernise its military to focus less on internal matters and more on China's periphery, with an emphasis on capability to fight local hi tech wars, but is still focused on homeland defence, rather than global reach.

Second, China's perceptions of vulnerability, especially a blockade, drive much of its economic as well as military doctrines.

Third, the US's de facto military-first approach may pass its sell-by date over the next few years as military superiority in the war with China is lost, which may even lead to the type of economic-military integration reforms like those pursued by China.

Fourth, the EU and other power centres have an important role to play in avoiding a Cold War II and in pursuing confidence-building measures to reduce the risk of conflict, as well as improving the maturity of Chinese foreign economic and political relations around the world.

It is difficult for all parties outside the Washington DC security elite, to assess whether the US does actually intend to pursue a greater level of economic separation, and press its allies to do the same, even if such a thing were politically possible in the US.

However, there must be considerable doubt as to whether any such approach would be successful, given US reliance on China's purchasing of US dollar denominated US government securities, and on Chinese imports, plus an as yet embryonic threat to the dollar's role as reserve currency; and other retaliatory measures.

An important tenet of European liberal-democratic traditions is that war should be a last resort, defensive only and proportionate. A war between the USA and willing allies, and China and its allies, from today's perspective almost certainly would not meet those three criteria. The global economic consequences would be very substantial and the loss of life unimaginable.

Thus if European nations perceive a drive to war in the US (or in China) there is likely to be some political 'push back', notwithstanding close transatlantic intelligence agency 'cooperation'. In practice, there could be considerable division in Europe in the wake of a perceived drive to war, something which does not escape the notice of Chinese and US security institutions.

On that basis it might be a solemn duty of those in Europe that support such 'war as a last resort' traditions, to promote, with allies, first confidence building measures and then a path to Chinese economic expansion which is globally beneficial and less likely to create a spiral towards conflict.

Chapter 12

A Greener Future
Christopher Gleadle

To create a future that is mutually 'greener', healthier, and more inclusive, there are many factors to be balanced in the EU's relationship with China. For, all actors' actions are interdependent and unless all nations focus on the same goals in a trusted, standardised, and coordinated manner, then what continues is no more than business as usual.

The EU and China – a matter of balance but it's complicated
China has become the world's second-largest economy. As a result, it has lifted nearly a billion people out of poverty. But this progress has been built upon a boom in energy from coal and has contributed to make China the world's largest emitter of CO_2. Furthermore, according to new international research, China placed 38.4 gigawatts (GW) of new coal-fired power capacity into operation in 2020 (three times the amount built elsewhere around the world) and has 247 GW of coal power under development.

Because of China's economic growth, it has become a major production source for products to the EU. It follows, that to repair the excesses of human activity on the climate, environment, and biodiversity – to 'green' the EU economy - there must be veracity in accounting for the impact of supply chains of which China is a major part.

Duly China does have an interest in pursuing a more sustainable and efficient path as the effects of climate change on Chinese agriculture, water, and food security as well as air and land pollution create tensions within the Chinese population, as well as with neighbours of, for example, Southeast Asia.

Accordingly, Xi Jinping posited "ecological civilisation" as a Chinese characteristic. He has stated that the Chinese government aims to have CO_2 emissions peak before 2030 and achieve carbon neutrality before 2060. Yet, China will do so with an emphasis on retaining high levels of economic growth and employment.

And, in the pursuit of a transition to clean energy upon which the European Green Deal is reliant, minerals, such as rare earths, for that energy transition, finds China as a major supplier of such minerals. This suggests China to has a strategic point of leverage. Also, an EU clean energy transition could see the EU becoming more independent and energy secure within its own borders. Hence, this could see a fall in energy requirements from outside of the EU, which may see global energy prices falling. As a result, since China is a large importer of energy, falling international energy prices could make running the Chinese economy cheaper and thus more competitive.

Furthermore, China has dominated the rare-earth market with subsidies to producers that kept prices very low for potential competitors to enter the rare-earth market. But this policy came at a cost since it caused unpopular environmental damage within those parts of China that processed these minerals.

However, since China is a major part of EU supply chains, the imposition of a Carbon Border Adjustment Mechanism (CBAM), due to be introduced by 2023, could mean Chinese carbon-intensive products losing comparative price advantage. This would encourage EU industry to source from other, 'greener' partners. Thus, pressure could be seen to be applied on China to commit to a more ambitious climate change and sustainability agenda. In contrast, COVID-19 has seen EU companies exploring greater localisation of their value chains and production processes, which would entail production specifically for the Chinese market within China.

Furthermore, CBAM could reduce opportunities for export-led development from China. For example, The Bank of Finland has estimated that, based on emissions embodied in EU-China trade and carbon border tax, a CBAM of US$28 per tonne of CO_2 on imports is equivalent to an average import tariff of 2 percent. As the carbon price increases, so would the effective tariff. Adding IMF estimates of a carbon price of around US$75 per tonne of CO_2 will be needed to restrain climate warming to 2 degrees, then the effective CBAM tariff would be around 6 percent.

Notwithstanding, commitments related to sustainability, including to effectively implement the Paris Agreement on climate change, fit neatly within China's own agenda. For, environmental threats have become a top concern in Beijing, partly because they have sparked discontent among the country's citizens. Thus, China has set itself a target of becoming carbon neutral by 2060, launched an emissions trading system and under new guidelines from the Ministry of Ecology and Environment made climate action part of local government performance evaluation – adding pressure on provincial and regional leaders to take the issue seriously.

But, while China may be able to meet its obligations under the Paris Agreement, local leaders are under constant pressure to deliver on pre-determined economic growth targets, which count more towards their personal evaluation than adhering to environmental standards. Consequently, the self-interest of local leaders could see the lowering of environmental standards unless they grasp the critical systems thinking to understand that economic growth, employment and tackling the multiple issues related to climate change are not mutually exclusive. Thus, systemically act upon climate mitigation, remediation, and adaptation to help meet economic and job creation targets essential to local leaders.

Also, current EU-China tensions see the EU-China Comprehensive Agreement on Investment (CAI) under strain. For example, the EU Commission has said that efforts to ratify the investment deal have been in effect suspended after tit-for-tat sanctions were imposed over China's treatment of its Uyghur population. Valdis Dombrovskis (commission's executive VP) has said that the current state of relations between Brussels and Beijing was "not conducive" for the ratification of the deal.

However, China's leaders surely feel confident that EU businesses will continue to invest in China having been encouraged by companies such as Volkswagen (largest brand in China by sales) to invest about €15 billion with three local joint ventures to build 15 different full-electric or plug-in hybrid models in China by 2025. Further encouragement may be gained from results of surveys on future investment plans, such as that conducted by the German Chamber of Commerce in China, which showed that 72 percent of companies are planning to increase investment in 2021 and that 96 percent have no plans to leave the Chinese market. Such insight bolsters notions that China does want to work with the EU. It wants to improve commercial relations, and that China does want EU companies to take part in its future development.

Moreover, at the 26th Conference of the Parties in Glasgow, November 2021, China will be in the spotlight in terms of specifying how it will bring its carbon emissions to a peak before 2030 and then reduce them. To achieve trusted carbon neutrality, the measures will have to be significant, start immediately, be carbon negative, and proven with transparent data trails for ensuring the veracity of reporting.

Raw material security will decrease dependence on China
The former Chinese leader Deng Xiaoping said in 1992 "the Middle East has oil; China has rare earths."

If China were to restrict exports of rare earths it would be worth remembering when in 2010, China did just that. Rare earth prices soared as the market panicked. Stockpiling took place. Then prices fell when the bubble burst. Within the EU the security of the supply chain and volatility of the price became concerns, which contributed to a growing amount of research on the fields of supply and price since the level of volatility experienced has highly negative consequences. Hence, on a positive note, many industries discovered they could do without rare earths, such as an electric motor that relies upon induction rather than magnets.

And, for the EU, securing access to critical raw materials can be achieved through several measures such as supply diversification, increased recycling volumes, substitution of critical materials and seeking a more systemised, holistic, balanced and sustainably viable transition pathway. For example, some raw materials have a high recycling potential, yet recycling rates remain generally low. This suggests the EU has an opportunity to create greater raw material security via increased investment into research and development for the integration of current and proven technologies where feedback loops can become dominant to create system optimisation and thus accelerate emissions and waste reduction. As a result, EU industry would reduce virgin material input, reduce impact as well as supply and price volatility, increase value chain security and performance, as well as generate recoverable and added value of waste through creating a secondary symbiotic marketplace.

However, rare earth elements do play an important part in the manufacturing of items that energise the global economy such as electric vehicles, wind turbines, smart phones, ceramics/glass, and one day, potentially, the spherical tokamak.

Accordingly, since China holds the single largest share of the world's known reserves of rare earths, China has a disproportionate share of mining production. Yet, it is interesting to note that, in the past, China has produced 98 percent of the world's raw rare earths, while in 2020, Chinese mines produced 110,000 tonnes of rare earths, which is approximately 55 percent of total global mining as other countries have raised production to lessen reliance on China to meet rising demand. But this does not mean Chinese funding is not behind rare earth extraction in other countries such as the state-owned China Great Wall Industry Corporation (CGWIC) funding approximately eighty percent of the Longonjo mine in Angola.

However, while the extraction of ores is the upstream part of the supply chain, processed minerals form the chain's midstream, while downstream uses the midstream products to manufacture goods such as magnets.

Such is the dominance of China in the rare earths supply chain, concentrates are still sent to China for processing since there are few downstream rare earth refining plants of scale outside of China. Exceptions are being planned, such as in the UK, which initially will focus on raw materials extracted from Longonjo. However, China did produce 85 percent of the world's rare earths refined products in

2020. And imports of rare earths to China are forecast to grow to 80,000 tonnes per year by 2030, up from an estimated 60,000 tonnes in 2021. Furthermore, China not only dominates the supply of rare earths but also demand, with currently 70 percent of global production consumed within the Chinese domestic market.

Biodiversity
Biodiversity is essential for the maintenance of planetary and human health, yet the interdependent drivers of biodiversity loss and spatial variation in their impacts need greater understanding.

For example, the planetary distribution of threatened and declining species (biodiversity loss) is subject to multiple stressors, with climate and human activities being a fundamental cause of that stress. Accordingly, there has been a large spatial variation in the distribution of threatened species over China's provinces. With increasing urbanisation and industrialisation, the expansion of construction and worsening pollution have led to habitat retreat or degradation. Consequently, high numbers of amphibians, mammals and reptiles are threatened as we see the biodiversity of Gansu, Guangdong, Hainan, and Shaanxi provinces being severely reduced.

Biodiversity loss disrupts many ecosystem processes, such as community structure and interactions, and can cause ecosystem malfunctioning, that ranges from reduced biomass productivity to weakening ecosystem resilience. This is because the interdependent nature of the earth's ecosystems creates feedback loops for zero waste systems. Thus, biodiversity loss degrades ecosystem health and the well-being of the human species. It follows, biodiversity loss is relevant to achieving the UN Sustainable Development Goals. This suggests that SDGs, far from existing in 17 silos, performance in meeting the goals is subject to performance of feedback loops. Action on one affects the many.

"intrinsic value of biological diversity, as well as the ecological, genetic, social, economic, scientific, educational, cultural, recreational and aesthetic values of biological diversity and its critical role in maintaining ecosystems that provide essential services, which are critical foundations for sustainable development and human well-being". Para 197, Rio+20

The EU and China have committed to international agreements such as the Convention on Biological Diversity (CBD) to reduce biodiversity loss. But targets in these agreements prove difficult to achieve due to lack of practical systemic implementation.

For example, of the multiple stressors to biodiversity loss, climate change receives greatest attention since it can change the composition, structure, and function of ecosystems as well as reshape the distribution of biodiversity. However, because many species and ecosystems are subject to multiple interdependent threats, it follows that climate change impacts on biodiversity will change in relation to other threats in any location over time. For instance, the Chinese Paddlefish, also known as Chinese Swordfish, is a reportedly extinct species of fish that was native to the Yangtze and Yellow River basins in China. On top of overfishing, a main cause of decline was the construction of the Gezhouba and Three Gorges dams that blocked spawning migration and thus caused the Paddlefish population to fragment.

China has many threatened species and biodiversity conservation priority areas are set out in the China Biodiversity Conservation Strategy and Action Plan (2011–2030). However, the acceleration of environmental change brings challenges to biodiversity conservation since regional variations such as climate, population, pace of economic development, or topography differ from one province to another. Thus, provinces need to integrate biodiversity protection and social development into a holistic sustainably viable plan. But creating balance between economic development and biodiversity is challenging for policy makers since priorities, targets, and skewed self-interest of decision makers clash. To set up an achievable biodiversity conservation plan the target setting for biodiversity conservation must be incorporated into regional sustainable development plans. This would provide insight to reconciling the relationship between multiple stressors and biodiversity over time. Accordingly, this would help set the 2030 global biodiversity target in the 15th meeting of Conference of Parties (COP15) to the CBD – to be held in Kunming, Yunnan Province, China, October 2021 (online) and face to face, April/May 2022.

Currently there is no coordinated integrated and holistic policy mechanism to halt the decline of biodiversity loss at the speed and depth needed.

Accordingly, to rapidly advance EU-China and international action to deliver the necessary and rapid decline of emissions as well as reverse the multiple stressors upon the biosphere there is a logic to uniting the COPs of Climate Change and Biodiversity into a more meaningful and integrated single conference.

Valuing Ecosystems in China
In the late 1990s, China suffered a series of natural disasters that were exacerbated by changes in ecosystems that were brought on by resource extraction and degradation. For example, in 1997, water extraction for human use exacerbated drought along the Yellow River. This was followed in 1998, when the Yangtze flooded. The flooding was intensified due to deforestation upstream. The floods killed 3,600 people, inundated 5 million hectares of crop land and are believed to have cost US$36 billion. In 2000, results of overgrazing and desertification led to dust storms in northern China that covered Beijing seven times in one month. Costs were estimated at US$2.2 billion.

Prompted by these disasters, in 2018, the PRC enshrined the concept of 'ecological civilisation' in its constitution, which emphasises the need for people to engage with nature in ways that allow people to live well and within the bounds of the biosphere. It is recognised that this requires sectoral reforms, spatial planning, technological innovation, ecosystem conservation and restoration and regulation. Additionally, there has been significant investment in cross-regional payments for ecosystem service schemes (PES), known in China as 'eco-compensation' programmes. The programme aimed to reduce soil erosion, deforestation, and flood risk by restoring forests and grasslands. Consequently, there is evidence that suggests the conversion of land through this payments programme has sequestered significant amounts of carbon, reduced soil erosion into the Yangtze and Yellow Rivers, and reduced flood risk.

Furthermore, in China, Gross Ecosystem Product (GEP) has been developed as a measure of the value of flows of ecosystem services since large-scale loss of natural capital and the consequent reduction in the flow of ecosystem services point to the urgent need for better metrics of ecological performance, and the systemic integration of this information into decision making. Therefore, just as GDP provides a useful summary of economic activity (consumption), GEP provides a helpful summary of the aggregate value of the contributions of nature to society. The development of GEP within China could provide a useful template to account for the value of natural capital worldwide.

Furthermore, China's National Ecosystem Assessment assessed the status and trends in terrestrial ecosystems, ecosystem quality and ecosystem services between 2000 and 2010. Seven ecosystem services were mapped for China's land area: food production, carbon sequestration, soil retention, sandstorm prevention, water retention, flood mitigation and provision of habitat for biodiversity. These services are supplied by China's ecosystems, which include forests, wetlands, croplands and grasslands.

The European Green Deal and China

The European Green Deal sets out a plan with the aim to make Europe climate-neutral by 2050. This implies turning climate and environmental challenges into opportunities across all policy areas and sectors of the economy and making the transition just and inclusive.

However, to achieve a climate neutral economy not only requires the participation of industry, but it also requires a transformation of entire and all value chains, of which, China is a major part.

And, while the two-dimensional 'circular economy' offers great potential, optimisation is held back since 'CE' still has waste streams and misbehaviour between functions over time, thus misses feedback loops. Consequently, current 'green' pathways are too slow, inadequate, and unlikely to achieve the stated aims since they fail to deliver the precipitous decline in emissions needed today.

For example, errors in carbon accounting are a cause of concern since climate impact can be seriously under reported. For instance, stemming from the Kyoto Protocol of 1997 that defined wood, or biomass, as a renewable energy source equal to wind and solar, has led to the EU, along with the UK (biomass now accounts for 12% of energy generation), and others, committing to burning forest biomass to replace coal. But burning wood produces more emissions than coal per unit of electricity made. The EU Commission's own Joint Research Centre states: "burning forest biomass is not carbon neutral because burning emits carbon simultaneously, while forests need decades, if not centuries to regrow to offset emissions." Thus, trusted carbon-neutrality cannot happen from burning wood pellets if the emissions and reduction of biodiversity services are not accounted for from that deforestation.

And, if we are to avoid a temperature rise of 3 or 4 degrees, then within a few decades, all nations together will need to transform our civilisation from one that currently pumps out 40 billion tons of carbon dioxide into the atmosphere each year, to one that produces a net removal of tens of billions. Thus, current net-zero policies will not keep warming below 1.5 degrees since they offer protection for business as usual, and not the climate. We need large and sustained cuts to CO2 emissions now! And the only way to achieve that is doing more with what we have and working together to integrate known and proven technologies (high-tech, low-tech and biotech).

Furthermore, verified decarbonisation of value chains must be just and fair and equip workers with new skills and help communities dependent on industries to manage the transition. A spherical economy (considers the application of feedback loops and holism) supports decision making in three-dimensions over time. As a result, decision makers will now understand the consequences of and between decisions to drive down emissions today. This will help modernise both the EU's and China's economies as well as draw benefit from the opportunities of an efficient, comparable, and authentic low-carbon, low-waste / zero-waste economy domestically and globally.

The current EU Green Deal action plan does include a 'sustainable products' policy that will ensure that products are designed to reduce environmental and social impacts throughout their life cycle, based on comparable and verifiable data. It will prioritise reducing and reusing materials before recycling them. Consequently, it will help foster a re-emergence of regenerative business models and set minimum requirements to prevent environmentally harmful products from being placed on the EU market. It will strengthen the extended producer responsibility as well as support consumers to choose, reusable, durable and repairable products. For example, it will introduce a 'right to repair' into EU consumer law aimed at halting built-in obsolescence of devices.

It follows that to revisit and reimagine old and well proven business models based on renting and sharing goods and services will play a role to be sustainable, viable and affordable.

EU and China tackling impact
About half of total greenhouse gas emissions and more than 90 percent of biodiversity loss and water stress come from resource extraction and processing of materials, fuels, and food. The EU's industry, while accounting for 25 percent of GDP, accounts for 50 percent of the EU's greenhouse gas emissions. Industry remains too 'linear' - too wasteful. Thus, industry and finance miss huge value opportunities from not operating as a sphere economy that would change behaviour and action to one that mirrors the creation of planetary resources.

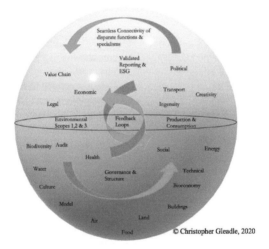

© Christopher Gleadle, 2020

Sphere Economy applies a holistic three-dimensional systems perspective over time to decision making. This enables consideration of alternative ways to govern the provisioning of resources not only at points of activity but along and across value chains. Thus, issues of equity and valuation of capital – economic, human, and natural – are visualised to help temper protectionist reactions that are detrimental to that capital. Thus, reduce risk.

Sphere Economy leapfrogs the two-dimensional circular economy since it includes feedback loops within decision making in a manner similar to the abundance-creating feedback loops of the Biosphere. By this action risk, waste, emissions, and impact are better understood and can be better audited for comparability.

Sphere Economy tackles multiple issues simultaneously accelerating action toward an equitable and authentic net-zero world. It implies making three dimensional decisions in a three-dimensional world.

"Sometimes it is not about things but the relationship between things"

An EU-China sustainably viable product policy (see: The 5 Essential Steps to Sustainable Viability) could reduce waste significantly as processes and technologies can emerge from systemic integration across value chains, in which waste and emissions can be avoided or transformed into valuable resources. In parallel, EU and Chinese companies could benefit from a robust and integrated single market for secondary symbiotic raw materials and by-products.

Consequently, for the EU Green Deal to work for everyone and be a point of leverage in the EU-China relations, a greater depth of critical systems thinking will give access to the strategic security question of the supply of sustainable raw materials necessary for clean technologies, digital, space and defence applications. A sphere economy approach will accelerate the diversification of supply from both primary and secondary sources to help accelerate a 'green' transition to happen.

We need industries - including SMEs - to take their role in this transition. An integrated industrial strategy will aim to enable EU businesses – big and small – to innovate and develop clean solutions while creating new markets.

Competition and Climate Change

It is natural that both China and The EU engage in a competitive struggle for market shares, resources, customers, and technological leadership. Systemic rivalry is revealed as a contrast between two differing ideologies: China's authoritarian party-state led capitalism on one hand and the EU's liberal-democratic market economy on the other. It follows with China's often aggressive 'wolf warrior' diplomatic behaviour we regularly see EU policymakers and diplomats pull climate change off the shelf when asked for examples of areas in which Europe and China remain partners.

The reality of the EU-China relationship is doggedly complicated. For robust climate action, only coordinated and harmonised EU-China action will help protect Europe from dangerous levels of climate change as it will China. It follows, the EU cannot safeguard its people from the worst impacts of climate change – extreme weather events, migration crises, and supply chain shocks, amongst others without action by China to address climate change in a similar manner. Conversely, the same truth holds for China, which has huge highly populated regions that are extremely vulnerable to the impact of climate change. Literally, we are all in this together. And there's the opportunity.

What Beijing prioritises in the five-year plan from 2021 will shape global emissions for decades to come. And, as the EU's own climate actions begin to reshape the European economy, new areas of competition with China will naturally emerge. Thus, climate action will increasingly intersect with questions of geopolitical and geo-economic interest. This suggests that climate policy and the broader complexity of the EU-China relations cannot be separated as the two are interdependent. Therefore, The EU and China will increasingly have to balance the growing competitive dimension with the need to co-ordinate to achieve ambitious climate protection.

Sustainably Viable Competition

The EU and China - with all other nations – face the same climate issues, and together must be clear for what constitutes credible, viable and just climate governance. To define clear benchmarks will help bring clarity to where nations meet, or not, such governance. This can help, for example, ensure that the EU does not legitimise climate inaction or human rights violations under the veil of cooperation. For surely, the only way to keep humanity safe is an immediate and sustained radical cuts to greenhouse gas emissions in a socially just way.

Managed in a sustainably viable manner competition can ignite a race to the top and drive innovation in both the development of new green technology and the integration of existing and proven technology that can drive down emissions today. To misunderstand the interdependence of bilateral cooperation and risk trade tensions could jeopardise robust climate action and risk failure to meet the aims of the Paris Agreement and EU carbon neutrality by 2050 on the one hand and China attaining its goals of emissions peaking by 2030 and goal of carbon-neutrality by 2060.

The green energy sector, CBAM, innovation and intellectual property need to be tackled together since they are interdependent. Accordingly, coordinated climate planning would visualise the value of holistic EU-China action. It will require the two partners to break down silos and build a unified literacy across the interdependent economic, trade, digital, connectivity, environmental and human rights communities.

And, if a steeper decarbonisation pathway for the EU requires a significant rise in carbon prices, which could, in turn, increase the risk of carbon leakage, The EU needs to address this risk head-on to ensure that, over the coming decade, EU businesses make the capital investments needed to shift towards cleaner, spherical production. The CBAM proposed by the European Commission would be a good step in both directions and facilitate discussions with China, and other nations, to present CBAM as a multilateral proposal.

Other measures would be to look at bridging fragmented specialisms and infill the knowledge gaps that will bring the diverse range of measures together as a whole. This could be a particular focus for the Horizon Europe research and innovation framework, which can provide financial support as well as foster international research to enhance Europe's position in the competition with China.

Alongside fostering close cooperation on preserving and strengthening multilateral climate governance frameworks, these propositions could feed into discussions for relevant international standards-setting bodies.

For example, China's central bank has revealed that it is co-operating with the EU to converge green investment taxonomies. Yi Gang, the governor of the People's Bank of China, has said that, in co-ordination with global partners, the primary goal of the central bank over the next five years is to implement and standardise a green finance system. This came just days after the EU's Sustainable Finance Disclosure Regulation came into force for fund institutions operating or selling products in Europe. He further spoke about the need to move towards competitive neutrality. And even went so far to say that China should consider applying the principle of competitive neutrality to SOEs as part of a solution to solve "structural problems in the Chinese economy".

Currently, China's fund industry lags the EU's when it comes to developing a standardised framework for ESG (Environmental, Social and Governance) and green finance. For example, according to AMAC's (Asset Management Association of China) latest report (February 2021) only 40 per cent of 37 sampled retail fund companies reported that "green investing" has been incorporated into their strategic planning. However, ESG and green finance is progressing quickly as a framework for environmentally focused investment standards. Accordingly, it is likely to be one area where Chinese and EU authorities can most easily find common ground toward action for carbon neutrality.

It follows, that the EU should also look to enlarge the International Platform on Sustainable Finance (IPSF) to include new members, such as the US. Apart from helping to reduce the risk of fragmentation in standards, extended engagement with China and other leading actors could help support a robust sustainable finance agenda under the G20. Accordingly, the EU, in cooperation with the UK, as president of COP26, and with the Biden administration, could present a coordinated front on climate expectations of China.

Furthermore, an integrated Connectivity Strategy would build on the existing EU Asia Connectivity Strategy and widen its regional scope to include the Western Balkans and Africa. Chinese investment in the infrastructure and energy sectors is highly significant for these regions' capacity to manage a green transition. Therefore, from both a geopolitical and a climate perspective, it is in the EU's interest to provide help to these countries to compete. By adopting a holistic spherical sustainably viable approach that incorporates climate, digital, trade, finance, and diplomacy efforts, the EU could create a compelling alternative to other connectivity strategies.

Concurrently, China in its 14th Five Year Plan (FYP) sets an 18 percent reduction target for "CO_2 intensity" and 13.5 percent reduction target for "energy intensity" from 2021 to 2025. And, for the first time, it also refers to China's longer-term climate goals within a five-year plan and introduces the idea of a "CO_2 emissions cap"; although it does not go so far as to set one.

Additionally, the 14th Five Year Plan specifies that China should strive to increase the storage and production of oil and gas and accelerate the construction of a natural gas pipeline network. But given the need to tackle air pollution and cut CO_2 intensity, and considering the government's focus on developing its rural areas, its No. 1 document for 2021 lists promoting natural gas to enter rural areas as part of the clean energy infrastructure project. In the current FYP, gas seems likely to benefit from its role as a transition fuel. Yet, longer-term, it could become unpopular as China looks to cut carbon emissions precipitously, and where the opportunities for integration between high-tech, low-tech and biotech will enable China's rural areas to address multiple issues such as energy security, agricultural productivity, transport, soil, water, biodiversity, waste, and desertification, amongst others, in a carbon efficient manner.

Conclusion
There is much to be learned from each other. From that combined knowledge can come greater wisdom to tackle multiple planetary and social stressors - such as climate change, environmental degradation, air quality, land and land use change, biodiversity loss, water stress, energy security, food, and so on - simultaneously to deliver climate justice.

But to grab this achievable goal, it will require the EU and China, with all international partners, to break the cycle of fear and greed upon which business as usual is based, and embrace trusted, holistic, harmonised, inclusive, and thus spherical sustainably viable action on innovation and policy making: to do more with what we have and precipitously reduce emissions today and not at some vague point in the future that goes unmeasured without a robust and standardised environmental return on investment.

Chapter 13

Digital revolution: Can we avoid the Tech War between the US and China?

Lord Tim Clement-Jones

The climate of Sino-British relationships has changed greatly since I first started going to mainland China in 2002. For most of the past 20 years there has been a great emphasis on moving the relationship forward in investment and trade, in the hope - at least by the business community - that China's reform and opening up policies started by Deng Xiaoping in 1979 would lead to a more rules-based approach as well as economic change.

On a visit in 2013, the All-party Parliamentary China Group (APPCG) led by Richard Graham MP, had a briefing with other APPCG members in Shanghai from the British Consulate General about the Chinese online platforms. It was clear that platforms such as Baidu, Alibaba, Alipay, Tencent and We Chat rivalled anything the West had to offer, and this all seemed quite unthreatening at the time. I also remember vividly going to Qingdao the following year with Sir Vince Cable who was then Secretary of State for Business Energy & Industrial Strategy to forge links with Chinese creative industries and promote IP protection.

I was a very willing member at the time of Huawei's international advisory board believing that this was a legitimate way to promote UK China business with a reputable Chinese tech company. The UK became the first G7 member to sign up to China's new competitor to the World Bank, the Asian Infrastructure Investment Bank.

China described its relations with Britain during the Cameron premiership as going through a "golden era". All the talk was of "Win Win" investment and of Britain being an important destination for Belt and Road collaboration. As a consequence, the level of investment by Chinese investors over the past 20 years has grown exponentially: it now stands at an estimated £135Bn invested in critical infrastructure, property, and shares in FTSE 100 companies. China is now the UK's biggest import market.

The UK - China relationship was in marked contrast to the US approach, which under President Obama, developed a much less user-friendly approach to Chinese investment. Huawei, for example, found itself blocked from government contracts and barred from making acquisitions through the US's Committee on Foreign investment (CFIUS) process in attempting to buy 3M, a maker of antihacking computer software, as early as 2008 and later, in 2011, from acquiring 3 Leaf, the cloud technology firm.

Since then, the geopolitical climate towards Chinese technology has cooled in many countries such as the UK, many parts of Europe, Australia and India - with Italy potentially withdrawing from Belt and Road membership. The cooling effect is a result of China being seen to erode the rule of law in Hong Kong, human rights violation in Xinjiang and security threats from digital technology.

Jeremy Cliffe of the New Statesman has memorably described the way China works at the moment as "Capitalist software operating on Leninist hardware". It is the latter which is becoming increasingly visible and which is impacting on China's international relationships.

The recent UK Parliamentary vote instigated by Nusrat Ghani MP in April 2021 to declare that China is committing genocide against the Uyghurs in Xinjiang - although non-binding on the Government - is a clear indication of the change of sentiment. Indeed, in March 2021 the UK Government itself has applied Magnitsky sanctions on four senior Chinese officials involved in the abuses in Xinjiang province. For better or worse, and to a lesser extent across the EU, having diverged for a decade, driven by the prospect of loosened intelligence ties, the UK, along with others such as Australia, has changed course to align itself much more closely with the China policy of successive US administrations.

This convergence as described by, America becoming more realistic on China from a hard line, with Europe becoming more realistic from a soft line by Robin Niblett, the director of Chatham House (Royal Institute of international Affairs). It is a mistake to think American foreign policy always changes with a new administration. Not having Trump tweeting at 6am is a relief for many of us, but Joe Biden is proving to be as hard-line over security issues and relations with China as his predecessor. At the Carbis Bay Summit in June 2021 it seems he pressed other G7 members to take a tougher line on China and greater commitment to his infrastructure alternative to the Belt and Road initiative the "Build Back Better World Partnership" (B3W), which significantly includes digital technology. Vaccine diplomacy by the G7 has had the same motivation to counter Chinese influence.

The US approach has in recent times resulted in a ban on the export of semiconductors to China. Additionally, the questioning of the operation of Bytedance owned Tik Tok is unlikely to change. The Biden administration has placed investment controls on technology that aids surveillance and repression and there are bills in Congress proposed with the explicit aim of countering tech competition from China. In turn, China is retaliating, using the supply of rare earth minerals, important in the manufacture of many digital devices as a counter. It has imposed export controls on technology such as 3D printing, drones, and voice recognition.

The UK now has its own legislation - the National Security and Investment Act (NSIA) - which is designed to do a similar job to CFIUS. The NSIA identifies 17 "sensitive sectors" where notification to and approval from a new Investment Security Unit will be required that includes Advanced Robotics, Artificial Intelligence, Computing Hardware and Quantum Technologies. Accordingly, the Secretary of State for Business, Energy and Industrial Strategy will have the power to prohibit or reverse certain transactions which they believe pose a national security risk or to impose conditions to the transactions. Furthermore, after the progressive hardening of policy, we have also seen the passage of telecommunications security legislation to ensure that equipment provided by telecoms suppliers deemed "high risk" - in other words Huawei - are removed from our 4 and 5G infrastructure by 2027 and a 5G diversification strategy for telecoms networks is being put in place.

An even clearer indication of a change of government policy towards China is the Integrated Review of Security Defence Development and Foreign Policy, set out in Global Britain in a Competitive Age published in March 2021. Among other things, this describes the context as defined by geopolitical and geoeconomic shifts, such as China's increasing power and assertiveness, internationally systemic competition, including between states, and between democratic and authoritarian values as well as systems of government and rapid technological change. China is regarded as a systemic competitor whereas Russia is described as a threat.

Technological competition is the new battleground

At the heart of this competition are AI and other tech research and development. Technological competition is the new battleground. Consequently, over the past year, the head of MI5, Ken McCallum, the former head of MI6, Sir Alex Younger, and the Director General of GCHQ, Jeremy Fleming, have warned of the cyber, technological, and scientific dangers posed by Chinese competition and actions in terms variously of cybersecurity, quantum computing, the design and freedom of the internet, and the security of emerging technologies such as smart cities.

The creation of the National Cyber Security Council back in 2016 and more recently ARIA (the Advanced Research and Invention Agency), the new Technology Office for Science and Technology Strategy and the National Science and Technology Council is part of the UK's response to this technological and cybersecurity challenge.

There is no doubt that China is already among the most advanced countries in AI - indeed a leader in some AI tech. China's State Council in 2017 issued the New Generation Artificial Intelligence Development Plan, which seeks to build an AI industry worth nearly US$150 billion to make China "the world's primary AI innovation centre" by 2030. China is also making massive strides in other areas such as cryptography, 5G electric vehicles and genomics; not forgetting China's desire for supremacy in quantum computing.

Concern is compounded over the use to which applications such as facial recognition and emotion AI are being put to use as forms of society control within China in general, and in Xinjiang in particular. In most recent times COVID health status has been used as a cover for longer term intervention.

Indeed, the prevailing view is that Xinjiang is being used as a test bed for surveillance technology linked to Chinese companies—particularly Huawei, Hikvision, Dahua, and ZTE, which then via the Belt and Road Initiative, which involves infrastructure projects and loans, supply AI surveillance technology in numerous countries. The Belt and Road Initiative itself is increasingly seen as an aggressive China forward policy rather than the use of soft power. There is also great western suspicion that China is using its membership of global standards setting bodies, such as the International Telecommunications Union and United Nations Industrial Development Organisation to further its own competitive ambitions.

Then of course there are the over 120,000 - mainly postgraduate - Chinese students who are an important source of income for UK universities and to date have been seen as a soft power advantage for the UK. Their main area of study is in science and technology, especially computer science. The Higher Education Policy Institute recently calculated that Chinese students contributed £2 billion annually in tuition fee income to UK universities and another £2bn across the economy as a whole.

But in a recent report "The China question: Managing risks and maximising benefits from partnership in higher education and research" from King's College London's Policy Institute, Jo, Lord Johnson, the former Higher Education Minister, and others, have sounded caution over university science and technology collaboration. He has made several recommendations on the management of risks arising from UK university and research systems' relations with China; the central one of which is:

"The government should include HE policy in a flexible and pragmatic whole-of-government approach to China, enabling a principled defence of UK interests and values. Science and technology are international enterprises, characterised by global collaboration, as well as global competition. A tension will always exist between the benefits and risks of collaboration. Given the evident benefits of working with China and the clear value of people-to-people links created through international study, severing ties would be unwise. Instead, the UK must manage and mitigate contingent risks, real or perceived."

In practice this welcome pragmatism involves steering clear of postgraduate teaching and research partnerships with Chinese universities in sensitive technology areas. Given the importance of Chinese students to UK and EU universities, there is no appetite to go beyond this, indeed some universities welcome the enforced clarity now surrounding the basis on which relationships can be built.

US investment, taken as a whole, is ahead on total R&D spending, but China is well ahead of the EU. And in terms of supercomputers, well ahead of both. As a result, in the US both the current administration and the previous administration have been criticised for not organizing and investing to win the technology competition against what is described as "a committed competitor." The National Security Commission on Artificial Intelligence Report chaired by Eric Schmidt, the former CEO of Google, described AI competition with China as a National Emergency, asserting that China could replace the US as an AI superpower.

There is also pressure - partly as result of the COVID PPE procurement issue - to reduce supply chain dependence on China. The White House has recently produced a set of reports entitled "Building Resilient Supply Chains, Revitalising Manufacturing and Fostering Broad-based Growth". They cover semiconductor manufacturing; large-capacity batteries, such as those for electric vehicles; critical minerals and materials; as well as pharmaceuticals and advanced pharmaceutical ingredients.

It is now clear that the US and China are increasingly in a massive struggle for technological supremacy. This will hugely impact world trade. As a result, it will be impossible for European countries, including the UK, not to engage.

No institution has had a more sudden change of approach to China than the EU. In December 2020 Ursula Von Der Leyen the President of the Commission hailed the new Comprehensive Agreement on Investment as " a values based trade agenda", when it was clearly thought that trade with China and geopolitics could be separated. Six months later the emphasis is on President Xi's "authoritarian shift", with the European Parliament in the face of the retaliatory sanctions by China on EU diplomats, members of the European Parliament and academics working at European think-tanks voting against the deal, so bringing the EU much closer into alignment with the US.

European Commission President Ursula von der Leyen and Josep Borrell, the EU foreign policy chief, indicated the Commission's shift in approach in a letter to leaders of the EU member states in April 2021: "The reality is that the EU and China have fundamental divergences, be it about their economic systems and managing globalization, democracy and human rights, or on how to deal with third countries. These differences are set to remain for the foreseeable future and must not be brushed under the carpet."

Values in technology
So what should our approach going forward be? As China makes a journey towards a tighter autocracy, there is growing Western consensus about the need to provide the contrast. As the EU Commissioner responsible for Digital, Margrethe Verstager, the Executive Vice President of the European Commission

for "A Europe Fit for the Digital Age" and former Competition Commissioner, said at the Cogx Festival this year we [EU] "need an alliance of democracies to underpin the values in our technology."

So, if the West - say a newly constructed D11 alliance - is to succeed in an international tech partnership it needs to be values driven. The Biden administration clearly gets this imperative even if it is less enthusiastic about tech regulation. But we do need to develop a joint approach to matters such as AI and data governance, tech competition and antitrust action and regulation of content online.

Luciano Floridi, professor at the Oxford Internet Institute, says traditional analogue sovereignty, as he calls it — which controls territory, resources, and people — remains a necessary function of modern states. But that is now insufficient. It must also reach an accommodation with digital power, which controls data, software, standards, and protocols and is mostly in the hands of global tech companies. Moreover, there needs to be a supranational element to digital sovereignty to be effective.

The EU itself has argued for the concept of "Digital Sovereignty" designed to reduce its dependence on foreign technology - both US and Chinese - and to increase its competitiveness. It is true that a single major actor can have an influence. The General Data Protection Regulation (GDPR) adopted in the EU in 2018 has had a global impact on global data usage standards and its AI regulation proposals may do the same but the fact is that this kind of digital sovereignty approach, as Floridi argues, will need to extend much more broadly.

This year, in a national response, the US enacted its National AI Initiative. The EU likewise published its Coordinated Plan on Artificial Intelligence, and the UK announced a forthcoming National AI Strategy. Internationally the strategic response of the West has been to create the Global Partnership on AI, initially a Franco /Canadian initiative, supported by the G7 and OECD (but belatedly by the US), to: "support the responsible and human-centric development and of use of AI in a manner consistent with human rights, fundamental freedoms, and our shared democratic values."

A group of legislators from the G7 put what they see as the technology imperative more starkly in a letter to their heads of government in January 2021:

"The platform technologies of quantum computing, artificial intelligence, and 5G deployment are set to radically change our global economy over the coming decades. The power inherent in these technologies cannot be overstated. While these technologies have the potential to improve the lives of citizens across the globe, they must be developed around core principles that safeguard user data. The PRC has taken the lead in developing some of these future industries – at times to the detriment of other nations through unfair or even illegal means. The Free World must avoid becoming dependent on a country that rejects market principles and democratic values. A coordinated partnership amongst our countries to lead the development of these technologies and set global norms and standards for their use is thus essential to make full use of their potential without compromising our security and interests."

At the same time however it seems that NATO is resisting calls for an international convention on the prohibition on AI-enabled and autonomous weapons systems. In prospect there is a further tightening of rules around technology-related business transactions which are considered by the Department of Commerce to pose a national security threat.

As relations between the west and China have soured a new breed of "wolf warrior" Chinese diplomat is very much in evidence. Foreign media correspondents such as the BBC's China correspondent John Sudworth are no longer welcome in Beijing nor indeed are some UK Parliamentarian's having been denied visas to visit.

Yet in the face of deteriorating relations, President Xi's response to international criticism has been to say that Beijing must build a more sophisticated "strategic communicative system with distinct Chinese characteristics" to lead global public opinion. With the right communication tools, China would have more friends and be seen around the world as "credible, lovable and respectable". The world must learn that the "Communist Party is truly striving for the wellbeing of the Chinese people, and understand why Marxism works, and why socialism with Chinese characteristics is good...We should better play the role of high-level experts, use important international conventions and forums, and make our voices heard through foreign mainstream media".

So where can we see constructive movement? Despite the constraints we need to be outward looking. Despite all the obstacles, the UK Government has declared the China market as more important than any other market. It is one thing to assert our values and desire to be competitive, it is quite another to adopt a consistently hostile stance to trade and investment in general. As the G7 legislators quoted above themselves said: "We continue to want constructive relations with the PRC based on reciprocity, transparency, and accountability."

Going forward the best way of engaging with China and Chinese investment is to avoid sourcing from sensitive provinces and not dealing with issues that could give rise to the sort of national security concerns that Huawei did. With the new National Security and investment legislation and dynamics around trade, businesses will have to be politically advertent and look at whether the technological sector they seek investment in, or to invest in, in partnership with overseas investors, is potentially sensitive. They may need to consider the market guidance which is being produced as a direct result of the cross-party representations made by myself and others and think carefully, geopolitically, about, which way the wind is blowing.

Repatriation of supply chains will become an issue beyond the US. These things ebb and flow. Over the 20th century, they expanded, shrank, and expanded again. But, especially because of Brexit, the pandemic and people's understanding of how the vaccinations were manufactured – and as a result of our new, much poorer relationship with China – repatriation is going to be much higher up the EU agenda. The Biden administration shortly after taking office set in train a supply chain review for four critical areas: rare earth minerals, semiconductor chips, electric vehicle batteries, and medical products, designed to establish "strong, resilient supply chains", not only through domestic manufacture but with allies such as Taiwan, Japan, South Korea, Australia, and some Latin American countries. Other Western countries and many tech businesses will no doubt take notice, with supply chains in sensitive tech sectors perhaps being split: one for products sold in China and another for the rest of the world. Taiwan, particularly in terms of the manufacture of telecoms networking gear, servers and integrated circuits looks like being the largest beneficiary. The dislocation and cost involved will be considerable however.

Tackling Global Challenges in collaborative competition
The major opportunity going forward, I believe, is for the West and China to work together on climate action, particularly in the adoption of green technologies. China has set an emission peak for 2030,

and achievement of carbon neutrality in 2060. These targets, on any basis, will be hard to achieve. But if there is any chance of achieving the targets set, China, will need to change the nature of its current economic growth towards a much more sustainable model. This could be the UK's opportunity through COP26 and partnering in green technologies which could make a global impact on climate action.

Robin Niblett in his shrewd analysis of post Brexit UK foreign and trade policy "Global Britain, Global Broker: A blueprint for the UK's future international role" says; "At a minimum, the UK needs to be a leading member of the group of countries protecting and supporting liberal democracies and standing up for rules-based international collaboration. It can also be a broker helping to connect democratic and nondemocratic governments in initiatives to tackle shared global challenges, from climate change to health resilience and equitable growth."

As he asserts, Britain can use its chairmanship of COP 26 to good effect, and this applies particularly to our relationship with China. There is some indication that pragmatism and principle can be combined, and the UK could perform this kind of role in the digital era. From recent read-outs of UK and China Foreign Minister contact it is clear that there are tensions but still the willingness to trade and mutually invest. The importance to both of a constructive UK-China relationship to tackle global challenges such as climate change and global health is clear. China will remain an important economic and technological powerhouse, trading and investment partner. But we need to pick and choose where we cooperate, and we compete, and that will require much improved navigation skills both on the part of business and government.

Chapter 14

China And Global Multilateral Institutions
Professor Michael Mainelli

The Hanse versus The Empires
The UK, Multi-Lateral Institution, and Relations with the EU, USA & China

"J'ai entendu vos points de vue. Ils ne rencontrent pas les miens. La décision est prise à l'unanimité."
"I have heard your points of view. They do not match mine. The decision is therefore unanimous." General Charles de Gaulle (1890-1970)

Multi-Multi-Lateral Institutions
Any political commentary must strike a balance between near-term irrelevance and long-term platitudes. The objective of this chapter is to explore the potential relationship of the UK and multi-lateral institutions with the 'Empires' of the EU, the USA, and now China. The conclusion is that UK engagement with multi-lateral institutions should play a much bigger role as it seeks a mutually-beneficial and harmonious world order with existing and emerging super-powers.

A quick definition of multi-lateral institutions and some examples are in order. Three or more nations can form a multi-lateral institution (MLI) to work on issues that relate to all the countries. There are a lot of MLIs. Examples include widely-based international institutions such as the United Nations (UN) on relationships among nations, with 17 specialist subsidiary agencies that are also MLIs.[1]

There are numerous development banks, such as the Asian Infrastructure Investment Bank (AIIB), the European Bank for Reconstruction and Development (EBRD) or the African Development Bank (ADB); legal bodies, such as the International Criminal Court (ICC) and the International Court of Justice (ICJ); regional bodies, such as the Gulf Cooperation Council (GCC) or Association of Southeast Asian Nations (ASEAN); groups, such as the Commonwealth Nations or Group of 77 developing world caucus; alliances, such as the North Atlantic Treaty Organisation (NATO) or Collective Security Treaty Organisation; interest bodies, such as the Organisation of the Petroleum Exporting Countries (OPEC) to harmonise policies on oil and gas or Organisation For Economic Cooperation & Development (OECD) on economics and taxation; let alone wide initiatives such as Belt & Road.

There are also organisations, such as the C40 group of cities on climate change, that involve devolved governments. There are trade associations that are on the edge of governments, e.g. International Organisation for Standards (ISO) of national standards bodies, or International Air Transport Association (IATA) of airlines. Some people go so far as to include various non-governmental organisations, e.g. Greenpeace or WWF on the environment.

---

1 FAO: Food and Agriculture Organisation, ICAO: International Civil Aviation Organisation, IFAD: International Fund for Agricultural Development, ILO: International Labour Organisation, IMF: International Monetary Fund, IMO: International Maritime Organisation, ITU: International Telecommunication Union, UNESCO: United Nations Educational, Scientific and Cultural Organisation, UNIDO: United Nations Industrial Development Organisation, UNWTO: World Tourism Organisation, UPU: Universal Postal Union, WHO: World Health Organisation, WIPO: World Intellectual Property Organisation, WMO: World Meteorological Organisation, and World Bank Group of: IBRD: International Bank for Reconstruction and Development, IDA: International Development Association, IFC: International Finance Corporation.

10 Types Of People In The World – Those Who Understand Bilateralism, And Those Who Don't

Governments have three basic methods to deal with other governments on issues. Unilateralism means dictating terms. Bilateralism implies a series of specific and unique agreements between two nations. Multilateralism means trying to organise several nations around some general principles of conduct, and then putting in place a structure to govern those principles and nations' conduct. Clearly, power symmetry or asymmetry features highly in a nation's bias towards one form. A dominant nation will tend towards unilateralism. Where unilateralism doesn't work, then bilateralism between dominant nations is common. Multilateralism is favoured by smaller nations to control the larger ones through force of numbers.

After World War II, the United States, unusually for a highly-dominant nation that could have wielded unilateral power, favoured a new world order based around multilateralism. There were some bilateral agreements, for example SALT, and even unilateral agreements, for example with Japan, South Korea, or Taiwan, but by and large the United States tried to work through multilateralism with other nations. For nearly seven decades multilateralism was believed to allow the United States to engage with more countries more effectively, efficiently, and consistently. The cost was assumed to be that at some points United States interests might be subordinate to groups of smaller nations.

Recent United States administrations have been less 'compromising' on many topics, as evidenced by the rising number of sanctions on other nations and individuals. The United States has moved towards bilateralism at a time when other countries, notably China but to a lesser degree India, Brazil, and Russia, also appear to prefer working bilaterally rather than working through MLIs and supporting the role of MLIs in international relations. Perversely, many international policy tools, perhaps especially sanctions, work best in a multilateral environment.

A Multiplicity Of Manicheists

In the 3rd century, the Prophet Mani taught a universal religion based on what we now call dualism. Everything is good or evil, black or white. The Cold War promoted a Manichean view of the world. On 5 March 1946, at Westminster College in Fulton, Missouri, Winston Churchill delivered his "Sinews of Peace" speech declaring that an 'iron curtain' had descended across Europe. The Western side of the wall was white, the Eastern side black. Manichean thinking dominated international relations for decades. In 1949, when the Communists under Mao Zedong defeated Chiang Kai-shek's Nationalist armies, China was deemed to fall on the black side of the iron curtain.

I was a child of the Cold War. When I studied international relations at Harvard my teachers were of the realpolitik school, such as Henry Kissinger, steeped in the Cold War. Yet Stanley Hoffman taught us to avoid being ensnared by any single doctrine, emphasising the difficulties and responsibilities of state-craft. Edwin O Reischauer taught us to look to the long-term for Asia, Japan, Korea, and 'China would be back'. In 1981 Ronald J Hill at Trinity College Dublin taught 'when the Soviet Union dissolves', and we scarcely believed him. He compelled us to study the 'Stans' because they would be nations again. We were warned not to fall for Manichean deceptions.

We have had other Manichean deceptions, developing versus developed, North versus South, or knowledge versus labour economies. Manichean deceptions blind us to hybrid viewpoints or nuanced complex groupings. Manichean polarities have been applied to the EU. Some fear a 'superstate', others its imminent collapse. I first went to China in 1983 when it was 'communist' – and have seen nearly four decades of miraculous economic transformations on numerous visits since. These transformations are not due to communism, nor are they due to free markets, nor capitalism. Similar Manichean extremes have been applied to China from the Warring States and the Qin Empire, to the Three Kingdoms, Sixteen Kingdoms, Ten Kingdoms, to today.

There are multiple world views of course. Four familiar views in international relations might be:

· Ideological – a set of ideas that set out an all-encompassing view of the world, often based on a theory, e.g. liberalism or communism, or values, e.g. liberty, equality, free speech, self-determination, peace;

· Realpolitik – in an anarchic world, hard and soft power can deliver national objectives;

· Institutionalism – MLIs can pool sovereignty for mutual interest, thus providing a rules-based system to resolve disputes and deliver common objectives;

· Constructivism - agency and structure are mutually constituted, thus objectives are achieved by spinning and using deep and elaborate webs of relationships among institutions and individuals that engender trust.

Ideologists are often theorists working in think-tanks and policy units. Front line security and intelligence agencies are realpolitik. Diplomats and international agencies promote institutionalism, perhaps especially MLIs. Cultural services and exchange programmes are constructivists, connecting people and building relationships beyond state institutions.

Liberalism is an ideology. The ideology of liberalism affirms three traditional ethical liberal values of individual rights, freedom of speech, and protection of property. To those three add three practical liberal values of limited government, free markets, and free trade. The international state is supposed to limit freedom of choice as little as possible. To all of these six values, add tolerance, as in US poet Robert Frost's definition of a liberal - "A liberal is a man too broadminded to take his own side in a quarrel." Liberalism benefits by being recursive about tolerance. Liberalism recognises, in a loose parallel with Gödel's Incompleteness Theorem, that there is no all-encompassing view of the world, even itself.

A Multiplicity Of Objectives & Issues

Nations might strive to attain a multiplicity of objectives, but some basics are security, rule of law, economic success, health, education, environmental satisfaction, equality, and care for the poor & elderly. Perhaps more simply, prosperity, security, and freedom of choice. Not far off the UK's 2018 National Security Review conclusion of a "Fusion Doctrine" combining economic success with security and influence.

Nations are drawn into a multiplicity of issues while pursuing objectives, but also by geography, neighbours, natural disasters, or events. Conflict in the international sphere manifests itself in competition for resources, e.g. natural resources, taxation, debt relief. Cooperation in the international sphere arises where there is common benefit in mutual action, e.g. climate change, refugees, pandemics, foreign aid, competition and anti-monopoly policy.

The Hanse versus The Empires

The Hanse, or Hanseatic League, was an economic and defensive confederation comprising up to 200 free towns and cities in northern Germany and neighbouring areas around the North Sea and the Baltic, spanning seven modern nations. Traditionally dated to a protective alliance formed by Lübeck and Hamburg in 1241, the Hanse reached the height of its power in the 1300's and held its last official assembly in 1669. If you will, it was an early Belt-Road Initiative. Kings Lynn in Norfolk was a Hanse town; London was not, though it was a trading post, a kontor.

The Holy Roman Empire lasted a thousand years, from 800 to 1806. It was a rollicking affair, a multi-ethnic complex of territories in Western and Central Europe that developed during the Early Middle Ages. Voltaire used the Holy Roman Empire as an unsatisfying case study of the concept of a republic, quipping, ["This body which called itself and which still calls itself] the Holy Roman Empire was in no way holy, nor Roman, nor an empire".[2] A sweeping generalisation might be that trade was seen as an instrument of the Empire.

There are some Manichean deceptions here. The Hanse had an interesting symbiosis with the Holy Roman Empire. Many cities often owed allegiances to the Empire, round the back, so to speak, of local kingdoms. The Hanse acted colonially in the Shetland Isles controlling dried codfish exports. Similarly, the Empire was not homogeneous and consisted of numerous principalities frequently pursuing radically different economic and trade policies. But hopefully the mists of time allow us to use these myths to clarify the fog of today's relations.

The Hanse calls to EU sensibilities across the centuries. The Hanse's vibrant legend of freely trading cities inspired Adam Smith and the Founding Fathers of the USA in developing their views of free trade. There are periods in Chinese history comparable to the Hanse and the Empire. The Ming Dynasty Admiral Zheng He and his famous Treasure Ship voyages of the early 1400's were Hanseatic, but were followed by a long period of closed borders and Imperialist Hǎijìn, 海禁, or sea bans. China has long described itself as Zhōng guó, 中国, the Middle Kingdom. In part, this implies a central role working with other kingdoms.

I wish to use 'Hanse versus Empires' as a metaphor for a world where either government attracts trade, the Hanse, or where government directs trade, the Empire. The Hanse was an MLI, and the Hanseatic approach would be to support Institutionalism. Imperialists believe that trade is an extension of the state. Imperialists are Realpolitik adherents. Government trumps trade. Hanseatics believe that to trade is to be human. Trade is a human right, a traditional liberal viewpoint. Trade trumps government.

Trade Moves

As a Past Master of the Worshipful Company of World Traders, I believe trade promotes prosperity and peace in line with our Company motto, "commerce and honest friendship with all". Game theorists and economists who study trade relations come down overwhelmingly to the conclusion that, under ideal conditions, unfettered trade is best. There are good reasons why 'free' trade theory rapidly turns into 'fair' trade discussions. Ideal conditions don't apply in the real world. Trade creates numerous issues stemming from a basic definition of a nation state, "a monopoly on the use of force in a geographic area", such as:

- security and defence issues such as the recent debate over Huawei, but also organised crime and trafficking;
- security of supply chains;
- control of immigration and types of immigrants, e.g. anti-money-laundering;
- consumer protection;
- environmental protection;
- cyber, the modern world's cyber geography doesn't fit nature's geography.

---

2 « Ce corps qui s'appelait et qui s'appelle encore le saint empire romain n'était en aucune manière ni saint, ni romain, ni empire. » *Essai Sur L'histoire Générale Et Sur Les Mœurs Et L'esprit Des Nations*, Chapter 70 (1756).

From Adam Smith onwards, thinkers have increasingly recognised that commerce is about much more than making money. Commerce is social interaction where people trade ideas, opinions, knowledge, or merchandise. Trade reaps economic benefits from specialisation and comparative advantage, creates prosperity, distributes success and wealth, and collectively enriches all our societies and communities. Trade is a force for good, but trade is not an intrinsic 'good'.

'Hanse versus Empires' is not a rehash of the 'globalisation polarisation' debate. Much analysis of British polarisation or USA polarisation has focused on the urban versus the rural, or David Goodhart's 'Somewheres', who feel strong local and national attachments, versus 'Anywheres', global villagers who value autonomy and mobility. On trade, you can be a rural Hanseatic, or a rural Imperialist, likewise an urban Hanseatic or an urban Imperialist.

Equally, much analysis focuses on central versus local tensions, or federalism versus confederalism. Any community has sub-communities, and governments need to encompass the span of communities within their geographic area, often with constituent sub-governments. One can remark that the EU is a confederation that has shown a tendency to move towards federalism. One could remark that the UK has increasing federalism but remains awkwardly centralised. One might suggest that China is politically centralised but economically has many confederal aspects. Again, on trade, you can be a centralist Hanseatic, or a local Hanseatic, likewise a federal Imperialist or a confederal Imperialist.

When I studied international relations, trade and industry were frequently seen to be subservient to the state, tools of statecraft. Since the 1970s we've seen a transformation in trade. Until recently trade had been left more and more to get on with itself, and got on with it indeed. Trade as a % of GDP, thus taking population growth into account, has risen from 27% in 1970 to 60% in 2019, a 220% rise in all of our lives over the past half century. Alongside technology, the rise in trade has powered most of our increasing economic well-being. It also powered the rise of multi-lateral institutions. Over the past few years, the pendulum of trade appears to be reversing its swing, moving from Hanseatic freedom to a tool of the Empires.

Sum Figures

Trade statistics can be ropey. Some WTO estimates place the scale of non-monetary trade at 25% to 40% of global trade. That's an enormous error bar just to begin with. Trade goods statistics have physical customs inspection reference points, though one still observes the Rotterdam Effect, the inflation of trade statistics due to the inclusion of quasi-transit goods. In 2017, the Netherlands recorded £6 billion less in exports to the UK than were recorded in UK imports. In turn, the UK reported £3 billion more in exports to the Netherlands than the Netherlands recorded as imports. Then we turn to services. Services export data are taken mostly from polls – and we've seen the accuracy of polling data lately. Foreign direct investment (FDI) figures are subject to too many vagaries and distortions to mention. And then over 1,200 adjustments to published GDP data, but we have what we have.

China and the EU are net exporters, while the USA and UK are net importers. Germany on its own is roughly the sixth largest exporter and importer to China. The UK is roughly the fifth largest export market for China, but only the 20th import market. China has pursued a traditional, export-led strategy to move to a market economy, to bring in know-how, to take advantage of comparative advantage. China's economy is rapidly moving to a more service-based economy with greater global financial services integration. There is a rebalancing of offshoring, onshoring, and supply chains.

The EU is the UK's largest trading partner. In 2019, UK exports to the EU were 43% of all UK exports and 52% of all UK imports. Financial & business services (a category which includes legal, accounting, advertising, research and development, architectural, engineering, and other professional and technical services) accounts for 55% of UK services exports, about 20% of total UK exports, and 42% of the UK's exports to the EU. Though a net exporter, the EU runs a large trade deficit with China, but the EU pursues a different strategy.

The 'London Effect'?

Professor Anu Bradford at Columbia Law School highlights the 'Brussels Effect'. In short, the EU's clout is via standards and regulation. First, with a single market about a fifth of global GDP, multinationals have to enter EU markets. Second, the EU prides itself on tough regulation, e.g. consumer data rights, food, the environment, so firms know they have to follow EU leadership on standards. Third, reinforcing the first two, firms often lobby their own governments to follow EU regulations. Some of the EU's skill in international standards derives from needing to handle 27 national interests at all times. Bradford posits that a post-Brexit UK will be just as cowed by this reinforcing triangle of pressure as the USA and China already are.

However, the UK might create the 'London Effect' in financial services. The UK's strength is as a deal centre and financial & business services exporter. The three 'Empires', China, EU, USA, are big trading partners with each other, facing much rebalancing ahead. A special UK strength has been capital allocation, as a FDI springboard to Europe, first for the Commonwealth, since the mid-1980s for the USA, then Japan, and latterly China. Part of firms' balancing of their balance sheets includes equity and debt, but also insurance. The UK is also a place for balancing global balance sheets, via patent boxes, inter-company transfers and holding companies. FDI and financial and business services go together well. UK financial services standards could become the international norm. Financial exchanges are commercial MLIs, so think of stock exchange public listing rules as a way of 'exporting' values of governance and fair play.

Small nations often have outsize financial centres: think Singapore, Zurich, Geneva, Dublin, or Amsterdam, let alone offshore centres around the world from Jersey, Guernsey, and the Isle of Man, to Gibraltar, Luxembourg, Cayman Islands, or Mauritius. As someone who travels the world advising countries and cities on establishing financial centres, what people value is stability and tolerance. Anecdotally, in the 1990s the Japanese coined a term for London's financial services, the 'Wimbledon Effect'. London hosts the Wimbledon tournament successfully, but rarely wins. Basically, the UK could thrive by providing the financial services 'tennis courts', highly successful despite a lack of native competition.

Smaller nations and centres try to emulate the Wimbledon Effect in, for example, Singapore, Monaco, Zurich, or Luxembourg. Multinationals frequently do their financial work in these foreign cities despite having no operational work in the same country. A French pharmaceutical company and a Japanese pharmaceutical company can structure a deal over a Malaysian plant in London, not in France, Japan, or Malaysia. On the contrary, I've never seen a deal in New York City, Tokyo, or Beijing where there is no indigenous USA, Japanese, or Chinese local business.

Certainty About How The Rules Of The Game Are Improved

As long as everyone is treated fairly, native and non-native, and the local jurisdiction isn't going to do something short-term or populist – typically a tax grab, retroactive, windfall, wealth, or financial transaction taxes – but rather becomes known for stability and sense, offshore centres do well. Despite its location and a bumpy start in the 1970s, the Isle of Man derives over 35% of its gross national income from international financial services based on a stable legal & regulatory environment plus specialist talent. The island certainly won't make rash decisions about financial services regulation or taxation as it would harm itself too greatly.

'Rule of law' is fundamental to Hanseatic approaches. Foreign trade is attracted to centres where all traders are treated fairly. The attraction of the City of London is based on the renown of its legal system, judges, arbitrators, and mediators. Unsurprisingly, numerous competitive financial centres have established zones of English law, complete with international arbitration centres.

Government officials frequently state that "business wants certainty". This is balderdash. Businesses thrive on uncertainty. If there was certainty, there would be no need for markets. All quantities and prices would be known. There would be no change and no opportunity to compete. Businesses realise that the rules of the game need to change and improve over time, or there will be no progress. No, businesses want certainty about how the rules of the game change or will change.

Politicians do not shine on 'certainty'. Certainty over how the rules will change requires a process that looks ahead, for example following a strict consultation, recommendation, drafting, revision, implementation timetable every so many years. Instead modern politicians react to most crises with instant legislation. Often these crises are media generated crises and the responses are designed to garner votes rather than solve a systemic problem.

Large firms do think these things through. When multi-nationals relocate they frequently look at the % of GDP taken by government rather than look at specific tax rates. At a high % of GDP taken by government then government must get the money via taxation of many forms. The corporate tax rate isn't the most important. Operationally too, firms take capricious governments into account:

"Pharma firms have cleverly placed manufacturing sites around the world, including in small countries such as Belgium and Switzerland which can quickly produce more vaccine than these countries could ever want." [The Economist, "Bullseye - An Effective Covid-19 Vaccine Is A Turning Point In The Pandemic" (14 November 2020), pages 21-24.]

Paradoxically, a UK separate from the EU and its policies might be seen as more stable for EU, USA, and Chinese firms. The UK could look forward to a surge of financial work from Chinese firms undertaking FDI with London as a springboard to the EU, and as a more neutral, and skilled, location for EU firms structuring work in China. The UK could assist 'onshoring' by the Empires, or the UK could look forward to a surge of multi-national deals as Belt-Road Initiative (BRI) or Build Back Better World (B3W) projects are hatched and grown in the neutral professional and financial 'tennis courts' of the City of London.

But it is never hard to find things to fret about. USA, Japanese, and some Chinese firms have taken justifiable offence at locating in the UK over the past few decades, in order to gain access to Europe, only to have access pulled out from under them despite assurances over Brexit making no difference. FDI inflows to the United Kingdom are falling.

Taking Back Control

I style the City of London as 'the world's coffeehouse'. The UK is a connector delivering financial & business services to support trade. The UK needs to sell the virtues of Hanseatic open borders and liberal values of limited government interference, free markets, free trade, individual rights, freedom of speech, and protection of property. In theory this shouldn't be hard, not least as these are traditional British values, often politically associated with the traditional liberal party of a century ago. Let the Imperialists structure their Empires as they will, but when they need to connect with each other then Hanseatic Britain is there. Connecting 8 billion people is sufficient work for 67 million.

Empires have tendencies to control trade and services, restrict immigration, restrict capital flows, manage exchange rates and enact industrial policies. Empires are run by bureaucrats and lawyers, whereas Hanseatic nations are run by traders and engineers. So, a Hanseatic UK that put free trade first might choose to:

- work to strengthen, and reform, MLIs, starting with the UN and its 17 agencies;
- treat all comers fairly, with minimal industrial policies, no state aid, no cartels or monopolies, finding ways for all comers to have a fair chance;
- be a model nation for swift, efficient, and secure working and student visas;
- simplify the tax structure so people can pay easily and fairly, perhaps finally implementing land value taxation while reducing corporation tax to stimulate commerce;
- promote a gold standard of the EU's General Data Protection Regulation as an export tool, which is what global consumers want when they think about it; work too on reducing trans-action friction by making e-signatures the standard for international commerce in line with eIDAS, the Federal ESIGN Act, and BankID;
- recognise that there is no such thing as weak encryption, the cornerstone technology of all digital finance, there is only strong encryption or no encryption, and that strong cyber defences are essential;
- strengthen and simplify anti-money-laundering;
- lead the world on trade-friendly climate targets, establish a MLI for international emissions trading, and perhaps issue a binding sovereign policy performance bond tied to our net-zero 2050 target where, similar to an inflation-linked bond, the UK pays more interest if it fails to adhere to the net-zero reduction pathway.

A Hanseatic strategy would promote the principle of least interference with trade. Leaving the EU lifts constraints that might have impeded the UK brokering between Empires. The UK has a fantastic opportunity to explore the many facets of trade and follow a new model. But economics is not everything. The choice is very much in the hands of the British people.

Recently, there have been disturbing moves to violate international law, weaken encryption, increase state aid, flip-flop on technology defence, undermine data protection. The National Security and Investment Bill strengthens the UK's ability to intervene in mergers and acquisitions, but application might emulate the USA's Foreign Investment Risk Review Modernisation Act (FIRRMA) and its commercial interference too slavishly. The Subsidy Control Bill, likewise, had better control subsidies, not excuse them.

Think Small, Successfully

One awkward question is whether the UK, with a population of 67 million, may actually be too large to adapt, too susceptible to populism, and not amenable enough to self-discipline. National economies of scale peter out more quickly than people imagine. Large countries have diseconomies of scale too. For every still-competitive USA or underway China, there remain Indian or Brazilian comparators of inefficiency and disorder.

Some of the world's most competitive nations are the small nations, Denmark, Sweden, Switzerland, Finland, Singapore, Ireland, Israel, or the Netherlands. James Breiding believes similar success characteristics are forged because these countries are 'too small to fail'. Success requires them to adapt to the world and be disciplined about competitiveness, quality, and sustainability over the long-term. The largest of these countries, the Netherlands, has a population of 17 million, barely a quarter of the UK's.

Successful small countries are fair and open. They signal stability and rule of law. Empires need fair Hanseatic ports for their own purposes. Going forward, might the UK be simultaneously too large and too small, or can it have the best of both, quiet small country success plus economies of scale? The UK needs to think big, yet emulate small. Some MLI work might develop city-to-city connections over nation-to-nation. Professional bodies, a traditional UK strength throughout the Commonwealth, are another MLI tool to be used more often.

Values Versus Trade

The post-Brexit world could be the UK's oyster. China needs to expand its investment in Europe. The UK should be China's preferred offshore platform for Europe, and beyond. The EU needs to expand its investment in China. UK skills, combined with stability and independence, ought to make the UK the EU's preferred offshore platform for China, and beyond. This Hanseatic role should be attractive to the UK and, done well, could soon make the UK indispensable to China, the EU, and the USA.

It's not hard though to bump up against issues that conflict with values: Tibet, Hong Kong, Taiwan, South China Sea, Xinjiang; Crimea, Georgia, NordGas, fishing rights, Libya; Guantanamo Bay, prison populations, capital punishment, election integrity, global warming. On China, at the annual Chancellor's 2021 Mansion House speech (1 July 2021) the Rt Hon Rishi Sunak MP said, "... people on both sides argue either that we should sever all ties or focus solely on commercial opportunities at the expense of our values ...". He rightly counselled a mature relationship pursuing trade and links within a framework of national resilience, understanding the need to take a principled stand on issues that contravene values. "After all, principles only matter if they extend beyond our convenience."

Willy Brandt's "Wandel durch Handel", "change through trade", belief has taken flak recently for imprecision on the location of 'red lines' and how to enforce them. There certainly will be almost no change without trade, in its widest sense. It is very much in the interest of Hanse nations to give the responsibility of drawing and policing red lines firmly to specific MLIs. Using MLIs, a nation can amplify the projection of its values, while simultaneously structuring domestic responses to red line transgressions, and maintaining trade more consistently through times of dispute.

Re-engaging Through MLIs

The EU was the UK's most important multi-lateral institution, until Brexit ended 47 years of membership. Paradoxically, the UK's departure from its primary multi-lateral institution means it should push much harder from inside many more MLIs if it hopes to engage successfully with the three current big blocs and nations, the EU, USA, and China, let alone emerging strong nations such as Brazil, India, Indonesia, or even a restructured Russia.

MLI engagement is a big strategic answer to a Hanseatic place in the world, but it's hard in modern politics to hold any long-term strategy when short-term cheap wins beckon. This chapter is not a polemic on the many threats that appear to have arisen due to complacency on the part of 'the West', perhaps punctuated by the 'fall of the wall' in 1989. However, it has been some time since there was a clear restatement of the values of western liberalism by a leading figure or a leading nation.

Discussion among the intelligentsia assumes a serious erosion of trust, increasing difficulty establishing what is true, and that populism reigns where principles don't pay. A liberal approach should be to redouble selling the better world of prosperity, security, and freedom of choice we want to build, long-term, together. MLIs are beacons towards that better world. A lot of work lies ahead to make those beacons shine more brightly.

> *"The principle of Toryism is mistrust of the people, qualified by fear;*
> *The principle of Liberalism is trust in the people, qualified by prudence."*
> William Ewart Gladstone (1809 – 1898), British Prime Minister (Liberal) at Chester

Chapter 15

Summation
Paul Reynolds

Summaries

Kerry Brown's chapter on Chinese governance describes a labyrinthine set of structures and processes which constitute the prima facie 'top-down' system; or perhaps more realistically, the Party's bargaining and negotiation system, across the whole of China. It has the formal institutions of a top-down command and control approach, but in practice appears to be an informal consultation and benefit-sharing arrangement within the Communist Party.

What is a remarkable feature of Chinese governance that emerges from the chapter is how tiny, relative to the size of the Chinese population, is the Communist Party central political elite, and indeed how the proportion of those employed in governmental organisations including state enterprises and sub-national government, is significantly less than the USA, and half that of France.

At least in structures and staffing, the Chinese political system does not conform to Western stereotypes of a vast bureaucratic state in which nothing is legal unless expressly stated as so. If that is the assumed feature that some countries are attempting to emulate in order to achieve high economic growth, they are copying the wrong thing.

Yeow Poon's chapter on the nature of changing Western perspectives on China sets out the different facets of historic and recent negative perceptions and Sinophobia, leading to suspicions of a 'world domination' agenda. Western perceptions of China, it suggests, are rooted in observations made through the prism of European supremacy, and through individualistic ideologies which emphasise personal liberty.

As such, the chapter argues, China has a more communitarian and cooperative culture relative to Western countries.

The chapter also expresses some alarm at the recent rise of Sinophobia and racism in the UK, as a consequence of the more recent anti-China political rhetoric.

On the economic front, the chapter contrasts the current commercial demonisation of China with the willing transfer of manufacturing capacity to China over decades by Western corporations; facilitated by Western elite structures which are focused on capital market gains and destructive short-termism. It concludes that a more empathetic approach to China by the West will be more beneficial for both sides, compared to rising antagonism.

Vince Cable's chapter on the Chinese economy accepts that China is on its way to becoming the world's largest economy, but expresses doubts about the solidity of the China 'growth model' based both on questionable data reliability (eg plans taken as historic fact) and on economic vulnerabilities.

First among the latter is the sustainability of such high levels of investment relative to GDP over such a long period, and the resultant low returns, which lead to high enterprise-level and bank/shadow bank debt. This chapter suggests that a surfeit of corporate cash is leading to a real estate bubble.

This astute analysis raises many questions about how China's economy has continued to grow despite all the imbalances, vulnerabilities and bottlenecks. The chapter does not, as has often been the case, predict imminent collapse.

In this chapter the Chinese economy is described as 'state-led'. Whilst this is useful as shorthand for describing a key prima facie difference between the Chinese and 'Western' economic systems, this can easily be misinterpreted. Defining 'state-led' is not easy, especially in the sense of how much US and EU economies are in practice state-led, and to what extent in practice the Chinese economy is not state-led, depending on definitions.

Many important questions are raised by this, including whether Chinese economic growth comes from it being state-led, or from other factors such as economic liberalisation, the manner of infrastructure financing, risk-return systems, the ease of debt financing, low labour cost or even having 450 million internal economic migrants.

Laurence Vandewalle's chapter explores the changing nature of the Chinese Communist Party leadership, and the policies and neo-Maoist slogans of Xi Jinping.

The chapter discusses the extent and speed of control assumed quickly by Xi Jinping after 2012, the highly selective Party-only anti-corruption campaign against senior rivals like Bo Xilai and the mechanisms he has deployed to move away from the collegiate style of Hu Jintao.

Whilst slogans and ideological tenets of the China model still refer to 'Chinese characteristics', (implying the model is therefore not duplicable), under Xi Jinping there seem to be a cautious move away from this, the chapter explains.

For the 'China model' to be exportable, the Chinese characteristics thus have to be de-emphasised. The suspicion expressed is that Xi Jinping wants to show, globally, that its China socialist model is superior to liberal democracy.

This is indeed enlightening. Xi Jinping came to power as leader on a platform which expressed (or implied) criticisms of his predecessor. One component was that military and civilian governance should be merged, especially at senior levels, in order to project power internationally, and another was that senior communist cadre corruption had become out of hand.

Merlene Toh Emerson's chapter takes a broad sweep across the BRI landscape and all its complexities.

The chapter sets out the obstacles, risks and vulnerabilities of the BRI project, especially how it has become the defining project of the Xi Jinping era. It also explores the economic, political, security and psychological benefits of the project to China. A key vulnerability is clearly the scope for overstretch in financial capacity and in the ability of China's officials and company executives to manage all the multiple financier projects of indeterminate returns.

Most notable in this chapter is the discussion of the geopolitical reasons behind the initiative. The key motives are considered such as the fear of the limits to growth, especially in the East, in a non-democratic country, the need for secure oil supplies and trade routes that are not maritime, overcoming the vulnerability to blockade (eg via the Malacca Straits), and the need to lock in economic relationships in the face of potential threats from the USA.

Two rarely-heard motivations cited are the desire under Xi Jinping to internationalise the Renminbi without operating through US-led financial infrastructure and institutions; and the desire for a global communications backbone to rival that of the US and UK, and without being dependent on Western-led networks and technology.

The future of BRI is assessed in the light of rival projects and initiatives from Europe, the US and elsewhere.

Phil Bennion's chapter first considers the demographic changes which have occurred in China as a result of economic growth, and the way that the communist leadership has adapted to those changes. Key to this, it explains, is the recognition by the Communist Party that the political psychology of China's success for the masses, is just as important as the mass psychology over the 'inevitability' of Western 'decline'.

The chapter alludes to the abandonment of Peaceful Rise, after Xi Jinping came to power, and how this set off a train of events leading to more frosty relations with Beijing.

The political problems precipitated by poor human rights in China are set out clearly, including problems in relations with neighbours due to the detention of hundreds of thousands of Uyghurs in Xinjiang, losing the moral high ground in international and multilateral institutions, and ensuring that economic relations with neighbouring BRI countries are highly instrumental.

The chapter also examines other international relationships, as with Russia, Japan and the ASEAN countries, painting a picture of Chinese foreign politico-economic management which has a long way to go before power matches responsibility.

Such a shortcoming could indeed lead to war, as the chapter hints at, since declining trust and misinterpretations in both civilian and military matters (on both sides) carry very significant dangers.

Andrew Leung's chapter on Hong Kong follows the extraordinary events in the 'Special Economic Region' over the last couple of years, with widespread protests, often violent, over the National Security Law which came into force June 2020, and over preceding political events.

The chapter explains that the 2020 National Security Law was passed by the National People's Congress in Beijing, and it is linked to Article 23 of the quasi-constitutional 'Basic Law' - which followed the return of Hong Kong to the Chinese mainland from the UK in 1997.

Many China analysts have linked Beijing's tough line on the National Security Law in 2020 and 2021 with Xi Jinping's neo-Maoist approach to order and security, wanting to put an end to the long sequence of protests which have scuppering key security and mainland-integration legislation.

It also laments growing inequality, housing unaffordability, and hints at discrimination against native Hongkongers who are poor speakers of Mandarin.

What is a memorable and notable feature of the chapter is its description of external influences behind the various Hong Kong protest movements, parties and factions, especially CIA and the US, allegedly using Hong Kong as a base to undermine the mainland.

Juli Minoves' chapter on the dilemmas of Taiwan starts with a solid historical narrative explaining how Taiwan came to be uniquely a prosperous quasi-nation-state with all the trappings of statehood (and global hi-tech exports), but not recognised as a nation-state by most of the world, amidst historical claims from mainland China's PRC.

The chapter interestingly paints a picture of a mainland China much more sanguine about Taiwan (or its own nomenclatures) than 'Western' narratives might suggest, even after democratisation. It refers to Chairman Mao's view that it might be resolved over '100 years', and to the likely negative impact of war on mainland economic growth on which much of the Communist Party's legitimacy rests. This suggests that China can live with the status quo as long as necessary.

By implication, changes to the status quo such as Taiwan voting for independence, or the US stationing nuclear weapons on the island, may turn out to be counter-productive and have negative effects for both mainland China and Taiwan. The chapter also suggests that while developments in Hong Kong may retard further economic integrationist measures between Taiwan and the PRC, the historical-legal parallels are insufficient to draw conclusions about the PRC's attitude to Taiwanese universal suffrage.

Discussing the contrast between economic liberalisation in both countries and political and social liberalisation in Taiwan only, the chapter concludes with a number of future scenarios, including political 'liberalisation' (eg democratisation decentralisation) in China as a potential path to future unity.

Humphrey Hawksley's article on China and its neighbours takes the reader on a vivid contemporary tour of China's historical 'balancing acts' at its periphery.

These include the South China Sea and tussles with the Philippines, Indonesia, Vietnam, Japan and others; Taiwan; relations with Pakistan and India, Sri Lanka, Russia, and complex relations with mainland ASEAN nations with significant Chinese communities, some of which are described as 'vassal states'.

The chapter convincingly questions the depth of relations between China and its neighbours, and suggests that in more recent years China's supposedly closer relations with its neighbours are more instrumental and narrowly economic, than warm and fluid.

This raises questions about the consequences of either continuing Chinese influence as its economy grows further, or of any hiccup in China's growth leading to a retrenchment and withdrawal of investment programmes.

One is left with the impression that China's relations with neighbours are coordinated somewhat ineffectively, and the limited resources of the Chinese central government in foreign relations are revealed by the lack of control over the projection of Chinese power amongst its neighbours.

Emil Kirchner's chapter on China-EU relations is notable for its clear motivation to seek cordial and pragmatic relations with China. The chapter expresses regret that the situation for the Uyghurs in Xinjiang, and the situation in Hong Kong, plus the difficulties presented by the SARS-Cov2 pandemic, South China Sea and tensions over Taiwan have all led to mistrust.

Importantly, the chapter sets out areas where cooperation is assumed to be still mutually beneficial, including the environment and climate-related emissions, piracy in the Gulf of Aden, terrorism and above all trade.

However, the chapter sets out more general areas which are problematic such as human rights, China accepting the global economic and judicial system and China's divide and rule approach to member states versus the EU, for example on BRI.

The chapter examines the progress of the EU-China Comprehensive Agreement on Investment (CAI), and the pressures from the USA and European Parliament at least to reconsider some of the provisions.

The chapter makes reference to commercially-led EU-China cooperation over piracy in the Gulf of Aden. However, as it has turned out, this has been something of a cover for China to establish a large military base at Obock, Djibouti, reportedly staffing up to 10,000 military personnel; more than double the size of the large multi-agency US base at Camp Lemonnier a short drive away.

Thus similarly, the beneficial cooperation over terrorism, discussed in the chapter, has also been used by China to position alleged mass incarceration in Xinjiang as 'joining the West in its War on Terror' and in its so-called battle with religious Islamic extremism.

Paul Reynolds' chapter explores the prospects for a Cold War II, which it suggests is unlikely, or even a 'hot war', which it says is more likely.

It also considers a number of undercurrents that impact upon the prospects for a future process of (US-Soviet style) 'confidence-building measures' to avoid war.

The chapter asserts that self-fulfilling anticipation of war, may have already begun. For example, the PLA has been acutely aware of China's economic vulnerability to blockade for decades, and is alarmed by US bases in North Australia and East Timor. China's responses include pipelines via Myanmar and a large new base well situated to block the Straits of Mandeb en route to the Suez Canal in retaliation. One notable observation in the chapter is that US foreign relations tend to be military/security first and economics second, quite the reverse in China's case. If relations are viewed in this way, it concludes, whilst China is expected soon to be the world's number one economic power, the US is likely to remain the world's number one military power for some time; creating a time window for potential US military action in the eyes of 'China hawks' in Washington DC.

Given the direction and acceleration of global climate change and biodiversity loss, *Chris Gleadle's* wide-ranging chapter on China and 'green' issues more easily overcomes the 'sovereignty' objections of the Chinese government when internal Chinese policy is being discussed. In climate change the whole world is affected.

This chapter sets out the size of the problem in both carbon emissions and biodiversity loss, placing much emphasis on rapid and continuing emissions growth arising from its dash to avoid energy short-ages as the economy has expanded. The consequent reliance on fast-tracked coal-fired electricity generation, mostly state or quasi-state, has meant that China has been not just the world's engine of economic growth, it has even more been the world's driver of rising carbon emissions that fuel climate change.

The chapter sets out, by contrast, the plethora of current and future environmental measures, structures, conferences, formal programmes and institutions being established by the Chinese government to address the problems.

In EU/UK-China relations the chapter emphasises the imperative of reforming the supply chains between Europe and China, in order to reduce emissions, with European measures that include import substitution, emission-related levies on imports (which it calculates at 6%+ equivalent), environmental assessments made by importers and other such remedies.

Lord Clement Jones' chapter on the hi-tech sectors, contrasts the more frosty China-Western economic relationship in tech sectors today with the more free-flowing relations of 20 years ago.

Ten years ago, or even little more than five years ago, the chapter explains, cooperation in hi tech sectors was focused more on problem solving and easing investment obstacles, for example in intellectual property protection, or technology transfer problems in 'compulsory' joint ventures.

The UK's experience is provided as a clear example of this shift, when, during the period 2010-2015 the UK joined the AIIB and the author of the chapter sat on the International Advisory Board of Huawei.

There are some difficult policy questions raised by this chapter. For example, if China's technological development is starting to outpace the West, especially the USA, then it is not very clear how separation and restrictive measures will halt that, and whether it will be tokenistic.

Will confidence-building measures emerge, returning hi-tech sectors to the 'Golden Era' of 5-20 years ago, or will matters continue to deteriorate and end up like an enhanced CoCom or Wassenaar Arrangement; both of which were the subject of campaigns for liberalisation by the late Lord Paddy Ashdown in the 1980s?

Michael Mainelli's chapter on the relevance of multilateralism in relations between China and the rest of the world deftly weaves ancient historical insights into modern polemics, referencing adherence to liberalism as an 'ideology', and arguing in favour of free trade, alluding to the Hanseatic League.

The chapter counsels against seeing the world as black and white, in assessing the impact of China, and encourages nuance and deeper understanding in policymaking, recognising many different taxonomies – from types of multilateral institutions to types of world outlook.

Reference is made to the role of financial services in London, post-Brexit, and the great opportunities presented, including from China, in contrast to the fall in inward FDI to the UK in the production of physical goods for export post-Brexit, asserting that as a result the world could be the UK's oyster.

Some very interesting thoughts for further discussion are raised by this chapter. For example, the choices facing countries like China in its involvement in multilateral institutions is a complex one, given that many multilaterals (like the EU) start out with an intention to serve a small number of early members. China is not the first country to face this latecomer problem.

Conclusions

When taken together these 15 chapters, diverse in topics and outlook, may represent something of a constructive challenge to standard 'Western' assumptions about how China's power has grown; and consequently where it is likely to go in the future.

The grand sweep of the book sheds much light on the roots of recent developments within China, and about China's future relations with the rest of the world over current horizons. The book looks past the domestic popular narratives of China within leading Western countries, offering some unique insights.. China is clearly not a socialist country, by most criteria, despite the PRC government's protestations and apparent Western acceptance of such a self-designation.

Counter-intuitively here are perhaps advantages both to the West and China of designating China as a socialist country. For the USA there are WTO rules on 'socialist' subsidies, and a need to present China as something different; 'the other'. For China there is a need for perceptions of continuity from Mao's time, and the desire to portray the Communist party as concerned for the interests of the poor and paternalist in outlook. It may follow that the Party wishes to convey that economic success is due to socialism of one kind or another, vaguely connected, flatteringly, to the character of Chinese people. Such a position may be more supportive to the Party than for example a combination of economic liberalisation, infrastructure investment, ease of debt finance, cadre privileges and low wages.

Is there a subtext in these chapters of a deep Western 'fear' that, notwithstanding China being a single party state, many of the core economic and governmental reforms they implemented over 40 years are entirely available to 'Western' countries?

There may be some underlying discomfort that at least economically, if China is systemically much closer to being a Singapore or a Qatar than a Cuba or a North Korea, there's really nothing 'Chinese' about it at all.

There is a very important question as to whether the rather scant Western analyses of China's actual economic system, as it works in practice, rather than the 'theory plus aggregated data' approach, result in part from the perceived scope it has to challenge the Western status quo and upset dominant interests back home.

China left behind its Maoist economic planning more than 40 years ago. A social safety net is largely absent. Government is relatively small. The central Communist Party elite is tiny, and its remarkable growth-led reduction in poverty is largely a by-product of enrichment by a huge cadre of Communist Party members across the provinces, and thus not the primary aim; ie 'Adam Smith with Chinese characteristics?'

This 40 year process has occurred against a background of nationalist aims for China's status as an important world power, facilitating exports physically and legislatively, in a myriad of ways, almost at all costs. Export-led growth led to investment-dependent growth, based to a great extent on trade facilitation.

It seems that the aims of these endeavours, after the legitimising effects of the post-1949 'unification' began to wane, is to strengthen Party legitimacy by 'permitting' annual economic growth, above all else.

Politically however, as the chapters above illustrate, the most extraordinary achievement is more the pursuit of relative economic liberalisation ('liberalisation' especially if you are a Party member or connected similarly), without any other sort of liberalisation; political, social or otherwise. It is this which has been such a stunning feat, and is a sustained balancing act to behold. One can see how Singapore is something of a model.

In any case, while the Chinese leadership may obsess about the fate of the USSR, even during the Mao era China never had a state monopoly command system that controlled all economic activity. At local level China never railed against small businesses or called them 'speculators'. Anyone crossing the Amur/Heilong Jiang River from Russia to China at any time from 1990 to 2020 will attest to the stark differences in day to day economic life.

In places where the nationalist (Han) narrative has less of a purchase, this balancing act of economic liberalisation, but no other type of liberalisation, has been harder to achieve. In Hong Kong this has, eventually, meant keeping the economic liberalisation, but rolling back the existing relative political and social liberalisation. A clash. The difficulties of this balancing act are thus magnified in its imposition in Hong Kong.

In this book there is frequent reference in some way or other to the Chinese 'economic model'. Exploring further this concept is instructive.

China's economy is often called 'state-led'. It's good shorthand, but can be misleading ... and subject to confirmation bias.

What is state and what is private in China are very much more fuzzy than in Europe or the USA. Many companies are called private when they are majority state-owned, and larger 'private' companies have Party Committees in parallel to 'international style' corporate governance; with close connections to state banks and 'shadow banks'. However it is common for them to have deliberately complex structures so that decision making is 'quasi-private'. This system partially explains both the ease of investment-finance access, but also the worrying China-wide problem of very low average returns on investments; where data is available.

Xi Jinping's international ambitions have led him cautiously to evangelise about the China economic model, implying it is exportable and duplicable for countries wishing to emulate Chinese economic growth. What is the point of 'Xi Jinping Thought' if it cannot be defined and applied? 'Cautiously' is inserted here because any model has to be defined, and thus demystified, which is risky for the Party.

The oft-used 'Chinese characteristics' phrase in the China model has a nationalistic flavour, almost implying economic success rooted in Han DNA. However, defining, codifying, and positioning the model as transferable to other countries rather removes the nationalistic 'Chinese characteristics' aspect of Chinese economic growth, and may raise questions over some of its less admirable features. If Chinese economic growth is unique, with a racial or cultural basis, under a 'Chinese socialism' system, then why is Taiwan more prosperous?

Two internal balancing acts of the Chinese Communist Party, i) economic liberalisation versus other liberalisations, and ii) an exportable model versus a 'unique' Chinese system, certainly look skilfully managed.

Economic growth imperatives have a major effect on things like enforcement of environmental rules. Lax implementation of regulation (eg in the environment) stems from the perceived need to prioritise economic growth above all to sustain legitimacy, and keep all the provincial cadres on board.

When implementation of globally-showcased environmental pledges in China clashes with economic growth, the latter always seems to prevail. In early August 2021, for example, the Chinese National Development Reform Commission announced that 53 closed coal mines in Inner Mongolia, Shanxi and Xinjiang would immediately reopen 'for one year'. Given the threat to growth from energy shortages that loom over the next decade, it looks unlikely that the 'for one year' part of the announcement will be adhered to.

Threats to the legitimising effects of growth also have a major impact on Chinese governance institutions, and indeed on the rise of Xi Jinping.

As is customary, Xi Jinping rose to power on the basis of criticisms of his predecessor: in this case Hu Jintao, who rose to power with the backing of Zheng Bijian, the inventor of 'Peaceful Rise' doctrine. Xi Jinping, however, focused on internal and external vulnerabilities and threats to growth, especially econo-military ones like a blockade threat, and the consequent need for faster and less collegiate decision-making.

Internally a key question concerned whether growth be maintained, east of the 'Heihe–Tengchong Line', at least without social and political reforms. This vulnerability lies behind the Belt and Road initiative and a need to expand non-maritime trade across the Asian land mass.

BRI and Xinjiang oil both lie behind the treatment of the Uyghurs, addressing a perceived vulnerability. Blockade risk also lies behind the Chinese military base at Obock in Djibouti, providing the scope if needed to block access to the Suez canal in retaliation for any threat of Malacca Straits blockade. The perceived blockade threat also underpins China's assertive approach to the South China Sea and the need for bases to help combat potential blockade threats. Hu Jintao's 'peaceful rise' seems now to rest in peace. If BRI fails, Xi Jinping fails, and despite the senior-party-only corruption purges, there are still plenty of Hu Jintao supporters around in the wings. BRI is central.

All of these factors have had a major impact on the response of the US and Europe to the Xi Jinping era. Just five years ago cooperation led the way, economics was key, and nearly all the issues were civilian ones. Not anymore.

Now the relationship, especially US-China, is more military-led and confrontational on both sides. The US, UK and Allies have warships in the South China Sea, the terrible treatment of the Uyghurs is called genocide, and Huawei is societas non grata. In the engage-versus-contain dilemma the Western dial has moved away from 'engage' (where it was for 35 years) and moved suddenly towards 'contain'. Under US pressure a major China-EU investment agreement, hailed by both sides as a great success, has stalled. Whilst Cold War II is very unlikely due to economic integration, which was absent between the West and USSR, a gradual de-coupling over two decades or more looks a significant possibility, as does war.

Economics will probably keep the relationship going for now, and ensure a new Cold War II is a just a tabloid headline to be retailed. However, the spiral of mutual suspicion and military-led thinking could result in a kinetic confrontation, if provoked. Suspicion that war is planned and inevitable can be self-fulfilling.

At present it doesn't ultimately matter so much whether it is true as China alleges that the CIA is behind protests in Hong Kong, or whether the Uyghurs are being induced to be Wahhabis and separatists by Saudi Arabia, to scupper BRI, or whether there is a US plan to install nuclear cruise missiles in Taiwan. Neither in the end does it matter so much whether China is expanding its stockpile of nuclear weapons, taking over Africa or trying to control all major ports in the world. With escalation towards war in mind, it is what is perceived on both sides that matters. And it matters to the world. De-escalation is thus a fair objective to pursue, and it requires confidence-building measures on both sides, of the type seen between the US and USSR in the 1980s.

By comparison with the consequences of a major war, the confidence-building measures required and their broader positive consequences look attractive. However they have to address a broad and interdependent set of underlying issues.

These include the scope for a blockade, the financial securities balance between the US and China, nuclear weapons and their targets, destabilisation in Xinjiang, internationalisation of the Renminbi, the treatment of the Uyghurs, Hong Kong political freedoms under the Basic Law, military dimensions of the Taiwan issue and so on. New institutions may be needed to reach a holistic way forward, if both sides are willing.

Importantly, cooperation within multilateral institutions will also be essential for de-escalation. This means addressing the Chinese perception that international institutions and international law itself are tools of US policy.

In this, the Chinese leadership will need to recognise that global and regional institutions do change, and that there is a quasi-Darwinian process at play; for example NATO acquired its prominent position pretty much by accident. US puppeteering is often exaggerated, and the US clearly benefits from some of the exaggerations and has disincentives to disavow them. Contrary to Western implications, no such multilateral organisations are cast in stone or will exist in perpetuity.

The opportunity therefore is for the West to engage China even more in the current processes of reform underway in all multilateral and regionals, including the WTO, NATO, ASEAN and even the SCO and AIIB. Chinese ambitions over the last 10 years to build institutions that parallel existing international bodies, especially in finance, are obviously not conducive to confidence-building and avoiding Cold War II.

Where has the debate gone about how Europe and the US can compete more vigorously with China, especially economically? Germany has fared best and VW is one of the biggest brands in China. However, competition is global and long-term plans to compete more effectively with China, similarly, are a rarity these days.

The deeper roots of this problem are made more stark by considering Japan's economic success in the 1980s and 1990s and the West's response.

In the 1980s and 1990s Japan was considered the world's great economic success. As an ally of the West the focus was on the things that Japan did better than the West. These included the role of the state in both promoting and regulating commerce. At the corporate level US and European firms copied 'Just in Time' manufacturing, 'core competences', kaizen (continuous improvement), and other practices.

There was reduced Western focus on the less favourable aspects of the Japanese economic system, and its ally status no doubt helped. These included the Keiretsu share-crossholding system and the obsession with corporate asset ownership, which reduced investment and caused a property bubble.

This 'selective learning' over the Japanese economic system has not happened with China, no doubt partly because the reality of the Chinese system is hardly known at all. This is partly because they can be opaque due to hidden Party control, partly because China is not an unthreatening ally like Japan. With a bit of schadenfreude, the West seems to believe that the jury is still out on whether the Chinese economic system is really successful or not.

Selective learning from China is one thing. Another is the more general drive towards deeper reform in the US and Europe which might have been precipitated by China's economic rise. A lack of understanding about China's system, in the way that the West understood Japan, carries the danger that the West will 'copy the wrong thing' if it copies at all.

The West, instead of playing to its strengths and understanding both the underlying strengths and weaknesses of the Chinese politico-economic system, may even mistakenly emulate authoritarianism, one party rule, politicised courts, extreme state surveillance or even the mythical 'state-led economy'.

If Western policy becomes even more military-led due to Xi Jinping's approach, the West might give up on the benefits of 'healthy competition' and attempt elimination of an economic competitor by military means. This would be catastrophic for all sides.

The world might hope that the soft power 'Peaceful Rise' Weltanschauung of Zheng Bijian may yet regain prominence in China once more.

Selected Bibliography

Chapter 2

1   https://www.carnegiecouncil.org/publications/archive/dialogue/1_03/articles/515
2   https://www.psychologicalscience.org/observer/geography-of-thought
3   http://www.martinjacques.com/articles/civilization-state-versus-nation-state-2/
4   The Rich History of China's Islam | Newlines Magazine
5   Discrimination against LGBT populations in China - The Lancet Public Health
6   https://buildingstatecapability.com/2017/05/10/how-did-china-create-directed-improvisation/
7   https://en.wikipedia.org/wiki/Yellow_Peril#United_Kingdom
8   First world war's forgotten Chinese Labour Corps to get recognition at last | First world war | The Guardian
9   Apology plea for Chinese seamen deported from Liverpool - BBC News
10 Compulsory repatriation of Chinese seamen in Liverpool - Timeline - Mix-d: Museum (mixedmuseum.org.uk)
11 YouGov Poll on Racism in the UK (carg.info)
12 https://en.wikipedia.org/wiki/The_End_of_History_and_the_Last_Man
13 https://www.todayonline.com/world/id-side-rich-china-over-fickle-us-malaysias-mahathir-mohamad
14 https://www.brainyquote.com/quotes/lee_kuan_yew_711055
15 https://en.unesco.org/courier/2018-4/human-rights-and-cultural-perspectives
16 https://www.un.org/en/sections/issues-depth/human-rights/ for a list of all types of human rights
17 Why Tunisia's Promise of Democracy Struggles to Bear Fruit - The New York Times (nytimes.com)
18 China has inspired us since Enlightenment (sciencenordic.com)

Chapter 3

1   Angus Maddison. Monitoring the World Economy 1820-1992. Paris, OECD 1995.
2   Ezra Vogel. Deng Xiaoping and the Transformation of China. Belknap Press, Cambridge Mass. 2001
3   George Magnus. Red Flags: Why Xi's China is in Jeopardy. New Haven CT Yale University Press 2018
4   Elizabeth Economy. The Third Revolution: Xi Jinping and the New Chinese State. Oxford University Press 2019
5   Thomas Orlik. The Bubble that Never Pops. New York. Oxford University Press 2020
6   Nicholas Lardy. The State Strikes Back: the End of Economic Reform in China. Peterson Institute for International Economics 2019
7   Stein Ringen. The Perfect Dictatorship: China in the 21st Century. Hong Kong University Press 2016 p.39
8   Kerry Brown. The World According to Xi; Everything You Need to Know About the New China. London I B Tauris 2018
9   Douglas Fuller. Paper Tigers, Hidden Dragons; the Political Economy of China's Technological Development. Oxford University Press 2016
10 Kai-fu Lee. AI superpowers: China, Silicon Valley and the New World Order. Boston, Houghton, Mifflin, Harcourt 2018
11 Peter Norman and Greg Autry. Death by China: Confronting the Dragon – a Global Call to Action Prentice Hall 2011
12 David Autor, David Dorn and Gordon Hanson. The China Syndrome: local Labour Market Effects of Import Competition in the USA. NBER Working Paper No.18054 2012
13 Bob Davis and Lingling Wei. Superpower Showdown: How the Battle Between Trump and Xi Threatens a New Cold War. Harper Collins 2020
    Matthew Klein and Michael Pettis. Trade wars and Class Wars. New Haven CT Yale University Press 2020
14 Kishore Mahbubani. Has China Won; the Chinese Challenge to American Primacy. Public Affairs. New York 2020
15 Petros Mavrodis and Andre Sapir China and the WTO; Why Multilateralism Still Matters. Princeton University Press 2021
16 Graham Alison. Destined for War: Can America Escape the Thucydides Trap. Boston. Hughes, Mifflin, Harcourt. 2017

Chapter 4

1. Fifth plenary session of the 19th Central Committee of the CPC
2. See the works of Thomas Piketty, in particular his second book 'Capital et ideologie' (2020) that could not be published in China due to discussion of wealth inequalities. For example Piketty states that the share of China's wealth held by the richest 10% of the population was about 40 to 50 % in the early 1990s a level of inequality below Sweden; by 2018 this had grown to nearly 70% close to that of highly unequal societies.
3. Until 2020 when Sun moved to the NPC as he had reached the age limit, and became as the deputy chair of the Financial and Economic Affairs Committee
4. Including when touring Jiangxi in May 2019 and Guangzhou in 2020
5. For example Hou Xin, Yuan Dong, Zhang Baocheng and Ma Xinli were arrested on 31 March 2013 see Human Rights Watch's statement published on 3 April 2013
6. A significant number of Chinese think that it was the American military that brought the virus to Wuhun during the World Military Games in October 2019. That idea was widespread by MFA spokesperson Zhao Lijian on his 'personal' Twitter account in March 2020.

Chapter 5

1. OECD Business and Finance Outlook 2018 https://www.oecd.org/finance/Chinas-Belt-and-Road-Initiative-in-the-global-trade-investment-and-finance-landscape.pdf
2. https://www.yidaiyilu.gov.cn/
3. https://www.chathamhouse.org/2020/08/debunking-myth-debt-trap-diplomacy
4. https://www.cfr.org/report/chinas-belt-and-road-implications-for-the-united-states/
5. https://www.cfr.org/article/belt-and-road-tracker
6. https://thediplomat.com/2019/07/which-countries-are-for-or-against-chinas-xinjiang-policies/
7. https://www.imf.org/en/News/Articles/2019/04/25/sp042619-stronger-frameworks-in-the-new-phase-of-belt-and-road
8. https://www.ponarseurasia.org/central-asia-s-autocrats-geopolitically-stuck-politically-free/

Chapter 7

1. Hong Kong has more US dollar millionaires this year, as calmer streets boost confidence and perception of wealth, South China Morning Post, 23 September, 2021 Hong Kong has more US dollar millionaires this year, as calmer streets boost confidence and perception of wealth | South China Morning Post (scmp.com) (accessed on 14 June, 2021).
2. Hongkongers identifying as 'Chinese' at record low; under 10% of youth 'proud' to be citizens – poll, Hong Kong Free Press, 28 June, 2019 Hongkongers identifying as 'Chinese' at record low; under 10% of youth 'proud' to be citizens - poll | Hong Kong Free Press HKFP (hongkongfp.com) (accessed on 13 June, 2021)
3. Explainer: what is Benny Tai's "10 steps to burn with us", The Standard, 6 January, 2021, Explainer: what is Benny Tai's "10 steps to burn with us" | The Standard (accessed 13 June, 2021)
4. An 'ugly plot' by the 'Democrats' in Hong Kong, Henry Litton, John Menadue's Public Policy Journal, 25 January, 2021 An 'ugly plot' by the 'Democrats' in Hong Kong - Pearls and Irritations (johnmenadue.com) (accessed on 13 June, 2021)
5. Tiny Apartments and Punishing Work Hours: The Economic Roots of Hong Kong's Protests, New York Times, 22 July, 2019 Tiny Apartments and Punishing Work Hours: The Economic Roots of Hong Kong's Protests - The New York Times (nytimes.com) (accessed on 13 June, 2021)
6. 'In 2014, many of the student protesters at Occupy Central were trained two years before they took it to the streets. They were described as Weapon of Mass Destruction to challenge the Chinese government', quoted in BBC documentary. Dim Sum Daily, 16 August, 2019 Hong Kong protesters trained at Oslo Freedom Forum before anti-extradition protest, past speakers include Denise Ho, HK singer and political activist and Al Qaida affiliated White Helmet, Raed al-Saleh - Dimsum Daily (accessed on 14 June, 2021)
7. Hong Kong media baron denies CIA connection, Financial Times, 29 August, 2014 https://www.ft.com/content/f1cb693e-2f44-11e4-a79c-00144feabdc0 (accessed on 14 June, 2021)
8. Hong Kong Basic Law, Wikipedia Hong Kong Basic Law - Wikipedia (accessed on 14 June, 2021)
9. Hong Kong national security law, Wikipedia, Hong Kong national security law - Wikipedia (accessed on 14 June, 2021)

10   2021 Hong Kong electoral reform, Wikipedia, 2021 Hong Kong electoral reform - Wikipedia (accessed on 14 June, 2021)

11   Understanding CCP Resilience: Surveying Chinese Public Opinion Through Time, Harvard Kennedy School Ash Centre for Democratic Governance and Innovation, July 2020 final_policy_brief_2021_edits.pdf (harvard.edu) (accessed on 14 July, 2021)

12   HK vs China GDP: A sobering reality, Hong Kong Economic Journal, 9 June, 2017 HK vs China GDP: A sobering reality EJINSIGHT - ejinsight.com (accessed on 14 June, 2021)

13   Guangdong-Hong Kong-Macau Greater Bay Area, Wikipedia Guangdong-Hong Kong-Macau Greater Bay Area - Wikipedia (accessed on 15 June, 2021)

14   Belt and Road Initiative, Wikipedia Belt and Road Initiative - Wikipedia (accessed on 15 June, 2021)

15   China to overtake US as world's biggest economy by 2028, report predicts, The Guardian, 26 December, 2020 China to overtake US as world's biggest economy by 2028, report predicts | China | The Guardian (accessed on 14 June, 2021)

16   The Future is Asian - Global Order in the Twenty-First Century, Parag Khanna, Weidenfeld Nicolson, London, 2019

17   Developing countries set to account for nearly 60% of world GDP by 2030, according to new estimates, OECD, 16 June, 2010 Economy : Developing countries set to account for nearly 60% of world GDP by 2030, according to new esti mates - OECD (accessed on 15 June, 2021)

18   2 years after mass protests rocked Hong Kong, will unrest return to city's streets as Beijing tightens grip?, South China Morning Post, 16 June, 2021 2 years after mass protests rocked Hong Kong, will unrest return to city's streets as Beijing tightens grip? | South China Morning Post (scmp.com) (accessed on 16 June, 2021)

Chapter 8

Bregolat, Eugenio. The Second Chinese Revolution. New York: Palgrave MacMillan, 2015.

Bregolat, Eugenio. La Segunda Revolución China. Barcelona: Destino, 2007.

Brown, Kerry. China's Dream – The Culture of Chinese Communism and The Secret Sources of Its Power. Cambridge: Polity Press, 2018.

Brown, Kerry. The World According to Xi. London: Tauris, 2018.

Brown, Kerry and Kalley Wu Tzu-hui, The Trouble With Taiwan – History, the United States and a Rising China. London: Zed Books, 2019.

Diamond, Larry. Developing Democracy Toward Consolidation. Baltimore: The Johns Hopkins University Press, 1999.

Dickson, Bruce J. The Party and the People – Chinese Politics in the 21st Century. Princeton: Princeton University Press, 2021.

Economy, Elizabeth C. . The Third Revolution – Xi Jinping and the New Chinese State. New York: Oxford University Press, 2018.

Esplin, Rachel Odell and Eric Heginbotham, "Don't Fall for the Invasion Panic", in Rachel Esplin Odell and Eric Hegin botham; Bonny Lin and David Sacks; Kharis Templeman; Oriana Skylar Mastro, "Strait of Emergency? Debating Beijing's Threat to Taiwan", Foreign Affairs Volume 100, 4 July/August 2021 and September/October 2021

Fell, David. Government and Politics in Taiwan 2n. ed. London: Routledge, 2018.

Fisichella, Domenico. Totalitarismo – Un regime del nostro tempo. Roma: Carocci editore, 1987.

Friedrich, Carl J. and Zbigniew K. Brzezinski. Totalitarian Dictatorship & Autocracy. New York: Praeger, 1972.

Gilley, Bruce "Deng Xiaoping and His Successors (1976 to Present)" in William A. Joseph, ed. Politics in China, An Introduction. New York: Oxford University Press, 2010.

Goldstein, Steven M. . China and Taiwan. Cambridge: Polity Press, 2015.

Hermet, Guy. Totalitarismes. Paris: Economica, 1984.

Joseph, William A. ed. Politics in China, An Introduction. New York: Oxford University Press, 2010.

Kissinger, Henry. On China. New York: Penguin Books, 2012.

Linz, Juan J. . Sistemi Totalitari e Regimi Autoritari – Un'Analisi Storico-Comparativa. Soveria Mannelli: Rubbettino, 2006.

Linz, Juan J. and Alfred Stepan. Problems of Democratic Transition and Consolidation, Southern Europe, South America and Post-Communist Europe. Baltimore: The Johns Hopkins University press, 1996.

Macridis, Roy ed. . Foreign Policy in World Politics, States and Regions. Englewood Cliffs NJ: Prentice Hall, 1989.

Manthorpe, Jonathan. Forbidden Nation: A History of Taiwan. New York: St. Martin's Griffin, 2009.

Spellman W.M. . Monarchies 1000-2000. London: Reaktion Books, 2001/2012.

Topol, Sarah A. . "Is Taiwan Next?", The New York Times Magazine. August 4/5, 2021.

Whiting, Allen S. "Foreign Policy of China" in Roy C. Macridis, ed. Foreign Policy in World Politics, States and Regions. Englewood Cliffs NJ: Prentice Hall, 1989.

Wolf, Margery. Women and the Family in Rural Taiwan. Stanford: Stanford University Press, 1972.

Chapter 8 - Digital References

Economic Cooperation Framework Agreement https://www.ecfa.org.tw/

Ministry of the Interior ROC Taiwan https://www.moi.gov.tw/

National Statistics Republic of China (Taiwan) https://eng.stat.gov.tw/point.asp?index=9

United Nations Digital Library https://digitallibrary.un.org/?ln=en

US Congress https://www.congress.gov/

US National Archives Catalog www.archives.gov

Chapter 10

Christiansen, T., Kirchner, E., and Wissenbach, U. (2019). The European Union and China, Macmillan.

Delamotte, G. (2020). Dealing with China: A European Perspective, Vol. 27, issue 2, 2020, pages 109-123.

Dorussen, H., Kirchner, E., and Christiansen, T. (2018). Security Cooperation in EU-China Relations: Towards Convergence?, European Foreign Affairs Review, Vol. 23, issue 3, pages 287-304.

European Commission and HR/VP, (2019) EU-China – A Strategic Outlook, Strasbourg, 12.3.2019, JOIN(2019) 5 final.

European External Action Service 2020. The Sinatra Doctrine. How the EU Should Deal with the US–China Competition, Brussels, 27 August. Available at: https://eeas.europa.eu/headquarters/headquarters-homepage/84484/sinatra-doctrine-how-eu-should-deal-us%E2%80%93china-competition_en.

Garcia-Herrero, A. (2021) Europe's disappointing investment deal with China: Why rush a deal that is so inherently

complex?, Bruegel, 4 January. Available at: https://www.bruegel.org/2021/01/europes-disappointing-invest
ment-deal-with-china.

Jenkins, R. (2019). How China is Reshaping the Global Economy: Development Impacts in Africa and Latin America.
Oxford: Oxford University Press

Kirchner, E. (2019). China and the European Union, Oxford Research Encyclopedias Politics, Online Publication,
December. DOI: 10.1093/acrefore/ 9780190228637.013.1131

Kirchner, E., Christiansen, T., and Dorussen, H. (Eds). (2016). Security Relations between China and the European
Union, Cambridge: Cambridge University Press.

Schneider F. (2018). China's Digital Nationalism. Oxford: Oxford University Press.

Chapter 11 - Further reading

Chinese Strategy, Military Forces, and Economics: The Metrics of Cooperation, Competition and/or Conflict.
Anthony H Cordesman, Center for Strategic and International Studies, updated 18th Sept 2018

China and the US. Anthony H Cordesman and Max Malot, Center for Strategic and International Studies, 2020

Global Strategy 2021: An Allied Strategy for China   Matthew Kroenig and Jeffrey Cimmino, Scowcroft Center for
Strategy and Security, 2020

The US-China Rivalry as Seen in the Cold War's Rear View Mirror. Ian Li NTU Singapore
https://thestrategybridge.org Oct 2019

What War with China Could Look Like. Todd South www.militarytimes.com Sept 2020

The New Great Game at Sea. Geoffrey F. Gresh. Texas National Security Review, December 2020

The Rise of China and the Future of the International Political System.
http://crossworks.holycross.edu/political_science_student_scholarship/2 May 2015

The Rule of Law and Maritime Security in the South China Sea. Douglas Guilfoyle. International Affairs 95/5 Sept 2019

Rethinking China's Rise. Xiaoyu Pu and Chengli Wang. International Affairs 94/5 Sept 2018

The Great Chinese Surprise Xiangfeng Yang International Affairs 96/2 March 2020

The Future War Studies Community and the Revolution in Military Affairs. Kai Liao International Affairs 96/5 Sept 2020

The China Model and the Global Crisis Shaun Breslin. International Affairs 87/6 Nov 2011

Geopolitics and Policy Paradigms in China and the United States. Mark Beeson and Kujian LI International
Affairs 91/1 Jan 2015

US-China Relations in a Multinodal World. Brantly Womack International Affairs 92/6 March 2016

Chapter 12 - Further Reading

The 5 Essential Steps to Sustainable Viability, Christopher Gleadle, 2018

The Economics of Biodiversity, The Dasgupta Review, Professor Dasgupta February 2021

Governing the Commons, The Evolution of Institutions for Collective Action, Elinor Ostrom, 1990

Robinson Crusoe, Danial Defoe, 1719

Acknowledgements

We would like to express our most sincere thanks to Jason Frazer, for his dedication to design and production of the book, and to Jo Hayes for her painstaking attention to detail in proofreading. Above all, we wish to express our deepest gratitude to all the authors for their help, encouragement and expertise that was generously given and without whom this book would not be possible.

Merlene Toh Emerson, Yeow Poon, Paul EM Reynolds, and Christopher Gleadle
Editorial Team
September 2021

Published by
The Paddy Ashdown Forum
London » Brussels
www.thepaddyashdownforum.org
info@thepaddyashdownforum.org

Design & Printing
Jason Frazer
London
itsjasonfrazer@gmail.com